C. Neill N.Y.

LT GEN. T. J. JACKSON.

From a Photograph taken a few days before his death.

Engraved for the Life of Jackson.

C.B. Richardson, Publisher.

THE LIFE

OF

STONEWALL JACKSON.

FROM

OFFICIAL PAPERS, CONTEMPORARY NARRATIVES, AND PERSONAL ACQUAINTANCE.

BY A VIRGINIAN.

Cooke, John Esten, 1830-1886.

"I have just received your note, informing me that you were wounded. I cannot express my regret at the occurrence. Could I have directed events, I should have chosen, for the good of the country, to have been disabled in your stead. I congratulate you on the victory which is due to your skill and energy."

LEE TO JACKSON, *at Chancellorsville.*

REPRINTED FROM

ADVANCE SHEETS OF THE RICHMOND EDITION.

NEW YORK:

CHARLES B. RICHARDSON,

596 BROADWAY.

1863.

RENNIE, SHEA & LINDSAY,
Stereotypers and Electrotypers,
81, 83, and 85 Centre-street,
New York.

R. CRAIGHEAD,
Printer,
81, 83 & 85 Centre-st.

TO THE READER.

This work has been written under disadvantages which entitle it to the liberal criticism of the reader. It was undertaken without thought of the probable activity of the summer campaign, and has been composed in bivouac—by the road-side—immediately before and after engagements—amid scenes and under circumstances which have rendered deliberate writing impossible. This, and my inability to correct the proof-sheets, should excuse the errors of the work.

All that I claim for the narrative is *truth*. This I think it possesses, and the merit is not trifling. Beyond its value as an accurate statement of events, derived in the main from official documents, I claim nothing for it—style least of all.

A religious paper has made an incredibly violent and insulting attack upon the work and the author, while the former was in press and the latter absent in the field.

To this attack I have no abusive epithets to utter in reply. The good people of the South shall judge between us.

Some of the material of this sketch is original; but the matter illustrating the official reports has been chiefly drawn from contemporary publications. A considerable number of these slips, some of them very interesting and curious, were unfortunately captured by the enemy about a month since. No MS. was lost, however; and the prediction of friends, that the work would probably be first published in New York, was not verified.

Constant movements, great events, and duties which could not be neglected, have made this book unequal to the great subject of which it treats. But the intention of the writer in composing it was an honorable and worthy one, as all who know him, he feels confident, will believe.

CAMP ——, July 21, 1863.

INTRODUCTORY.

"JACKSON is dead!"

Seldom have words penetrated more deeply to the heart of a great nation. The people of the Confederate States had begun to regard this immortal leader as above the reach of fate. He had passed unhurt through such desperate contests; his calm eyes had surveyed so many hard-fought battle-fields, from the commencement of the combats to their termination, that a general conviction of the hero's invulnerability had impressed every heart—no one could feel that the light in those eyes of the great soldier would ever be quenched. But that Providence which decrees all things wisely at last sent the fatal bullet: and the South is called upon to mourn the untimely death of one who seemed to his countrymen the chosen standard-bearer of liberty. After the battle of Chancellorsville, and while the wound of the famous soldier attracted to him the warmest sympathy and drew forth the earnest prayers of many thousands for his recovery, the journals of the land contained many notices of his services and genius, and his death was alluded to as a calamity too frightful to be contemplated. Well has one of these journals in speaking of Lee and Jackson said: "It is an honor to breathe the air they breathe. Together, they make up a measure of glory which no nation under Heaven ever surpassed. Other great leaders we have, to whom unstinted praise is due and everywhere gladly accorded; but the rays of their fame converge and accumulate but to add to the dazzling splendor that illuminates the names of Lee and Jackson.

"The central figure of this war is, beyond all question, that of Robert E. Lee. His, the calm, broad military intellect that reduced the chaos after Donelson to form and order. But Jackson is the motive power that executes, with the rapidity of lightning, all that Lee can plan. Lee is the exponent of Southern power of command;

Jackson, the expression of its faith in God and in itself, its terrible energy, its enthusiasm and daring, its unconquerable will, its contempt of danger and fatigue, its capacity to smite, as with bolts of thunder, the cowardly and cruel foe that would trample under foot its liberty and its religion.

"Jackson is no accidental manifestation of the powers of faith and courage. He came not by chance in this day and to this generation. He was born for a purpose. In this conviction, he rests serenely, awaiting the healing of his wounds; willing once more to hear the wild cheers of his men as he rides to the front; or, if that be denied him, content to retire from the field, a maimed, humble, simple Christian man. Civil honor, were it the highest in the gift of the country, could not add one cubit to the stature of his glory.

"Even should he die, his fiery and unquailing spirit would survive in his men. He has infused into them that which cannot die. The leader who succeeds him, be he whom he may, will be impelled, as by a supernatural impulse, to emulate his matchless deeds. Jackson's men will demand to be led in 'Stonewall Jackson's way.' The leader who will not or cannot comply with that demand, must drop the baton quickly. Jackson's corps will be led forever by the memory of its great chieftain."

Alas! the termination of his wound was fatal. The great soul has passed away from us: and we are left without his sagacious counsels, his splendid powers of execution; his unerring judgment, and that intuitive genius for war which made him, in his sphere, the first of living leaders, and ranked him with the greatest who have lived in all tide of time.

It is the life of this famous general that we now propose to write —a popular and unstudied record of his career—for the satisfaction of that honorable curiosity which his countrymen feel in relation to his services. Those services need no record indeed: for they are graven in imperishable characters on the tablets of every heart. But some portions of this great career may have been obscured amid the smoke and dust of these hot days of battle: and the object of these pages is to review them succinctly and furnish some personal details of the hero's character.

CONTENTS.

PAGE

To the Reader.................................... 5

Introductory 7

CHAPTER I.

Birth, Parentage, and Early Services in Mexico............ 13

CHAPTER II.

Professor at the Virginia Military Institute—Appointed Colonel in the Virginia Line.................................. 17

CHAPTER III.

Engagement at Falling Waters.......................... 21

CHAPTER IV

Battle of Manassas.................................... 25

CHAPTER V.

Jackson's Farewell to the Old Brigade..................... 32

CHAPTER VI.

The Winter Expedition to Romney....................... 35

CHAPTER VII.

The Battle of Kernstown............................... 39

CHAPTER VIII.

The Battle of McDowell................................ 43

CHAPTER IX.

PAGE

The Battle of Winchester.................................. 49

CHAPTER X.

The Battle of Cross Keys 62

CHAPTER XI.

Battle of Port Republic.................................. 68

CHAPTER XII.

Illustrations—Romney: Kernstown.......................... 73

CHAPTER XIII.

Illustrations—McDowell: Winchester...................... 81

CHAPTER XIV.

Illustrations—Cross Keys: Port Republic.................. 99

CHAPTER XV.

Jackson in June, 1862.................................. 107

CHAPTER XVI.

Cold Harbor.................................. 114

CHAPTER XVII.

The Retreat of McClellan to Malvern Hill.................. 121

CHAPTER XVIII.

Pope.................................. 135

CHAPTER XIX.

Cedar Run.................................. 147

CHAPTER XX.

Details.................................. 153

CHAPTER XXI. PAGE

The March to Manassas........ 159

CHAPTER XXII.

Jackson at Bay........ 173

CHAPTER XXIII.

Manassas: August 29, 1862........ 177

CHAPTER XXIV.

Manassas: August 30, 1862........ 183

CHAPTER XXV.

Invasion of Maryland........ 195

CHAPTER XXVI.

Sharpsburg........ 207

CHAPTER XXVII.

The Army Resting........ 219

CHAPTER XXVIII.

Fredericksburg........ 225

CHAPTER XXIX.

Winter Quarters at Moss Neck........ 236

CHAPTER XXX.

Hooker Advances........ 241

CHAPTER XXXI.

The Wilderness—Chancellorsville........ 247

CHAPTER XXXII.

"It is all Right"........ 262

CONTENTS.

CHAPTER XXXIII.

PAGE
Jackson, the Soldier and the Man 270

APPENDIX I.

Operations of General Jackson's Command from September 5th to September 27th, 1862.—Official Report 289

APPENDIX II.

"The Old Stonewall Brigade" 301

LIFE

OF

STONEWALL JACKSON.

CHAPTER I.

BIRTH, PARENTAGE, AND EARLY SERVICES IN MEXICO.

THOMAS JONATHAN JACKSON was born January 21, 1824, in Clarksburg, Harrison county, Virginia. His great grandfather, an Englishman by birth, emigrated to the western portion of Virginia; and Edward Jackson, grandfather of the General, was surveyor of Lewis county for a long time, representing it in the Legislature. His son, Jonathan Jackson, father of the General, moved to Clarksburg, where he studied and commenced the practice of law with his cousin, Judge John G. Jackson, acquiring considerable reputation, and marrying Miss Neal, a daughter of Thomas Neal, of Wood county. He, however, became embarrassed in his circumstances by going security for friends, and all his property was eventually swept away. When he died, in 1827, his children were left penniless. These children were four in number—two sons and two daughters—Thomas, the subject of this sketch, being the youngest, and at the time but three years old.

The child was thus left upon the very threshold of life to learn the hard lesson of poverty. But this lesson, thus early learned, bore ample fruits in a soil so rich and auspicious to the finer growth of the human soul. The young man was taught from the very commencement of his earthly career to make up by honest toil for the neglect of fortune, and instead of frittering away his time and faculties in the haunts of pleasure or the frivolous pursuits of youths generally, to turn his attention to the more ennobling aims of life, and fit himself for that career in which he was to secure his great fame.

Soon after the death of his parents he was taken to the home of an uncle in Lewis county, and remained at this place —the family homestead of the Jacksons, in which his father had been born—until he reached the age of seventeen. Here he labored on the farm in summer and went to school three months in the winter, gaining the rudiments of a plain English education—what he acquired subsequently was due to his stay at West Point, and his ultimate studies at the Virginia Military Institute. His habits of life, even at this early age, are said to have been grave and serious—his discharge of every duty conscientious and complete. He assisted his uncle in the management of the farm; and soon secured among the residents of the county a high character for industry, intelligence, and probity. His orphan condition excited great sympathy among the neighbors, who knew and respected the good character of the Jackson family; and every assistance was rendered him in his struggle to carve out his own pathway in life, and secure an honorable independence. A proof of this friendly sympathy is contained in the fact that at the age of *sixteen*, he was elected constable of the county of Lewis, the duties of which office he discharged with intelligence and credit.

The inclinations of the young man seem, however, to have pointed early towards arms as a profession. Some hereditary instinct of his family for war probably developed itself in the grave and serious youth—but to those who believe as we do that a mightier hand than man's shapes all human events, this early inclination will appear to have been the means of fitting him for the grand part he was eventually to have in the assertion of Southern liberties. It is certain that young Jackson found himself impelled toward a military career, and at the age of seventeen he set out for Washington on foot, to secure, if possible, an appointment as cadet at West Point. This he was enabled to do through the instrumentality of some political friends, and he entered upon his studies there in 1842.

In July, 1846, at the age of twenty-two, he graduated with distinction, was brevetted 2d Lieutenant, and immediately ordered to report for duty in Mexico, under General Taylor. He served under that commander until Gen. Scott took the field, when he was transferred to the command of the latter. His military career was distinguished, and his promotion rapid. In August, 1847, he was made 1st Lieutenant in Magruder's Battery; brevetted Captain "for gallant and meritorious conduct in battles of Contreras and Churubusco," August 20, 1847 (Aug., 1848), and brevetted Major "for gallant and meritorious conduct in battle of Chepultepec," September 13, 1847 (March, 1849). No other officer had so distinguished himself and risen so rapidly as the young Virginian. The unknown youth had, in this brief space of time, attracted the attention of his generals, and become one of the most promising young officers of the army.

The climate of the country had, however, told powerfully upon a frame at no time very robust. His health became so impaired that he was unable to discharge his duties—and, with the high sense of honor which marked his character, he, on the conclusion of peace, resigned his commission. (Feb. 29, 1852.) Returning to Virginia, he obtained a Professorship in the Virginia Military Institute, and continued in the performance of the important duties of this position until the breaking out of the present war. Soon after entering upon his duties at the Military Institute, he married Miss Junkin, daughter of the Rev. Dr. Junkin, Principal of the Washington College. This lady and her children died, and he was afterwards married to Miss Morrison, of North Carolina—his only living child, a daughter, but recently born, being the sole issue of this marriage.

Few records of the brief career of the young soldier in Mexico remain, tending to throw any light upon his personal character—that unique individuality which has since attracted to him the eyes of the whole world. The brief official recognition of his "gallant and meritorious conduct" remains; but beyond this we find little. His profound religious sentiments, it is however known, were at this time fully developed. He did not, like many other Christians, confine himself to barren faith, but actively exerted himself in the cause of God. He restrained all profanity in his camp, welcomed army colporteurs, distributed tracts, and endeavored to have every regiment in the army supplied with a chaplain. "He was vulgarly sneered at," it is said, "as a fatalist; his habits of soliloquy were derided as superstitious conversations with a familiar spirit; but the confidence he had in his destiny was the unfailing mark of genius, and adorned the Christian faith which made him believe that he had a distinct mission of duty, in which he should be spared for the ends of Providence." It would seem, indeed, that even at this early period of his life, he had fully embraced that doctrine of Predestination which undoubtedly marked his character very strongly in latter years. No intelligent person has ever attributed to him the vulgar and shocking sentiment of "fatalism"—but it seems certain that from an early period in his career, he espoused the Presbyterian doctrine of Providential supervision and direction of human affairs, to the fullest extent; and had but one feeling, which may be accurately summed up and expressed in the words, "Do your duty, and leave the rest to God."

It is said that while in Mexico, a battery of the enemy was pouring a storm of shot and shell down a road, along which he wished his men to advance. They remained under cover, out of the fire, shaken in nerve and fearing to venture forth. This was excessively distasteful and mortifying to their young commander, and leaving them, he advanced to the road, and calmly walked up and down among the plunging shot and shell, calling out coolly, "Come on—this is nothing—you see they can't hurt me!"

It will thus be seen that, either from native courage or that sentiment of predestination alluded to, young Jackson had already acquired the dauntless nerve and coolness which afterwards rendered him so famous.

The penetrating eyes of Napoleon, had he seen that youth, calmly walking amid the heavy fire of the enemy's artillery, and declaring coolly that it "could not hurt him," would have discerned much in his face—would have understood that this young man would "go far."

CHAPTER II.

PROFESSOR AT THE VIRGINIA MILITARY INSTITUTE—APPOINTED COLONEL IN THE VIRGINIA LINE.

Jackson remained at the Military Institute in discharge of his duties until the spring of 1861. Then the time for the full display of the great faculties of his soul came. Peace might have left forever hidden the profound and splendid genius of the man, but the bloody flower of war was about to burst into bloom, and the quiet, "eccentric" professor was to shape and mould the great events of a mighty period in the history of the world. Cromwell might have remained a brewer—Jackson an unknown professor; but for both of these iron souls Providence had decreed and shaped their work.

The year 1861 opened, big with portents. The air seemed to be filled with that mysterious electricity which preludes revolution and battle. Great events were on the march, and the minds of men were aroused and excited; all hearts beat fast with the ardor of the time. In January the "Star of the West" was fired upon in Charleston harbor, and Mississippi followed South Carolina, seceding from the Union. Florida, Alabama, Georgia, Louisiana followed in the same month, and military movements began at many points. Early in February Jefferson Davis was elected President of the Confederate States; and on the 4th of March Abraham Lincoln was inaugurated President of the United States. State after State seceded; a permanent Constitution of the Confederate States was adopted March 11, and on April 13th Fort Sumter surrendered to General Beauregard. From that moment the issue was clearly joined, and all intelligent minds perceived that it meant *civil war*. The Confederate States accepted it—marshalled their forces—organized for the general defence—and entered upon the great struggle with grave and serious hearts, but profound reliance on that God of Hosts who gives not the battle to the strong or the race to the swift, but upholds the righteous cause against all assailants, working its deliverance.

Up to the 17th April the galaxy of the Confederate States wanted one of its brightest luminaries. The Southern cross was yet without the central light which was to complete its glories. Virginia, the soul of revolution in the past—the proud, defiant, chivalric sovereignty which had been hitherto the first to throw down the gauntlet of resistance to oppression—Virginia, the mother of warriors and statesmen, remained inactive, lagging in the rear. Some day the causes of this phenomenon will be investigated, the actors in that drama delineated, and "every one shall have his own." Certain it is that the beautiful Virgin of the Virginia Shield hesitated long to lift the spear in defence of her chastity, and it was not until a brutal and insolent foe came in direct contact with her pure person that she woke to the danger, and raised her arm.

The Ordinance of Secession was passed on the 17th April, and the Virginia Convention took immediate steps to operate against the enemy in the Valley. It was a matter of primary importance to drive the Federal forces from Harper's Ferry, and secure the stores there, and this was promptly undertaken. We had only a few volunteer troops to move with against the U. S. regulars; but Virginia had a well-grounded confidence in the courage of her population, and the event of the movement was looked to with confidence.

With this month of April, 1861, again appears upon the scene the young soldier who had so greatly distinguished himself in Mexico, and since that time had been so quietly pursuing the beaten path of his duties at the Virginia Military Institute. Jackson was now thirty-seven years of age. He was scarcely known beyond the walls of the Institute in which he continued to perform his official duties with military regularity, and if the outer world heard of him at all, it was only through jests or witticisms directed against his peculiarities of character and demeanor by some of the students who, with the love of fun proverbial in their class, had much to say of the eccentricities and odd ways of "Old Tom Jackson." The universal tendency to caricature the peculiarities of a man of original genius is well known—to make fun of those very great traits which separate such men from the common-place mass of human beings—and Jackson received more than a fair share of this undesirable attention on the part of his students. He was a martinet in the performance of his duties—administered things in his department "on a war footing," and no doubt caused the volatile young men whom he taught, to regard him as a most unreasonable and exacting stickler for useless military etiquette and ceremony. But he was conscientious in this extreme attention to little things, and he was clearly right. The Institute was a *military* school—its chief value consisted in the habits of military obedience which it impressed upon the ductile characters of the youth of the Commonwealth—and Jackson no doubt regarded any relaxation of the rules of the establishment as tending directly to strike at the intentions of its founders, and destroy its usefulness. We have heard that he once continued to wear a thick woollen uniform late into the summer, and when asked by one of the professors why he did so, replied that he had seen an order prescribing that dress, but none had been exhibited to him directing it to be changed. This was the source of some amusement to the young gentlemen who had no idea of military "orders" and the implicit obedience which a good soldier considers it his bounden duty to pay to them. But was not Jackson right? Let the thousands who, in this bitter and arduous struggle, have been taught by hard experience the necessity of strict, unquestioning compliance with all orders, to the very letter, reply to the question.

Jackson thus remained a soldier as before—as strict in the performance of duty, and as exacting in regard to others, as if he was still in the field. It is certain, too, that his religious convictions had become strengthened and established as the controlling influence of his life. He had long since become a devout member of the Presbyterian Church, and was a most devoted and exemplary Christian—looking to God, and "lifting up hands of prayer" for guidance in all things from the supreme ruler of the universe. We shall have occasion, subsequently, to speak more particularly of this humble and devoted piety—of the profound submission of this great man's heart to the will of his Maker. Never has that unwavering trust deserted him, in the gloomiest scenes of the war; and in his last moments he said calmly that he had no repinings or regrets for the loss of his arm; it was God's will, and whether his life was spared or not, he submitted himself with humility and entire confidence to the mercy of his Redeemer.

Such was the man to whom the authorities of Virginia looked when war threatened her frontier and a stout-hearted leader was required to drive back the enemy. Gov. Letcher will live forever in history as the official who conferred the first military commission in the Southern army on Jackson. He appointed him Colonel, the Virginia Convention unanimously approved the appointment, and Jackson speedily proceeded to Harper's Ferry, and took command of the small "Army of Observation" there on the 3d of May, 1861. Upon the approach of this force, Lieut. Jones, commanding the Federal forces, attempted the destruction of the armory and government works, and evacuated the place, which was immediately occupied by the Virginia troops.

CHAPTER III.

ENGAGEMENT AT FALLING WATERS.

Jackson remained in command of the forces in the Valley until May 23d, when General Joseph E. Johnston, formerly Quartermaster-general U. S. Army, and an officer of tried experience and courage, arrived and took command. The force which Jackson thus surrendered the command of to General Johnston consisted of nine regiments and two battalions of infantry, four companies of artillery, with sixteen pieces without caissons, harness, or horses, and about three hundred cavalry. All were undisciplined, several regiments without accoutrements, and the supply of ammunition was entirely inadequate for active operations.

But the character of the men who commanded this volunteer force was a sure guaranty that all defects would speedily be remedied. Johnston was a thorough soldier, and had his whole heart in the cause; Stuart, who commanded the cavalry, was characterized by untiring energy, clear judgment, and extraordinary powers of moulding and infusing his own brave spirit into the hearts of his men; and Pendleton, who was in charge of the artillery, was an excellent officer, with a complete knowledge of military matters, derived from his early education at West Point. The deficiency in harness for the artillery was readily supplied by the use of ropes and farm gearing; the cavalry were taught that more depended upon stout hearts, strong arms and the *élan* of the true cavalier, than on the number or excellence of weapons; and into the ardent youths of the infantry was infused the stern courage, the unyielding fortitude, the daring, the obstinacy, the unshrinking nerve of Jackson. With Stuart in command of his cavalry, Pendleton in charge of the artillery, and Jackson to lead his infantry force, General Johnston had an auspicious augury of the splendid results which, in spite of its small numbers, the army would surely achieve. Jackson had already begun to mould his troops into that impenetrable phalanx which stood stern and unbroken afterwards, amid scenes of the most frightful carnage, and whose battle-flag, pierced with balls and torn with shell, has never yet gone down before the foe. There, in the valley, he organized and gave its character to that brigade which afterwards took his own name of "Stonewall," and, as the "Stonewall Brigade," is known now and admired for its unshrinking courage and unsurpassed efficiency throughout the civilized world.

The pause in the storm did not last very long. Early in June General Johnston was advised of the advance of Patterson with a heavy force, and he made arrangements immediately for the evacuation of Harper's Ferry. A glance at the map, and a very slight knowledge of the ground, will exhibit the necessity of this movement. Harper's Ferry is untenable by any force not strong enough to take the field against an invading army and hold both sides of the Potomac. It is in a triangle; its only strong position, in the rear of the town, being exposed to enfilade and reverse fires from the Maryland Heights; and the place is liable to be flanked with ease by an enemy, crossing at Williamsport or other point above—Leesburg or other point below. General Johnston had information from "the indefatigable Stuart," as he styles him, who observed the whole river front with his cavalry, from Point of Rocks to beyond Williamsport, that Patterson was within a few hours' march of the Potomac, and McClellan supposed to be advancing from Western Virginia to form a junction with him at Romney; and, in consequence of this intelligence, he wisely determined to evacuate a position which it "perfectly suited the enemy's views" to have him occupy, and retire to Winchester, his true base of operations, where all the great highways converged. Thence he could oppose McClellan advancing from Romney, and Patterson from Martinsburg—had the Valley to fall back along if necessary—but, better than all, the way was open to Beauregard, who might need his assistance at Manassas. The new field of operations was chosen with the eye of the true soldier—from a veritable trap General Johnston emerged into an open field, where he could advance or retire at will, free as a ranger of the prairie, to strike, or stand on the defensive; and this new position he hastened to occupy. Colonel, now Major-general, A. P. Hill was dispatched with two regiments *via* Winchester towards Romney; and Johnston, after sending off all the heavy baggage and public property, destroyed the bridges over the Potomac, and fell back towards Winchester. A flank movement from Charlestown towards Bunker's Hill, a small town on the Martinsburg turnpike, frightened General Patterson greatly. That commander retreated, and General Johnston marched to Winchester. He had scarcely arrived, when information reached him that Patterson was again advancing, and Jackson, with his brigade, was sent to the neighborhood of Martinsburg, to support Stuart's Cavalry. Jackson's orders were to destroy such of the rolling stock of the Baltimore and Ohio Railroad as could not be brought off, but, if the enemy appeared, to retire before him to Winchester.

The two men who have since attracted so many eyes to their great deeds, and whose friendship remained close and warm to the moment when one of them passed away, were now thrown together in front of the Federal army—Stuart with his cavalry, and Jackson with his infantry!—a dangerous combination, whatever the force of the enemy; and so, indeed, it proved. Stuart, living in the saddle, and watching the enemy with lynx-eyed vigilance, suffered no movement of Patterson's to escape him, and, on one occasion, surprised a whole company, who were so much startled and alarmed by the officer's stentorian command to "Throw down their arms!" that the men, too, fell on their faces. Finding the enemy advancing in heavy force, Jackson, in obedience to orders, fell back before him. It has never been the habit of General Jackson, however, to omit any opportunity of striking a blow at the enemy. Whether in advancing or retiring, one of his cardinal maxims has been to inflict all the injury possible upon his foe; and this practice he inaugurated at Falling Waters. At that point he turned upon the heavy column of Patterson, posted the 5th Virginia and Pendleton's Battery in a skilfully selected position, and engaged the advanced force of the Federal army in an obstinately contested fight. The artillery was handled admirably, under the direct supervision of Jackson, and the 5th Virginia fought like veterans. The ground was held stubbornly, heavy loss inflicted on the enemy, and the Federals held completely in check. It was only when he was about to be outflanked that Jackson slowly retired, bringing off forty-five prisoners, and scarcely losing a man.

The engagement at Falling Waters was the first which

took place between the two armies, and the augury of future success was auspicious. Jackson had retired in a way peculiar to himself, had felt the enemy with a roughness which gave them little desire for a repetition of the ceremony, and his men saw that in their silent leader they had to do with a thorough soldier, whose nerve and judgment were equally admirable, and in whose hands the force would be fought with consummate courage and skill. Jackson was always Jackson—in small things as in great—in the skirmish as in the great battle—and the same eagle eye which chose the ground at Kernstown, Port Republic, and Groveton, ran along the thin line and saw that all was right at Falling Waters.

CHAPTER IV.

BATTLE OF MANASSAS.

But we linger too long amid these early scenes of the great soldier's career. Mightier events were on the march, and the Federal government was marshalling its huge masses to hurl them upon the main body of the "rebels" at Manassas. Here Jackson was to display in their fullest extent those heroic qualities of stubborn courage and dauntless resolution which characterized him; to win the name of "Stonewall" which will cling to him forever; and to arouse that enthusiasm which in the latter months of his life rendered him the idol of the popular heart. He continued to march and countermarch in front of Patterson, whom Johnston was never in a condition to attack—the Federal force amounting to about 32,000; until, on the 18th of July, a dispatch reached Winchester, announcing that the Northern army was advancing on Manassas. Gen. Johnston was directed, if practicable, to send his sick back to Culpepper Court-house, and go to Beauregard's assistance.

The good judgment shown by Gen. Johnston in his evacuation of Harper's Ferry now became apparent. The road to Manassas was open, and he speedily took steps to reinforce the army of the Potomac. To be able to do this it was necessary first to defeat Patterson, or to elude him. The latter course was chosen, and intrusting the disposition of the cavalry to Stuart to cover the movement, Johnston left Winchester to be defended by the militia of the region in earthworks, and commenced his march by way of Ashby's Gap, toward the East. Stuart, posting a cordon of pickets from Smithfield, along by Summit Point and Rippon to the Shenandoah, completely concealed the change of base; and Johnston's little army wended its way towards Manassas.

The valley region will long be alive with the traditions of this great flank movement, and the spirit exhibited by the men. They had so often formed line of battle in front of Patterson, only to retire afterwards without fighting, that the troops nearly broke out in open murmurs against their commander. They did not know that frequently, when his bristling guns threatened the foe with their grim muzzles from every hillock, those guns were *without a single round of ammunition;* and that no one could be more disappointed at the necessity which existed for retiring than their general. Now, however, when the order for a rapid march came, the troops perceived in the air, so to speak, the long looked-for odor of battle. They snuffed it up eagerly; and went on their way actually dancing for joy, and with deafening cheers. Through Frederick and Clarke, past Millwood, wading the Shenandoah and toiling up the rough pathway at Ashby's Gap, they went upon their way, without rations, ignorant of their destination, but knowing one thing only, that the moment for *action* had arrived. On the way a message from Beauregard reached Johnston by an officer who killed his horse to carry it—"If you wish to help me, now is the time." Johnston hastened on—his troops half famished, but "game" to the last.

Stuart drew in his pickets; slowly put his little column in motion to cover the rear, and having passed last through the mountains, pushed on to the front again. At Piedmont the exhausted infantry was placed upon a train of the Manassas Gap Railroad—the cavalry and artillery continuing their march. Gen. Johnston reached Manassas about noon, on the 20th July, preceded by the 7th and 8th Georgia and Jackson's brigade—the President of the railroad assuring him that the remainder of his force embarked on the cars should arrive during the day.

The complicated and exciting details of the first great battle of Manassas need not be given in this memoir of one of the actors therein, prominent as he was among the heroic souls who upon that day rolled back the great tide of invasion, pillage, and rapine. Gen. Johnston being the senior in rank, took command of the entire forces, but owing to Gen. Beauregard's superior knowledge of the ground, approved all his plans, and directed their execution under Beauregard's command.

Jackson with his brigade was placed in rear of Gen. Longstreet near Blackburn's Ford, the scene of the battle of the 18th. Let us look at the composition of this force which was on that day to win the name of the "Old Stonewall Brigade," and niche itself in history forever. It consisted of the 2d Virginia, Col. Allen; the 4th Virginia, Col. James L. Preston; the 5th Virginia, Col. Harper; the 27th Virginia, Lieut.-col. Echols; and the 33d Virginia, Col. Cumming. It embraced the flower of the young men of the Valley of Virginia—the best and bravest youths of all the land—and was to show by its decimated ranks, and the entire disappearance finally of every one of its original officers, with what heroic courage it opposed its bosom to every danger. It was 2,611 strong; and was on the morning of the 21st posted, as we have said, in rear of Longstreet, behind the skirting of pines near Blackburn's and Mitchell's Fords.

From this position, however, Jackson was, at seven in the morning, ordered to move more to the left, between Bonham's left and Cocke's right, to support either in case the enemy attacked. He remained here until ten or eleven, when he rapidly pushed forward with his brigade to support Bee, Bartow, and Evans, whose commands, exhausted by their desperate contest during the whole forenoon, were mingled and in disorder. Taking position below the brim of the plateau, nearly east of the Henry House, and to the left of the woods occupied by the weary commands above mentioned, Jackson opened with his artillery, with great effect, and held the enemy in check until Gen. Johnston came up, with Gen. Beauregard, and took direct command of the shattered forces, which he led in person to the charge, the colors of the 4th Alabama at his side.

The presence of Johnston and Beauregard acted upon the forces like a charm. As they galloped up and down the lines, the men cheered wildly and seemed burning to renew the contest. A new line of battle was instantly formed—with Bee and Evans on the right; Jackson in the centre, with four regiments and thirteen pieces of artillery; and on the left, Gartrell, Smith, Falkner, Fisher, and other commanders of regiments or battalions. The force which thus confronted the overwhelmning columns of the enemy consisted of about 6,500 infantry and artillerists, and two companies of Stuart's cavalry. The enemy's force which now bore hotly and confidently down on the little band of Southerners, was by their own official history of the day, 20,000 infantry, seven companies of regular cavalry and twenty-four pieces of improved artillery, most of it rifled, while ours were nearly all smooth bore. Heavy reinforcements were held in reserve by the Federal commander; and as far as human intelligence could estimate the future, it seemed certain that the thin line of Southerners would be broken and annihilated by the mere weight of their opponents. But one serious element was left out of the calculation. The cause in which the men of the South fought—and the character of those forces, from the highest officer to the humblest private. On one side, the demoniac lust of spoil and rapine—a mad and infamous invasion of a great people's homes and firesides, with "Booty and Beauty" for the watchword: subjugation the result aimed at by their legions. On the other, a great race fighting in defence of their soil, their families—the very little ones at their knees—for freedom and home and sacred honor. They were led by Johnston, Beauregard, Jackson—those noble types of the mighty Anglo-Saxon race; and with such a cause and such leaders, the little band of Southerners were more than a match for their swarming foes.

It was now two o'clock in the afternoon. The enemy had full possession of the plateau upon which Robinson's and the Henry House were situated. It was necessary to drive them from it; and Gen. Beauregard gave the order for the entire right of his line, with the exception of the reserves, to advance. The Southerners rushed forward with wild cheers, and gained the plateau in face of a tremendous fire, Jackson's brigade piercing the enemy's centre, with the determined courage of veterans and carrying all before them. They suffered heavily, and the ground was strewn with some of the noblest youths of the South; but the plateau was recovered, and the Federal lines broken and swept back at all points. The splendid courage of the Southerners covered them with glory; but their triumph was short-lived. The enemy threw forward heavy reinforcements—attacked our exhausted lines; and by pure weight of numbers drove the Southerners back, retaking their guns and recovering all the ground which they had lost.

This was the turning point of the whole contest. If the enemy were left in possession of this vantage ground thus gained the struggle was over, and nothing remained for Beauregard but to withdraw his shattered and defeated columns in the best order possible before their victorious assailants. But such a thought never entered the brain of that great soldier or his comrades. It was "do or die"—victory or death; and the broken lines were again marshalled for a desperate and final struggle. Just as Beauregard had ordered forward his entire line, including all his reserves, and galloping forward, had taken command of them in person, reinforcements pushed forward by Johnston appeared upon the field, and a general attack of the whole force was made all along the line. The fighting which ensued was desperate—terrific. All thought but victory seemed to be discarded by the Southerners, and they charged madly over piles of dead, with a vigor and desperation which no opponents could resist. Jackson was everywhere in the thickest of the fight, cheering on his noble brigade, and holding it steady under the terrific fire which mowed down whole ranks of them and their comrades. A more desperate struggle has perhaps never occurred in the history of the world than that which took place on that field near Manassas, between the hours of half-past two and four o'clock, on the 21st of July, 1861—and the occasion was one to try the nerves of the stoutest heart that ever beat. The Southern leaders saw with irrepressible anguish the exhaustion of the troops, the waning fortunes of the day, and the countless reserves which the enemy hurled incessantly upon their thin and weary lines. Among these was the heroic Gen. Bee, in command of the 4th Alabama and some Mississippians who were nearly worn out by the terrible ordeal through which they had passed. Bee rode up and down the lines cheering on the men and beseeching them by all they held dear not to give way, when he met Jackson and said in the bitter despair of his heart, "General, they are beating us back." The face of the stern silent soldier betrayed no answering emotion. The keen eye glittered for an instant; the lips opened; and in the curt, peculiar tones of the speaker he said: "Sir, we will give them the bayonet." Bee seemed to gather new inspiration from the words; he galloped baek to the remnants of his command, and pointing to Jackson, called out to his men:

"*There is Jackson standing like a stonewall! Let us determine to die here, and we will conquer! Follow me!*"

The words echoed like a bugle blast in the ears of his brave troops—they rallied; and taking the head of the column, Bee charged the enemy, falling mortally wounded in the front.

It was just at this time that General Kirby Smith arrived with his fresh troops, which he had disembarked from the cars, and rapidly pushed forward towards the battle-field; and with his batteries he opened a destructive fire upon the enemy's right and centre. At half-past three the Federal forces were driven back on their left and centre, but formed a new and formidable line of battle in the shape of a crescent, from the Carter House across the turnpike to Chinn's house. They had lost heart, however, in the long and bloody struggle. Their leaders could not bring them up again to the contest. Before the resolute advance of our troops, mainly directed against their right flank and rear, they gave ground, were driven over the narrow plateau into the fields beyond, and the rout became general. Their torn and bleeding columns were pursued by our cavalry which, earlier in the day, under Colonel Stuart, had made a splendid charge upon a regiment of Zouaves, scattering and riding them down; and had this cavalry force been sufficient, but few of the routed forces of the Federals would have escaped to tell the tale of their reverses to the gaping citizens of Washington.

Thus terminated the hard-fought battle of Manassas, in which the army of the Shenandoah gained undying laurels. Jackson's men had fought with that matchless daring which has since made the name of the first brigade immortal; and, though painfully wounded in the hand, their great leader was filled with joy and pride. The country had gained a splendid victory against enormous odds; and although he did not then know it, Jackson had gained a name with which he is forever inseparably identified. When the heroic Bee exclaimed:

"There is Jackson standing *like a stonewall.* Let us determine to die here, and we will conquer," he unconsciously employed a term which thenceforth clung to Jackson more closely than his baptismal appellation. From that hot day of battle the leader of the men of the valley was known as "Stonewall Jackson"—his command as the "Stonewall Brigade." Many are ignorant, and few recall the fact that the great soldier was christened "Thomas Jonathan." His veritable christening in the popular heart was on that evening of Manassas, when Bee, about to surrender his great soul to his Maker, baptized him, amid blood and fire, "STONEWALL JACKSON."

CHAPTER V.

JACKSON'S FAREWELL TO THE OLD BRIGADE.

SUCH was the part taken by the thenceforward famous leader in the great battle of Manassas. He had held a subordinate position in the contest, and the force under his command was small; but the masterly handling of his troops, and the obstinate stand which they made, justified Jackson in the statement which he proudly made in taking leave of them soon afterwards: that they had decided the fate of the battle.

The morning of Jackson's fame had scarcely dawned, however. He had secured that immortal name which will forever characterize him; but the arena had been too limited for the full display of his splendid faculties, and few suspected the existence of those inexhaustible resources of strategy and daring which lay hid beneath the calm exterior of the silent Virginian. The time was soon to come, however, when these great faculties would blaze out before the eyes of the world, surrounding their possessor with a halo of almost dazzling splendor, and when the deeds of the man, Stonewall Jackson, would ring throughout the civilized world, making his very enemies bear tribute to the matchless genius which struck and overwhelmed them.

After the battle of Manassas, Jackson remained with his brigade near Centreville until the early part of October, having during that time made but one movement—in the direction of Fairfax Court-house, when Gen. Beauregard, by advancing and then falling back, endeavored to draw McClellan out of his earthworks. About the month of September, Jackson, who had been made a Brigadier-general before he left the Valley, was advanced to the rank of Major-general, and assigned to the command of the troops in and around Winchester, then threatened by a large Federal army under Gen. Banks. To his great sorrow, the old First Brigade, which he had so long commanded, was to stay behind with the main army, and there took place, at the camp of the brigade, near Centreville, on the 4th of October, one of those scenes which irresistibly excite the deepest emotions of the heart, and light up the page of history which records them.

On that day Jackson took leave of his old "First Brigade." The officers and men were drawn up as though in line of battle, and their commander appeared in front, as he had so often appeared before, when about to give the order for a charge upon the enemy. But now, no enthusiasm, no cheers awaited him. All knew for what purpose he came, and the sorrow which filled every heart, betrayed itself in the deep silence which greeted his approach. Not a sound along the line—not a hand raised in greeting—not a murmur, even, going to show that they recognized their beloved captain. The bronzed faces were full of the deepest dejection, and the stern fighters of the old brigade were like children about to be separated from their father.

Jackson approached, and mastering his emotion by an effort, said, in the short abrupt tones with which all were so familiar:

"I am not here to make a speech, but simply to say farewell. I first met you at Harper's Ferry in the commencement of this war, and I cannot take leave of you without giving expression to my admiration of your conduct from that day to this—whether on the march, the bivouac, the tented field, or on the bloody Plains of Manassas, where you gained the well-deserved reputation of having decided the fate of the battle. Throughout the broad extent of country over which you have marched, by your respect for the rights and the property of citizens, you have shown that you were soldiers, not only to defend, but able and willing both to defend and protect. You have already gained a brilliant and deservedly high reputation throughout the army of the whole Confederacy, and I trust in the future, by your deeds on the field, and by the assistance of the same kind Providence who has heretofore favored our cause, you will gain more victories, and add additional lustre to the reputation you now enjoy. You have already gained a proud position in the future history of this our second war of independence. I shall look with great anxiety to your future movements, and I trust, whenever I shall hear of the *First Brigade* on the field of battle, it will be of still nobler deeds achieved, and higher reputation won!"

Having uttered these words, Jackson paused for an instant, and his eye passed slowly along the line, as though he wished thus to bid farewell individually to every old familiar face, so often seen in the heat of battle, and so dear to him. The thoughts which crowded upon him seemed more than he could bear—he could not leave them with such formal words only—and that iron lip, which had never trembled in the hour of deadliest peril, now quivered. Mastered by an uncontrollable impulse, the great soldier rose in his stirrups, threw the reins on the neck of his horse with an emphasis which sent a thrill through every heart, and extending his arm, added in tones of the deepest feeling:

"In the army of the Shenandoah you were the *First Bri-*

gade! In the army of the Potomac you were the *First Brigade!* In the second corps of the army you are the *First Brigade!* You are the *First Brigade* in the affections of your general; and I hope by your future deeds and bearing you will be handed down to posterity as the *First Brigade* in this our second war of independence. Farewell!"

As the last words echoed in their ears, and Jackson turned to leave them the long-pent-up feeling burst forth. Three prolonged and deafening cheers rolled along the line of the old brigade; and no sooner had they died away, than they were renewed, and again renewed. The calm face of the great leader flushed as he listened to that sound, but he did not speak. Waving his hand in token of farewell, he galloped away, and the old brigade deprived of its beloved chief, returned slowly and sorrowfully to camp.

CHAPTER VI.

THE WINTER EXPEDITION TO ROMNEY.

JACKSON proceeded to Winchester, and taking command of the forces there, applied himself energetically to the work of organizing the raw levies from the surrounding country. Gen. Loring's command from Western Virginia was subsequently assigned to him—and he succeeded in regaining his old Stonewall Brigade, which returned to him, and went into camp near Kernstown, in the latter days of November.

On the 1st of January, 1862, Gen. Jackson sent out an expedition to Bath and Romney, where the Federal forces were committing the most wanton depredations, and ruling the whole region with a rod of iron. The day was exceedingly bright and beautiful—the air soft and balmy—and the men left behind them their overcoats, and even their blankets, expecting the wagons to follow and join them before these articles were needed. The wagons did not come up, however; and on the third day of the march, when, after winding about among by-ways and paths they had reached Unger's Cross Roads, the weather suddenly changed, and a freezing snow-storm came on. From Unger's three roads radiate—one to Romney, another to Martinsburg, and a third to Bath, better known as Berkeley Springs. The latter road was the one which Jackson now pursued.

This expedition is only remarkable for the great powers of endurance which it betrayed in the men; peremptory orders from the War Office at Richmond having arrested his further advance, almost before he had commenced the execution of the design which he had in view. The weather was really terrible. It has been truthfully said that Napoleon's passage of the Alps scarcely surpassed the march. Rain, snow, hail, sleet, beat upon the troops who were without tents, overcoats, or blankets, as has been stated; and had it not been for bivouac fires many of the soldiers must have perished. Subsequently, from the close proximity of the enemy not even fires were allowed, and the feet of some of the men froze to the soles of their boots. "I built a big fire," says a gallant young soldier whose notes of the march are before us, "and went to sleep by it; but waked up about 12 o'clock at night and found the fire out, and about three inches of snow over me." He, like the rest, had left his blankets, and this winding sheet covered that night the whole slumbering army.

The difficulties of the march were fourfold for the trains. The roads were covered with ice two inches thick, and so thoroughly glazed by the sleet that horses and men kept their feet only with the greatest difficulty. Men were slipping and their guns going off all along the line—"thousands fell flat every day," says an eye-witness—and both men and horses were often seriously hurt. The knees and muzzles of the horses were terribly injured—they were seen limping along, crippled and streaming with blood—but still Jackson pressed on. Wagon after wagon slid off and turned bottom upward, in spite of every attempt to steady them. One train of wagons and artillery took from daylight until 3 P. M., to pass a hilly point—heavy details of men steadying the animals, and almost lifting the vehicles along. Jackson, however, continued his march, his plans not admitting of delay; and soon came upon the advance of the enemy about six miles from Bath, in Morgan county. Here he had a sharp skirmish, the Virginians, under Col. Patton, driving the enemy back, and capturing about thirty prisoners. This was followed up by an attack on the force which held possession of the town, who were in like manner defeated and driven across the Potomac, which they were forced to wade on one of the coldest nights ever known in that region.

Jackson, having cleared the path thus far, now made a flank movement in the direction of Romney to fall upon the Federal force stationed there, and committing every outrage upon the citizens. His movements were rapid but not so rapid as those of the enemy. They were at least 12,000 in number, but had no desire to meet the Confederates, evacuating Romney and falling back before Jackson got within a day's march of the place. Large supplies were captured at Romney, to which Jackson now advanced, and the enemy in his front were completely dispersed. It behooved him to guard his communications however from attack, and leaving Gen. Loring at Romney, he returned with his old Stonewall Brigade to Winchester to watch the enemy toward Harper's Ferry.

Such was the position of affairs when the order above mentioned was sent to Gen. Loring to fall back from Romney. This he promptly did, and soon afterward the enemy were in possession of Moorefield. The facts of this expedition are little known. When they are fully set forth, as they doubtless will be some day, the movements and designs of Jackson will be understood and appreciated at their just value.

Operations during the remainder of the winter were not important, though Dam No. 5, on the Potomac, was completely destroyed, and the enemy to that extent damaged. A desultory warfare of pickets was kept up along the river—both armies awaiting the opening of Spring for serious military movements.

Early in March the enemy began to move, and Jackson received information that they were about to attack him at Winchester with an overwhelming force. Shields soon afterwards advanced, and Jackson offered battle to his advance force on two successive days. This was, however, declined, and the main body of the enemy having come up, Jackson, on March 11th, evacuated Winchester, slowly falling back before them. He had, as was usual with him, secured every thing in the shape of public stores, and none of the fruits of his expeditions fell again into the hands of the enemy. Trains, cars, engines from the Baltimore and Ohio Railroad had all been sent to the rear—and the men had been greeted with the unique spectacle of one huge railroad engine rolling slowly along the valley turnpike toward Staunton, drawn by forty-two horses. Nothing was thus left for the enemy, pressing now into Winchester, and Jackson's little army of about 3,000 men continued slowly to retire in face of the foe. Ashby with his cavalry held the rear, and obstinately disputed every inch of ground with the on-pressing enemy. Chew's battery supported him, and the roar of the guns was the "lullaby and reveille" of the little army.

CHAPTER VII.

THE BATTLE OF KERNSTOWN.

JACKSON crept slowly along up the valley, accelerating his motions as he proceeded. But on the 21st of March he received a dispatch from Ashby stating that the enemy had evacuated and fallen back from Strasburg. His resolution was promptly taken, and the men although greatly fatigued with their long march were, on the 22d, faced about and marched rapidly down the valley toward Winchester again, Jackson determined to press the enemy and divert from their intended march a body of about 15,000 men, under General Sedgwick, who were then moving by way of Snicker's Gap, to join the Federal force operating against Gen. Johnston; and his troops were accordingly pushed forward with the greatest possible rapidity toward Winchester.

They consisted of Ashby's cavalry, which, with Chew's battery, already held the front—Col. Fulkerson's brigade, consisting of the 23d and 37th Virginia and Shumaker's battery; Brigadier-general Garnett's brigade, consisting of the 2d, 4th, 5th, 27th, and 33d Virginia (the "old Stonewall Brigade"), and McLaughlin's, Carpenter's, and Waters' batteries; Col. Burks' brigade, consisting of the 21st, 42d, and 48th Virginia, and the 1st battalion Virginia regulars and Marye's battery. All the regiments except the 48th, which was the rear-guard, arrived within a mile or two of Kernstown, a place about two miles south of Winchester, by two o'clock on the afternoon of the 23d of March, and bivouacked there that night.

During the march information had reached Gen. Jackson from a reliable source, that the enemy were sending off their stores and troops from Winchester; and, after arriving near Kernstown, he learned from a source which had been remarkable for reliability, that the Federal force of infantry at Winchester did not exceed four regiments. A large body of the enemy was leaving the valley, and had already reached Castleman's Ferry (leading to Snicker's Gap) on the Shenandoah. Though it was very desirable to prevent the enemy from leaving the valley, Gen. Jackson deemed it best not to attack until the morning; but subsequently ascertaining that the enemy had a position from which his forces could be seen, he concluded that it would be dangerous to postpone it until the next day, as reinforcements might be brought up during the night.

After ascertaining that the troops, part of which had marched more than fourteen miles since dawn, and Garnett's and Burks' brigades, which had made a forced march of nearly twenty-five miles on the previous day, were in good spirits at the prospect of meeting the enemy, Gen. Jackson determined to advance at once.

Leaving Col. Ashby with his command on the Valley turnpike, with Col. Burks' brigade as a support to the batteries, and also to act as a reserve, the general moved with one piece of Carpenter's battery and Col. Fulkerson's brigade, supported by Gen. Garnett's to the left, for the purpose of securing a commanding position on the enemy's right, and, thus turning him by that flank, force him back from his strong position in front which prevented a direct advance. Soon after Carpenter brought up his other pieces, McLaughlin's and Waters' batteries also came forward; the eminence was reached; and the three batteries under their respective captains commenced playing upon the enemy whose position was now commanded. Jackson continued to advance his artillery, keeping up a continuous fire upon the enemy on his right—while Col. Echols with his regiment, the 27th, with its skirmishers thrown forward, kept in advance, and opened the infantry engagement, supported by the 21st, under Col. Patton, no other regiment of Gen. Garnett's command having come up. Well did these two regiments do their duty, driving back the enemy twice in quick succession. A severe wound compelling the noble leader of the 27th to leave the field, the command devolved upon the Lieut.-colonel, the dauntless Grigsby, whose officers and men behaved admirably.

Col. Fulkerson having advanced his brigade, consisting of the 23d and 37th, respectively under the command of Col. Taliaferro, and Lieut.-col. Carson, to the left of Col. Echols, judiciously posted it behind a stone wall, toward which the enemy were rapidly advancing, and opened a destructive fire, which drove back the Federal forces in great disorder, after sustaining a heavy loss, and leaving the colors of one of their regiments upon the field. This part of the enemy's routed troops having, to some extent, rallied in another position, were also driven from this by Col. Fulkerson. Soon after the 27th had been engaged, Gen. Garnett, with the 2d, 4th, and 33d Virginia, commanded respectively by Col. Allen, Lieut.-col. Ronald, and Col. Cummings, moved forward and joined in the battle, which now became general. The 1st Virginia battalion, P. A. C. S., under Capt. Bridgford, though it unfortunately became separated in advancing, was in the engagement; and from near five to half-past six P. M., there was almost a continuous roar of musketry, the enemy's repulsed regiments being replaced by fresh ones from his large reserves. As the ammunition of some of the Confederate troops became exhausted, noble instances were seen of their borrowing from comrades, by whose sides they continued to fight, as though resolved to die rather than give way. The troops were fighting under great disadvantages, but it was unfortunate that Gen. Garnett ordered his men to fall back, as the enemy's advance would otherwise have been retarded, and an opportunity afforded the reserves to come up and take part in the engagement. The advance of the enemy, consequent upon this movement, enabled them to turn Fulkerson's right and force him to fall back—but the presence of General Jackson soon counteracted this dangerous state of things. The 5th

Virginia was assigned a position which it held until the arrival of Colonel Burks, with the 42d, under Lieut.-col. Langhorne. Col. Burks and the officers and men of the 42d proved themselves worthy of the cause which they were defending, by the spirit with which this regiment took and held its position until its left was turned by the enemy, pressing upon the 5th as it fell back. Col. John Campbell was rapidly advancing with his regiment to take part in the struggle; but night, and an indisposition on the part of the enemy to press further, had terminated the battle, which had commenced about 4 o'clock in the afternoon. Leaving Ashby in front, Gen. Jackson fell back with the remainder of his command to the wagons, and bivouacked for the night.

The artillery had played its part well in the battle, but we lost two pieces—one belonging to McLaughlin's, the other to Waters' battery; the former from having upset when hard pressed by the enemy, and the latter from having its horses killed when on the eve of leaving the field which it had so well swept with grape as to have driven back the enemy from a part of it, over which he was pressing about the close of the battle. During the engagement, Col. Ashby, with a portion of his command, including Chew's battery, remained on the Confederate right, and not only protected the rear in the vicinity of the Valley turnpike, but also threatened the enemy's front and left. Ashby fully sustained his high reputation by the able discharge of the important trust confided to him by Jackson.

Owing to the exhausting march which the infantry had made since the morning of the day previous to the battle—between thirty-five and forty miles—many of them were left behind. Jackson's army, present on the evening of the battle, consisted of 3,087 infantry, of which 2,742 were engaged, and 27 pieces of artillery, of which 18 were engaged. Owing to the recent heavy duty and the extent of country to be picketed, only 290 cavalry were present to take part in the engagement. There is reason to believe that the Federal infantry on the field numbered over 11,000, of which probably over 8,000 were engaged. Their artillery engaged equalled or exceeded ours, and their cavalry force was larger. Our loss was 80 killed, 342 wounded. A few days after the battle a Federal officer stated that their loss in killed was 418. Their wounded, upon the supposition that they bore the same relation to their killed as ours, must have been such as to have made their total loss more than three times that of the Confederates. The wounded of Jackson's army received that care and attention from the noble women of Winchester which they knew so well how to give, and the dead were buried by the loyal citizens of the town. The hospitalities of Baltimoreans relieved the wants of the captured.

Though the battle of Kernstown did not enable Jackson to recover possession of Winchester, yet the more important object at the moment—that of calling back troops that were leaving the valley, and thus preventing a junction of Banks' command with other forces, was fully accomplished; and a heavy loss in killed and wounded inflicted upon an enemy greatly the superior of Jackson in numbers. Thus, though the field remained in possession of the enemy, all the most essential fruits of the battle remained in the hands of the Confederates.

CHAPTER VIII.

THE BATTLE OF M'DOWELL.

After the battle of Kernstown, Gen. Jackson retreated in the direction of Harrisonburg. His rear-guard, comprising Ashby's cavalry, Capt. Chew's battery, and from time to time other forces, was placed under the direction of Col. Turner

Ashby, an officer whose judgment, coolness, and courage, eminently qualified him for this delicate and important trust.

Although pursued by a greatly superior force under Banks, Jackson halted for more than a fortnight in the vicinity of Mount Jackson. After reaching Harrisonburg he turned toward the Blue Ridge, and on April 19th, crossed the South Fork of the Shenandoah, and took position between that river and Swift Run Gap, in Elk Run Valley. Gen. Ewell having been directed to join the main body, left the vicinity of Gordonsville, and on April 30th arrived with his division on the West of the Blue Ridge.

The main body of Banks' pursuing army did not proceed further south than the vicinity of Harrisonburg; but a considerable force under the command of Gen. Milroy was moving toward Staunton from the direction of Monterey—and, as Gen. Jackson was informed, on good authority, part of it had already crossed to the East of the Shenandoah Mountain, and was encamped not far from the Harrisonburg and Warm Spring turnpike. The positions of the two Federal armies were now such, that, if left unmolested, they could readily form a junction on the road just named, and move with their united forces against Staunton.

At this time Gen. Edward Johnson, with his troops, was near Buffalo Gap, west of Staunton; so that if the enemy was allowed to effect a junction it would probably be followed, not only by the seizure of a point so important as Staunton, but must compel Gen. Johnson to abandon his position, and might succeed in placing the enemy between him and Jackson. To avoid these results, Gen. Jackson determined, if practicable, after strengthening his own division by a union with Johnson's, first to strike at Milroy, and then to concentrate the forces of Ewell, Johnson, and his own against Banks. To carry out his design against Milroy, Gen. Ewell was directed to march his division to the position then occupied by Jackson, in Elk Run Valley, with a view to holding Banks in check, while Jackson pushed on with his division to Staunton. These movements were made. At Staunton Gen. Jackson found, according to his previous arrangements, Major-gen. Smith, of the Virginia Military Institute, with his corps of cadets ready to co-operate with him in the defence of that portion of the Valley.

On the morning of May 7th, Gen. Johnson, whose familiarity with this mountain region, and high qualities as a soldier, admirably fitted him for the advance, moved with his command in the direction of the enemy, followed by the brigades of Gen. Taliaferro, Col. Campbell, and Gen. Winder, in the order named. Encountering the enemy's advance near the point where the Staunton and Parkersburg turnpike intersects the Harrisonburg and Warm Springs turnpike, Gen. Johnson pressed forward. The enemy rapidly retreated, abandoning their baggage at Rodgers' and other points east of the Shenandoah Mountain. Atter the advance had reached the western base of the Shenandoah Mountain, the troops bivouacked for the night.

On the following morning the march was resumed, Gen. Johnson's brigade still in front. The head of the column was halted near the top of Bull Pasture Mountain, and Gen. Johnson, accompanied by a party of thirty men and several officers, with a view to a reconnoissance of the enemy's position, ascended Setlington's Hill, an isolated spur of the Bull Pasture Mountain, on the left of the turnpike, and commanding a full view of the valley of McDowell. From this point the position and to some extent the strength of the enemy could be seen. In the valley in which McDowell is situated, he observed a considerable force of infantry. To the right on a height were two regiments—but too distant for an effective fire to that point. Almost a mile in front was a battery supported by infantry. The enemy, observing the reconnoitring party, sent out a small body of skirmishers, which was promptly met by the men with Gen. Johnson and driven back.

For the purpose of securing the hill, all of Gen. Johnson's regiments were sent to him. The 52d Virginia being the first to reach the ground was posted on the left as skirmishers; and it was not long before they were engaged in a brisk encounter with the enemy's skirmishers whom they gallantly repulsed. Soon after this, three other regiments arrived and were posted as follows: the 12th Georgia on the crest of the hill and forming the centre of the line; the 58th Virginia on the left to support the 52d; and the 44th Virginia on the right near a ravine.

Milroy, having been reinforced during the day by Gen. Schenck, determined to carry the hill if possible by a direct attack. Advancing his force along its western slope, protected in his advance by the character of the ground, and the woods interposed in front of the Confederate forces, and driving our skirmishers before him, he emerged from the wood and poured a galling fire into our right which was returned, and a brisk and animated contest was kept up for some time—when the two remaining regiments of Johnson's brigade, the 25th and 31st, coming up, they were posted to the right. The fire was now rapid and well sustained on both sides; and the conflict fierce and sanguinary. In ascending to the crest of the hill from the turnpike, the troops had to pass to the left through the wood by a narrow and rough route. To prevent the possibility of the enemy's advancing along the turnpike, and seizing the point where the troops left the road to ascend the hill, the 31st Virginia was posted between that point and the town, and when ordered to join the brigade in action, its place was supplied by the 21st Virginia.

The engagement had now not only become general along the entire line, but so intense that Jackson ordered Gen. Taliaferro to the support of Gen. Johnson. Accordingly the 23d and 37th Virginia were advanced to the centre of the line, which was then held by the 12th Georgia with heroic gallantry; and the 10th Virginia was ordered to support the 52d, which had already driven the enemy from the left, and had now advanced to make a flank movement on him. At this time, the enemy was pressing forward in strong force on Jackson's extreme right, with a view of flanking that position. This movement was speedily detected, and met by Gen. Taliaferro's brigade and the 12th Georgia with great promptness. Further to check it, portions of the 25th and 31st Virginia regiments were sent to occupy an elevated piece of woodland on our right and rear—so situated as to fully command the position of the enemy. The brigade commanded by Col. Campbell coming up about this time was, together with the 10th Virginia, ordered down the ridge into the woods to guard against movements against the Confederate right flank, which they, in connection with the other force, effectually prevented.

The battle lasted about four hours—from half-past four in the afternoon until half-past eight. Every attempt by front or flank movement to attain the crest of the hill where our line was formed was signally and effectually repulsed. Finally, after dark, the enemy ceased firing and retired. Their artillery, posted on a hill in Jackson's front, was active in throwing shot and shell, up to the period when the infantry fight commenced; but, in consequenee of the great angle of elevation at which they fired, and the sheltered position of the Confederates, they inflicted no loss upon the Southern troops. Jackson did not bring up his artillery; there being no road to the rear by which his guns could be withdrawn in case of disaster; and the prospect of successfully using them did not compensate for the risk.

Gen. Johnson, to whom Jackson intrusted the management of the troops engaged, proved himself eminently worthy of the confidence reposed in him by the skill, gallantry, and presence of mind which he displayed on the occasion. Having received a wound near the close of the engagement, which compelled him to leave the field, he turned over the command to General Taliaferro. During the night the enemy made a hurried retreat toward Franklin, in Pendleton county, leaving their dead upon the field. Before doing so, however, they succeeded in destroying most of their ammunition, camp equipage, and commissary stores, which they could not remove. The loss of the Confederates in the battle of McDowell was 71 killed, and 390 wounded, making a total loss of 461. Among the killed and wounded were Colonel Gibbons, of the 10th Virginia; Col. Harman, of the 52d; Col. Smith and Major Higginbotham, of the 25th, and Maj. Campbell, of the 42d Virginia.

To prevent Banks from reinforcing Milroy, Mr. J. Hotchkiss, who was on topographical duty with the army, proceeded with a party to blockade the roads through North River and Dry River Gaps, whilst a detachment of cavalry obstructed the road through Brock's Gap. As the enemy continued to fight until night, and retreated before morning, but few of their number were captured. Besides quartermaster and commissary stores, some arms and other ordnance stores fell into the hands of the Confederates.

Leaving Lieutenant-colonel Preston, with a detachment of cadets and a small body of cavalry, in charge of the prisoners and public property, Jackson, with the main body of the army, preceded by a body of cavalry under Capt. Sheets, pursued the retreating enemy to the vicinity of Franklin—but succeeded in capturing only a few prisoners and stores along the line of march. The junction between Banks and Milroy having been prevented, and becoming satisfied of the impracticability of capturing the defeated enemy, owing to the mountainous character of the country, which was favorable to the escape of a retreating force, Jackson determined, as the enemy had made another stand at Franklin, with a prospect of being soon reinforced, that he would not attempt to press further, but return to the open country of the Shenandoah Valley—hoping to defeat Banks before he should receive reinforcements. Accordingly, on Thursday, May 15th, the army, after Divine service, to render thanks to God for the victory, began to retrace its steps.

CHAPTER IX.

THE BATTLE OF WINCHESTER.

FROM the pursuit of Milroy and Schenck toward Franklin, General Jackson returned to McDowell on the 14th of May. On the following day he crossed the Shenandoah Mountain and encamped that night near the Lebanon White Sulphur Springs. Here the troops were halted for a short time after their fatiguing marches, to enable them to attend Divine service, and to observe the fast recommended by the proclamation of President Davis. On the 17th May the march was resumed toward Harrisonburg.

In the mean time, while the pursuit of the Federal troops west of the Shenandoah Mountain was in progress, General Banks had fallen back to Strasburg, which position it was understood he was fortifying. General Jackson moved from Harrisonburg down the Valley turnpike to New Market, in the vicinity of which a junction was effected with Ewell's division, which had marched from Elk Run Valley. Leaving the Valley turnpike at New Market, General Jackson marched his forces, via Luray, toward Front Royal, with the hope of being able to capture or disperse the garrison at the latter place, and get in rear of Banks, or compel him to abandon his fortifications at Strasburg. To conceal this movement as far as possible from the enemy, General Jackson directed Brigadier-general Ashby, who had remained in front of Banks during the march against Milroy, to continue to hold that position until the following day, when he was to join the main body—leaving, however, a covering force sufficient to prevent information of the movement against Banks' rear from crossing the lines.

Jackson's command at this time embraced Ashby's cavalry;

the 1st ("Stonewall") Brigade, under General Winder; the 2d Brigade, Col. Campbell commanding; the 3d Brigade, Col. Fulkerson commanding; the troops recently under command of Brigadier-general Edward Johnson; and the division of Gen. Ewell, comprising the brigades of Gens. Elzey, Trimble, and Taylor; and the Maryland Line, consisting of the 1st Maryland regiment and Brockenbrough's battery, under Brigadier-general Geo. H. Stewart, and the 2d and 6th Virginia cavalry, under Colonel Flournoy.

On Thursday, May 22, Jackson moved with his entire command down the road leading from Luray to Front Royal—the advance, under Gen. Ewell, bivouacking about ten miles from the last-named place. Moving at dawn on Friday, the 23d, and diverging to the right so as to fall into the Gooney Manor road, Jackson encountered no opposition until he came within a mile and a half of Front Royal—when, about two in the afternoon, the enemy's pickets were encountered and driven in by our advance, which was ordered to follow rapidly. The 1st Maryland regiment, supported by Wheat's battalion of Louisiana Volunteers and the remainder of Taylor's brigade acting as a reserve, pushed forward in gallant style, charging the Federals, who made a spirited resistance, driving them through the town and taking some prisoners. The main force of the enemy now retired a short distance beyond Front Royal, and took position on a commanding height to the right of the turnpike. From this point they opened rifled artillery upon our troops as they advanced beyond the town. Col. Crutchfield, Chief of Artillery, placed some guns in position to dislodge them; and the 6th Louisiana was moved to the left through the woods, to flank their battery. But, in the mean time, Wheat's battalion and the 1st Maryland, Col. Bradley F. Johnson, advancing more directly, and driving in their skirmishers, the Federals retreated across both forks of the Shenandoah, attempting, in their retreat, to burn the bridge over the North Fork. Before they could fully accomplish their purpose our troops were upon them, extinguished the flames, and crossed the river—the enemy in full retreat towards Winchester, and our artillery and infantry in pursuit. The cavalry, under Gen. Ashby and Col. Flournoy, had crossed the south fork of the Shenandoah at McCoy's Ford, above the enemy's position, for the purpose of destroying the railroad and telegraphic communication between Front Royal and Strasburg; and also to check the advance of any reinforcements from Strasburg, or the retreat of any portion of the enemy in that direction from Front Royal. Colonel Flournoy kept a short distance west of that river, and having executed his orders, was now in readiness to join in pursuit of the retreating enemy. Delayed by difficulties at the bridge over the North Fork, which the enemy had made an effort to burn, Col. Flournoy pushed on with four companies of the 6th Virginia cavalry, and came up with a body of Federal troops near Cedarville, about five miles from Front Royal. This force consisted of two companies of cavalry, two pieces of artillery, the 1st Federal regiment of Maryland infantry, and two companies of Pennsylvania infantry, which had been posted there to check our pursuit. Dashing into the midst of them, Captain Grimsby, of Company B, in the advance, these four companies drove the enemy from their position, who soon, however, re-formed in an orchard on the right of the turnpike, when a second gallant and decisive charge being made upon them, their cavalry was put to flight, their artillery abandoned, and their infantry, now thrown into great confusion, surrendered themselves prisoners of war, —our whole loss being twenty-six killed and wounded.

While these occurrences were in progress, Gen. Ashby—who, after crossing at McCoy's Ford, had moved with his command further to the west, so as to skirt the base of the Massinutton Mountain—met with a body of the enemy posted as a guard at Buckton, in a strong position, protected by the railroad embankment. Ashby drove back and dispersed the enemy, but with the loss of some of his most valuable officers and men. Among them Captains Sheets and Fletcher. The infantry and artillery pursued but a short distance before darkness rendered it necessary to go into camp.

The results of this first day's operations, were the capture of about seven hundred prisoners, among them about twenty officers, a complete section of rifled artillery (10-pounder Parrotts), and a very large amount of quartermaster and commissary stores. The fruits of the movement were not restricted to the stores and prisoners captured. The enemy's flank was turned, and the road opened to Winchester. In the event of Bank's leaving Strasburg, he might escape toward the Potomac; or if Jackson moved directly to Winchester, he might move *via* Front Royal toward Washington city. In order to watch both directions, and at the same time advance upon him if he remained at Strasburg, General Jackson determined, with the main body of the army, to strike the turnpike near Middleton, a village five miles north of Strasburg and thirteen miles south of Winchester.

Accordingly, on the following morning, General Ashby advanced from Cedarville toward Middletown, supported by skirmishers from Taylor's brigade, with Chew's battery and two Parrott guns from the Rockbridge artillery, followed by the whole command, except the troops left under command of Gen. Ewell near Cedarville. Gen. Ewell, with Trimble's brigade, the 1st Maryland, and the batteries of Brockenbrough and Courtney, had instructions to move toward Winchester. Ashby was directed to keep scouts on his left to prevent Banks from passing unobserved by Front Royal. Brig.-gen. George H. Stewart, who was now temporarily in command of the 2d and 6th Virginia cavalry, had been previously dispatched to Newtown, a point further north, and nine miles from Winchester, with instructions to observe the movements of the enemy at that point. He there succeeded in capturing some prisoners and several wagons and ambulances, with arms and medical stores. He also advised Gen. Jackson of movements which indicated that Banks was preparing to leave Strasburg.

General Jackson accompanied the movement of the main body of the army to Middletown. Upon arriving there, he found the Valley turnpike crowded with the retreating Federal cavalry, upon which the batteries of Poague and Chew, with Taylor's infantry promptly opened; and in a few moments the turnpike which had just before teemed with life presented a most appalling spectacle of carnage and destruction. The road was literally obstructed with the mangled and confused mass of struggling and dying horses and riders. The Federal column was pierced, but what proportion of its strength had passed North toward Winchester Gen. Jackson had then no means of knowing. Among the surviving cavalry the wildest confusion ensued, and they scattered in disorder in various directions, leaving, however, some two hundred prisoners, with their accoutrements in our hands.

A train of wagons was seen disappearing in the distance toward Winchester, and Ashby, with his cavalry, some artillery, and a supporting infantry force from Taylor's brigade, was sent in pursuit. But a few moments elapsed before the Federal artillery, which had been cut off with the rear of the column, opened upon Jackson with the evident intention to cut its way through to Winchester. Our batteries were soon placed in position to return the fire, and Gen. Taylor was ordered with his command to the attack. After a spirited resistance, this fragment of the Federal army retreated to Strasburg, and from thence made its way through the mountains across the Potomac. A large amount of baggage fell into our hands at this point. Entire regiments, apparently in line of battle, had laid down their knapsacks and abandoned them.

Having become satisfied that the main body of Banks' army had already passed this point on its way to Winchester, our troops which had halted, moved on in pursuit in that direction. The large number of wagons, loaded with stores and abandoned by the enemy between Middletown and Newtown, plainly indicated his hurried retreat.

From the attack upon Front Royal up to the present moment, every opposition had been borne down, and there was reason to believe, if Banks reached Winchester it would be without a train, if not without an army; but, in the midst of these hopes, Gen. Jackson found that the infantry and cavalry under Ashby had abandoned themselves to pillage to such an extent that their gallant commander found it impossible to continue the pursuit. The artillery, which had pushed on with energy to the vicinity of Newtown, found itself, from this discreditable conduct, without a proper support from either infantry or cavalry. The relaxation in the pursuit was unfortunate, as the enemy was encouraged by it to bring up, about two hours later, four pieces of artillery, which were planted on the northern skirt of Newtown and opened on our batteries. Their fire was replied to by Capt. Poague's two rifled guns with skill and accuracy. When Gen. Jackson overtook the advance it was thus held in check by the enemy's artillery. Further movements were retarded until nearly dark, when the enemy retreated and the pursuit was renewed.

As Gen. Jackson advanced beyond Newtown the same profusion of abandoned Federal wagons, loaded with stores, met his eye, but he derived no benefit from this property, as the time lost during the disorder and pillage, and the consequent delay of the advance at Newtown, enabled the enemy to make arrangements for burning them. Shortly after leaving Newtown the advance was fired upon by a body of the concealed enemy, but they were soon driven off by the 33d Virginia, Col. Neff, and the march resumed.

On reaching Bartonsville, another ambuscade from the right, left, and front was encountered, and heavy firing kept up for some time. In repelling this, the 27th Virginia, Col. Grigsby; 2d Virginia, Col. Allen, and 5th Virginia, Col. Baylor, acquitted themselves gallantly. Skirmishing continued during the night, the enemy ambuscading from point to point.

So important did Gen. Jackson deem it to occupy, before dawn, the heights overlooking Winchester, that the advance continued to move forward until morning, notwithstanding the darkness and other obstacles to its progress. The other troops were permitted to halt for about an hour during the night. In the mean time, Major-general Ewell, with Trimble's brigade, the 1st Maryland, and Stewart's cavalry, which had now joined him from Newtown, and Brockenbrough's and Courtney's batteries, was advancing to Winchester by the turnpike from Front Royal to that place, and had occupied a position about three miles from the town, as early as ten o'clock in the night, and thrown forward his pickets about a mile in advance of his position.

As General Jackson approached Winchester, soon after dawn, the enemy's skirmishers were occupying the hill to the southwest, overlooking the town. He ordered Gen. Winder to seize that height as speedily as possible. The 5th Virginia was accordingly thrown out in advance as skirmishers, and the 2d, 4th, 27th, and 33d Virginia (the "old Stonewall Brigade") being placed in order of battle, the whole line was ordered to advance. This was done in gallant style, and the position on the crest secured, though the enemy made a resolute but unsuccessful effort to dislodge our troops from so commanding a position. Two Parrott guns from the Rockbridge artillery, and the batteries of Carpenter and Cutshaw were promptly posted on the height, to dislodge a battery of the enemy which was playing from the front with great animation and effect upon the hill. At this moment, a body of the enemy's sharpshooters were seen crossing the ridge to Jackson's left, between him and a battery which soon opened an enfilade fire on our batteries. Poague's guns were promptly turned to the left, which compelled the infantry to seek shelter behind a stone fence, from which their fire upon our cannoneers and horses, was, for a while, very destructive. By the well-directed guns of Carpenter and Cutshaw, the Federal battery in front had now become silenced, but the battery on the left still kept up a brisk and damaging fire. Withdrawing his battery to the left and rear, so as to avoid the exposure under which he was severely suffering, Poague opened his guns upon the enfilading battery of the enemy. He was also directed by Gen. Winder to throw some solid shot against the stonewall, under the shelter of which, their sharpshooters were pouring a fatal fire into our ranks.

During these operations, valuable officers and privates suffered; among them, Colonel J. A. Campbell, commanding the 2d Brigade, was wounded. Whilst the enemy's artillery was playing on Jackson's position, his infantry moved to the left, as if designing to gain possession of that portion of the hill immediately to the north. General Taylor was ordered to advance his brigade to the left, and check the movement. Promptly leaving the turnpike, he passed, under cover of the hill, in rear of Winder, and formed his line of battle in face of a heavy fire of artillery and musketry from the sharpshooters, the 10th Virginia infantry taking position on the left, and the 23d Virginia on the right of his line. Steadily, and in fine order, mounting the hill, and there fronting the enemy where he stood in greatest strength, the whole line magnificently swept down the declivity and across the field, driving back the Federal troops, and bearing back all opposition before it. In this gallant advance, all the troops of General Winder joined except those left as supports to the batteries. This successful charge being followed by the giving way of the whole Federal army, General Elzey, who had been in reserve on the Valley turnpike, was now ordered to pursue, and, eagerly uniting in the general advance, soon entered Winchester with the other troops. On the right, the attack under General Ewell was executed with great skill and spirit. The 21st North Carolina and the 21st Georgia gallantly drove back the advance force of the enemy; but the 21st North Carolina becoming exposed to a destructive fire from a Federal regiment posted behind a stonewall, after suffering severely in both officers and men, was forced to fall back. The 21st Georgia having succeeded in driving that regiment from its shelter, reinforced its brigade.

With the 1st Maryland on his left and Trimble's brigade on his right, General Ewell now moved toward the eastern outskirts of the town. That advance was made about the time that Taylor's brigade was so gallantly crossing the hill and charging toward the western side of the town. This simultaneous movement on both his flanks, by which his retreat might even have been cut off, may account for the suddenness with which the entire Federal army gave way, and for the slight resistance which it made in passing through the town. The Federal forces were now in full retreat. As General Jackson's army passed through the town in pursuit, they were received with the most enthusiastic demonstrations of joy by its loyal people, who, for more than two months, had been suffering under the hateful surveillance and rigors of military despotism.

Notwithstanding the fatiguing marches and almost sleepless nights to which the mass of General Jackson's troops had been subjected, they continued to obey his orders and press forward with alacrity. The Federal forces, upon falling back into the town, preserved their organization remarkably well; but in passing through its streets, they were thrown into confusion, and soon after debouching into the plain and turnpike to Martinsburg—and after being fired upon by our artillery—they presented the aspect of a mass of disordered fugitives. Never was there an opportunity where it was in the power of cavalry to reap a richer harvest of the fruits of victory. Hoping that his cavalry would soon come up, General Jackson pressed forward with his artillery and infantry for two hours, his purpose being, by the fire of his artillery to prevent the re-forming of the enemy. As nothing, however, was heard of the cavalry, and as little or nothing could be accomplished without it, in the exhausted condition of the infantry—between which and the enemy the distance was continually increasing—General Jackson ordered a halt, and issued orders for going into camp and refreshing the men. He had seen only some fifty of Ashby's cavalry prior to the pillaging scenes of the previous evening, and none at all since an early hour of the past night. The 2d and 6th Virginia regiments of cavalry were under the command of Brigadier-general George H. Stewart, of Ewell's command.

After the pursuit had continued for some distance beyond the town, and seeing nothing of the cavalry, General Jackson dispatched his aide-de-camp, Lieutenant Pendleton, to General Stewart, with an order "to move as rapidly as possible, and join him on the Martinsburg turnpike, and carry on the pursuit of the enemy with vigor." General Stewart's reply was "that he was under the command of Gen. Ewell, and the order must come through him." About an hour after the halt of the main body had been ordered by General Jackson, Brigadier-general George H. Stewart, with his cavalry, came up, and renewing the pursuit, pushed forward in a highly creditable manner, and succeeded in capturing a number of prisoners; but the main body of Banks' army was now beyond the reach of successful pursuit, and effected its escape across the Potomac.

Before reaching Bunker Hill, General George H. Stewart was joined by General Ashby, with a portion of his cavalry, their delay in coming up having been caused by a movement made to the left to cut off a part of the enemy's force. The cavalry pushed on to Martinsburg, where a large amount of army stores were captured; and there was reason to believe that if the pursuit on the part of the cavalry had been prompt and persevering, but a small portion of Banks' army would have escaped.

On the following day—the 26th of May—Divine service was held in the camps of the Southern army, and thanks were rendered to God for the success with which He had blessed their arms, and his continual favor implored—a duty which Gen. Jackson never failed to impress upon his troops. The men then rested; but, on the 28th, movements against the enemy were renewed. Early on the morning of that day, Gen. Winder, in order to make a demonstration toward the Potomac, left his encampment near Winchester with the 4th, 5th, 33d and 27th Virginia regiments—the ever-ready "old brigade"—and Carpenter's and Poague's batteries, and took up the line of march for Charlestown by way of Summit Point. When about four miles from Charlestown, he received information that the enemy were in possession of that place in heavy force: upon being advised of which, General Jackson ordered Ewell with reinforcements to his support. Notwithstanding the report of the large number of the enemy and the expectation of reinforcements in the course of the day, Gen. Winder moved forward continually toward Charlestown, and, as he emerged from the wood, less than a mile distant from the town, he discovered the enemy in line of battle, about fifteen hundred strong, and decided to attack them.

Upon the appearance of our troops, they were fired upon by two pieces of artillery. Carpenter's battery was immediately placed in position, supported by the 33d Virginia, and was so admirably served that, in twenty minutes, the enemy retired in great disorder, throwing away arms, blankets, haversacks, and accoutrements of every description. The pursuit was continued rapidly with artillery and infantry to Halltown. A short distance beyond that point, observing the enemy in position on Bolivar Heights, Gen. Winder returned to the vicinity of Charlestown.

On the following day, the main body of the army took position near Halltown, and the 2d Virginia was sent to Loudoun Heights—the Blue Ridge opposite Harper's Ferry—to drive the enemy out of the town and across the Potomac.

Meanwhile, Gen. Jackson had to guard against a serious peril which menaced him in the rear. One portion of the Federal army had been routed and driven to the river, but other heavy bodies were hanging on his rear and flank which it behooved him to prepare for. Shields was moving from Fredericksburg on his right, and Fremont from the south branch of the Potomac, near Romney, on his left, with the view of concentrating a heavy force in his rear and cutting off his retreat up the Valley. To avoid such a result, Gen. Jackson, on the 30th May, issued orders to all the troops, except Winder's brigade and the cavalry, to return to Winchester. Directions were given to General Winder to recall the 2d regiment from Loudoun Heights, and, as soon as it should return to its brigade, to move with his command, including the cavalry, and rejoin the main body of the army.

Before General Jackson reached Winchester, the enemy's cavalry had appeared at Front Royal, and Col. Connor, who held that town with the 12th Georgia and a section of Rice's battery, hastily and improvidently abandoned the place—permitting not only Federal prisoners then in our possession, but some of his own men to fall into the hands of the enemy. Quartermaster and commissary stores, which Jackson had captured at that place, and estimated at $300,000, were, however, destroyed before being recaptured by the enemy.

Early on the morning of the 31st of May, the 21st Virginia, Col. Cunningham commanding, left Winchester in charge of some 2,300 prisoners, and moved up the Valley toward Staunton. He was followed by the other troops then near Winchester, which, at that time, embraced Jackson's entire command, except the portion left with Gen. Winder. That night they encamped near Strasburg, and on the following morning, June 1st, Gen. Fremont, who was approaching by way of Wardensville, attacked Jackson's outpost in that direction.

As it was necessary for Gen. Jackson to maintain his position at Strasburg until Winder arrived with his command, Gen. Ewell was ordered with his division to hold Fremont in check. Other troops were subsequently sent to his support, and, after a spirited resistance, the enemy's advance fell back a short distance. Toward evening Winder arrived—part of his brigade, the 2d Virginia, having marched thirty-six miles. The command being thus united again, the retreat continued toward Harrisonburg.

The public property captured in this expedition—at Front Royal, Winchester, Martinsburg, and Charlestown—was of enormous value, and so large in quantity that most of it had to be abandoned for want of means of transportation. The medical stores which filled one of the largest storehouses in Winchester were fortunately saved; but in spite of the efforts of Major Harman, Chief Quartermaster, transportation for other stores of countless value could not be secured. Most of the instruments and some of the medicines, urgently needed at the time, were issued to the surgeons—the rest sent to Charlottesville and turned over to a medical purveyor. Two large and well-furnished hospitals, capable of accommodating some 700 patients, were found in the town, and left undisurbed, with all their stores, for the use of the sick and wounded of the enemy. Commissary supplies, consisting of upwards of 100 head of cattle, 34,000 pounds of bacon, flour, salt, sugar, coffee, hard bread, and cheese, were turned over to the proper officers, besides large amounts taken by the troops and not accounted for. Sutler's stores valued at $25,000, and for want of transportation abandoned to the troops, were captured. Quartermaster stores to the value of $125,185 were secured, besides an immense amount destroyed. Many horses were taken by the cavalry. Among the ordnance stores taken and removed in safety were 9,354 small-arms and two pieces of artillery with their caissons.

The official reports of casualties in the entire command during the whole expedition showed a loss of 68 killed, 329 wounded, and three missing—making a total loss of 400 men.

In addition to the 2,300 prisoners in Col. Cunningham's charge, there were found in the hospitals at Winchester about 700 sick and wounded of the enemy, and at Strasburg some 50—making the total number who fell into Jackson's hands about 3,050. Those left in the hospitals were paroled. Eight Federal surgeons, attending the sick and wounded at Winchester, were at first held as prisoners of war, though paroled, and the next day unconditionally released.

In his official report, from which we have taken the above narrative, Gen. Jackson declares that the main body of the troops acted in a manner worthy of the great cause for which they were contending; and adds, that as far as his knowledge extended, the battle of Winchester was "on our part a battle without a straggler."

CHAPTER X.

THE BATTLE OF CROSS KEYS.

JACKSON had thus out-fought, out-generalled, and triumphed over his foes, who were closing in upon his rear with the vain hope of intercepting and destroying him. They did not know the man with whom they had to deal—his sleepless vigilance, the execution following the conception, as thunder does the lightning—the profound and unerring military genius, which was so much more than a match for all his foes combined—the eye which pierced to the depths of all their plans and devices, and defied those enemies to entrap him.

He had accomplished his object, and he now set out on his return. Banks was driven ignominiously to the Potomac—his stores of countless value captured or destroyed; a tremendous blow had been struck, whose sound reverberated along the Valley—and Jackson had no longer any thing to keep him there. Converging columns were closing in on the flanks and rear of the weary lion; and he slowly retired, still full of "fight" and menace, toward the safer region of the upper Shenandoah, to renovate his forces for any other struggle which should be necessary.

Leaving Strasburg on the evening of the 1st of June, he continued to move up the Valley turnpike, the cavalry under Brigadier-general Geo. H. Stewart, bringing up the rear.

Fremont's advance, which had been hovering near the Southern army during the day, soon ascertained that the retreat had been resumed, and moved in pursuit during the night. Encountering our rear-guard, they were challenged, but replying "Ashby's cavalry" to the challenge, they approached so near as to make an attack. The 6th Virginia cavalry, which was nearest the enemy, were thrown into confusion, and suffered some loss; and this disorder was, to some extent, communicated to the 2d Virginia cavalry also. Its commander, Colonel Munford, soon re-formed it, however, and gallantly driving back the enemy, captured some of their number. From information received respecting Shields' movements, and from the fact that he had been in possession of Front Royal for more than forty-eight hours without effecting a junction with Fremont, as originally designed, Jackson became apprehensive that he was moving via Luray, for the purpose of reaching New Market, on his line of retreat, before the Confederates arrived there. To avoid this, he caused White House bridge, upon the assumed line of Shields' march, over the south fork of the Shenandoah river to New Market, to be burned—and also Columbia bridge, which was a few miles up the river.

On the 2d of June, the enemy's advance came within artillery range of Jackson's rear-guard, and commenced shelling it, throwing the cavalry and artillery into some disorder. This led Gen. Ashby to one of those acts of personal heroism and prompt resource, which strikingly marked his character. Dismounting from his horse, he collected from the road a small body of infantry from those who were fatigued and straggling behind their commands, and posting them in a piece of wood near the turnpike, he awaited the advance of the enemy's cavalry, pushing forward to reap the fruits of the panic produced by the shells. As they approached within easy range, he poured such an effective fire into their ranks as to empty a number of saddles, and check their further pursuit for that day. Having transferred the 2d and 6th Virginia cavalry to Ashby, Jackson from that time placed him in command of the rear-guard of the army. On the 3d of June, after the army had crossed the bridge over the Shenandoah near Mount Jackson, Ashby was ordered to destroy it, which he barely succeeded in doing, before the Federal forces reached the opposite bank of the river. Here Ashby's horse was killed, and he narrowly escaped with his life.

Jackson reached Harrisonburgh at an early hour on the morning of the 5th, and passing beyond that town, turned toward the east, in the direction of Port Republic. On the 6th, General Ashby took position on the road between Harrisonburg and Port Republic, and received a spirited charge from a portion of the enemy's cavalry, which resulted in the repulse of the latter, and the capture of Colonel Wyndham, with sixty-three others. Fearing that the Federals would make a more serious attack, Ashby called for infantry support; and the brigade of General George H. Stewart was accordingly ordered forward. In a short time the 58th Virginia became engaged with a Pennsylvania regiment, called the Bucktails, when Colonel Johnson, of the 1st Maryland, coming up in the hottest period of the fire, charged gallantly into its flank, and drove the enemy with heavy loss from the field, capturing Lieutenant-colonel Kane, commanding the regiment. In this skirmish, our infantry loss was 17 killed, 50 wounded, and three missing. Among the killed was the heroic Ashby. The name of this splendid type of Southern chivalry will live as long as the history of this, our great war for independence, and we need not pause to delineate his great outline upon the crowded canvas of our subject. It is there before the eyes of all the world—the chevalier upon his milk-white horse—the admired, the beloved, the peerless partisan of Virginia. Our feeble praise can add nothing to his fame, and we do not touch upon a theme which demands a separate treatment. It may, however, gratify some of our readers to see the words of General Jackson—words never before published—on the occasion of his death; to know, "under the hand and seal" of the immortal Jackson, what he thought of Turner Ashby. "An official report," writes General Jackson, "is not an appropriate place for more than a passing notice of the distinguished dead; but the close relation which General Ashby bore to my command for most of the previous twelve months, will justify me in saying that as a partisan officer I never knew his superior. His daring was proverbial; his powers of endurance almost incredible; his tone of character heroic, and his sagacity almost intuitive in divining the purposes and movements of the enemy."

Such are the words of Jackson upon Ashby—one hero's estimate of another. That epitaph shall remain the glory of Ashby "the heroic," while the grass grows and the water runs!

The main body of Jackson's command had now reached the vicinity of Port Republic. This village is situated in the angle formed by the junction of the North and South rivers, tributaries of the south fork of the Shenandoah. Over the larger and deeper of these two streams, the North river, there was a wooden bridge, connecting the town with the road leading to Harrisonburg. Over the South river there was a passable ford. The troops more immediately under the command of Jackson were encamped on the high ground north of the village, about a mile from the river. General Ewell was some four miles distant, near the road leading from Harrisonburg to Port Republic. Fremont had arrived with his forces in the vicinity of Harrisonburg, and Shields was moving up the east side of the south fork of the Shenandoah, and was then at Conrad's store, some fifteen miles below Port Republic. Jackson's position was about equidistant from both hostile armies. To prevent a junction of the two Federal armies, he had caused the bridge over the south fork of the Shenandoah, at Conrad's store, to be destroyed.

Intelligence having been received that Shields was advancing further up the river, a small cavalry force was sent down during the night of the 7th to verify the report, and gain such other information respecting the enemy as could be obtained. On the next morning the cavalry precipitately returned, announcing that the enemy were approaching The brigades of Gen. Taliaferro and Gen. Winder were soon under arms, and Gen. Jackson ordered them to occupy positions immediately north of the bridge. By this time the Federal cavalry, accompanied by artillery, were in sight, and after directing a few shots towards the bridge, they crossed South river, and dashing into the village, planted one of their pieces at the southern entrance of the bridge. In the mean time, the batteries of Wooding, Poague, and Carpenter, were being placed in position; and Gen. Taliaferro's brigade having reached the vicinity of the bridge, was ordered to charge across, capture the piece, and occupy the town. While one of Poague's pieces was returning the fire of that of the enemy at the far end of the bridge, the 37th Virginia, Col. Fulkerson, after delivering its fire, gallantly charged over the bridge, captured the gun, and, followed by the other regiments of the brigade, entered the town, and dispersed and drove back the Federal cavalry. Another piece of artillery, with which the enemy had advanced, was abandoned, and subsequently fell into the hands of the Confederates. About this time a considerable body of infantry was seen advancing up the same road; and our batteries opened with marked effect upon this force and the retreating cavalry. In a short time the infantry followed the cavalry, falling back to Lewis's, three miles down the river, pursued for a mile by our batteries on the opposite bank, when the enemy disappeared in the woods round a bend in the road.

This attack of Shields had hardly been repulsed before Ewell was seriously engaged with Fremont, moving on the opposite side of the river. The enemy pushed forward, driving in the 15th Alabama, Col. Canty, from their post on picket. This regiment made a gallant resistance, which so far checked the advance of the enemy, as to afford Gen. Ewell time for the choice of his position, at leisure. His ground was well selected on a commanding ridge, a rivulet and large field of open ground in front—wood on both flanks—and his line intersected near its centre by the road leading to Port Republic. Gen. Trimble's brigade was posted on the right, somewhat in advance of his centre—the batteries of Courtney, Lusk, Brockenbrough, and Rains in the centre. Gen. Stewart's brigade on the left, and Gen. Elzey's brigade in rear of the centre, and in position to strengthen either wing. Both wings were in the wood.

About ten o'clock the enemy threw out his skirmishers and shortly afterwards posted his artillery opposite our own. The artillery fire was kept up with great animation, on both sides, for several hours. In the mean time a brigade of the enemy advanced under cover on the right, occupied by Gen. Trimble, who reserved his fire until they reached the crest of the hill in easy range of his musketry, when he poured into them a deadly fire from his whole front, under which they fell back. Observing a battery about being posted on the enemy's left, half a mile in front, Gen. Trimble, now supported by the 13th and 25th Virginia, of Elzey's brigade, pushed forward for the purpose of taking it, but found it withdrawn before he reached the spot, having, in the mean time, some spirited skirmishing with its infantry supports. Gen. Trimble had now advanced more than a mile from his original position, while the Federal advance had fallen back to the ground occupied by them in the morning.

Gen. Taylor, of the 8th brigade of Louisiana troops, having arrived from the vicinity of the bridge at Port Republic; toward which he had moved in the morning, reported to Gen. Ewell about 2 P. M., and was placed in rear. Col. Patton, with the 42d and 48th Virginia, and 1st battalion Virginia regulars also joined, and with the remainder of Gen. Elzey's brigade was added to the centre and left, then supposed to be threatened. General Ewell, having been informed that the enemy were moving a large column on his left, did not advance at once; but subsequently ascertaining that no attack was designed by the force referred to, he advanced, drove in the enemy's skirmishers, and when night closed, was in position on ground previously held by the enemy.

CHAPTER XI.

BATTLE OF PORT REPUBLIC.

The engagement in which General Ewell's command thus defeated Fremont is generally known as the battle of Cross Keys. It was to be followed by a still more decisive action.

General Jackson had remained at Port Republic during the greater part of the 8th of June, expecting a renewal of the attack. As no movement, however, was made by Shields to renew the action that day, Jackson determined to take the initiative and attack him on the following morning. Accordingly, Gen. Ewell was directed to move from his position, at an early hour on the morning of the 9th, toward Port Republic, leaving General Trimble, with his brigade, supported by Col. Patton, with the 42d Virginia and the 1st battalion of regulars, to hold Fremont in check, with instructions, if hard pressed, to retire across the North river and burn the bridge in their rear. Soon after 10 o'clock, Gen. Trimble, with the last of the Confederate forces, had crossed the North river, and the bridge was destroyed.

In the mean-time, before five in the morning, Gen. Winder's brigade was in Port Republic, and, having crossed the south fork by a temporary wagon bridge, placed there for the purpose, was moving down the river road to attack the forces of Shields. Advancing a mile and a half, he encountered the Federal pickets and drove them in. The enemy had judiciously selected his position for defence. Upon a rising ground near the Lewis house he had planted six guns, which commanded the road from Port Republic and swept the plateau for a considerable distance in front. As Gen. Winder moved forward his brigade, a rapid and severe fire of shell was opened upon it. Captain Poague, with two Parrott guns, was promptly placed in position, on the left of the road, to engage, and, if possible, dislodge the Federal battery. Capt. Carpenter was sent to the right to select a position for his battery, but finding it impracticable to drag it through the dense undergrowth, it was brought back and part of it placed near Poague. The artillery was well sustained by our batteries, but it soon became obvious that the superiority in this arm was on the part of the enemy. Gen. Winder, being now reinforced by the 7th Louisiana, Col. Hays, seeing no mode of silencing the enemy's battery and escaping its destructive missiles, but by a rapid charge and the capture of it, advanced with great boldness for some distance, but encountered such a heavy fire of artillery and small-arms as greatly to disorganize his command, which fell back in disorder. The enemy advanced across the field, and, by a heavy musketry fire, forced back our infantry support, in consequence of which our guns had to retire. The enemy's advance was checked by a spirited attack upon their flank by the 58th and 54th Virginia, directed by Gen. Ewell and led by Col. Scott, although his command was afterwards driven back to the woods with severe loss. The batteries were all safely withdrawn except one of Captain Poague's six-pounder guns, which was carried off by the enemy.

Whilst Winder's command was in this critical condition, the gallant and successful attack of General Taylor, on the Federal left and rear, diverted attention from the front, and led to a concentration of their force upon him. Moving to the right along the mountain acclivity, through a rough and tangled forest, and much disordered by the rapidity and obstructions of the march, Taylor emerged with his command from the wood just as the loud cheers of the enemy proclaimed their success in front; and, although assailed by a superior force in front and flank, with their guns in position within point-blank range, the charge was gallantly made, and the battery, consisting of six guns, fell into our hands. Three times was this battery lost and won in the desperate and determined efforts to capture and recover it. After holding the battery for a short time, a fresh brigade of the enemy, advancing on his flank, made a vigorous attack upon him, accompanied by a galling fire of canister from a piece suddenly brought into position at a distance of about three hundred and fifty yards. Under this combined attack, Taylor fell back to a skirt of the wood, near which the captured battery was stationed, and from that point continued his fire upon the advancing enemy, who succeeded in recapturing one of the guns, which he carried off, leaving both caisson and limber. The enemy now occupied with Taylor, halted his advance to the front.

Winder made a renewed effort to rally his command, and succeeding, with the 7th Louisiana under Major Penn (the colonel and lieutenant-colonel having been carried from the field wounded) and the 5th Virginia, Col. Funk, he placed part of Poague's battery in the position previously occupied by it, and again opened on the enemy, who was moving against Taylor's left flank to surround him in the woods. Chew's battery now reported, and was placed in position and did good service. Soon afterwards, guns from the batteries of Brockenbrough, Courtney, and Rains were brought forward and placed in position. Whilst these movements were in progress on the left and front, Col. Scott, having rallied his command, led them under the orders of Gen. Ewell to the support of Gen. Taylor, who, pushing forward with the reinforcements just secured and assisted by the well-directed fire of our artillery, forced the enemy to fall back, which was soon followed by his precipitate retreat, leaving many killed and wounded upon the field. Gen. Taliaferro, who, on the previous day, had occupied the town, was directed to continue to do so with part of his troops, and with the remainder to hold the elevated position on the north side of the river, for the purpose of co-operating, if necessary, with Gen. Trimble, and preventing his being cut off from the main body of the army, by the destruction of the bridge in his rear. But finding the resistance more obstinate than he anticipated, Gen. Jackson sent orders to Taliaferro and Trimble to join the main body. Taliaferro came up in time to discharge an effective volley into the ranks of the wavering and retreating enemy. The pursuit was continued some five miles beyond the battle-field by Gens. Taliaferro and Winder, with their brigades and portions of the batteries of Wooding and Caskie, Col. Munford, with cavalry and some artillery, advancing about three miles beyond the other troops.

The Confederates captured in the pursuit about 450 pris-

oners, some wagons, one piece of abandoned artillery, and about 800 muskets. Some 275 wounded were paroled in the hospitals near Port Republic.

Whilst the forces of Shields were in full retreat and our troops in pursuit, Fremont appeared on the opposite bank of the south fork of the Shenandoah with his army, and opened his artillery on our ambulances and parties engaged in the humane labors of attending to our dead and wounded and the dead and wounded of the enemy. The next day, withdrawing his forces, he retreated down the Valley.

On the morning of the 12th, Col. Munford entered Harrisonburg, where, in addition to wagons, medical stores, and camp equipage, he captured about 200 small-arms, and also about 200 of Fremont's men, many of them severely wounded. The Federal surgeons attending them were released, and those under their care paroled.

In the battles of Cross Keys and Port Republic our loss in killed, wounded, and missing was 1,096, including the skirmish on June 6th; also one piece of artillery. No estimate was made of the enemy's killed and wounded in these engagements by Gen. Jackson, but their loss was unquestionably far greater than his own. In addition, 975 prisoners were captured between the 6th and 12th. The small-arms taken numbered about 1,000; and seven pieces of artillery, with caissons and limbers, fell into our hands.

On the 12th, Jackson recrossed South river, and encamped near Weyer's Cave: "For the purpose of rendering thanks to God for having crowned our arms with success," says Gen. Jackson, "and to implore his continual favor, Divine service was held in the army on the 14th." The army remained near Weyer's Cave until the 17th, when, having rested long for this command, it recommenced its march—this time for a new field of operations—on the banks of the Chickahominy.

CHAPTER XII.

ILLUSTRATIONS—ROMNEY: KERNSTOWN.

We have presented a concise narration of that great campaign of the Valley upon which Jackson's fame will rest as upon pillars of adamant.

We claim thorough accuracy for all the statements in relation to these battles; for the account is given almost entirely in the words of General Jackson's official reports. These reports are so full, so lucid, so exhaustive of all the main great facts and outlines, that they leave little to be desired; and in narrating the events of this portion of the famous soldier's career, we have shrunk from interrupting the history given, so to speak, under his own hand and seal, with any comments, additions, or coloring of our own.

Something, however, remains to be said in relation to these occurrences—some familiar details which could not, with propriety, be given in the official reports, may here be noted down. The subject is not unworthy of such minute attention. In relation to these great events, every detail, however trifling, is valuable. By his operations in this magnificent campaign, Jackson will be mainly estimated in that "after time" which sums up and passes judgment upon all human things without fear, favor, or the prejudices of the contemporary. In that grand career, extending over barely two years, but so crammed with extraordinary events, the names of Kernstown and McDowell, Winchester, and Port Republic, will outshine Cold Harbor, Manassas, Sharpsburg, and Fredericksburg. In these latter battles, he was one of General Lee's lieutenants, carrying out the orders of a commander-in-chief, under the eyes of that commander. In the Valley, he was commanding in the field—far away from the capital, and often without communication with any one. What he there accomplished was due to his own brain and nerve, and perfect soldiership. When the coming generations speak of Jackson they will delight to dwell upon the toiling, marching, thinking, fighting of those two or three months. Tradition will cluster around the least detail; and the great soldier will be inseparably associated, in every heart, with the beautiful region which he loved so well.

From the moment when he took command of the little "Army of the Valley," General Jackson based all his military operations upon the conviction announced in a letter to a friend, dated March 3, 1862: "*If this Valley is lost, Virginia is lost.*" His far-seeing eye at once discerned the long train of "woes unnumbered" which would follow the occupation of the Shenandoah Valley by the enemy, and every faculty of his soul was bent to the almost hopeless task of holding it against the strong column about to advance upon Winchester. His expedition to Romney had this design in view; and, perhaps, no portion of Jackson's military operations more accurately indicates his method of warfare than this:

"Please procure me," he wrote a friend on January 29th, "thirty-five miles of telegraph wire from this point to Romney."

The point was Winchester, and from that place he designed watching the roads to Harper's Ferry and Williamsport—able to communicate promptly with Loring at Romney, and direct his operations, or to move that force and his own either according to the preconcerted plan, or as subsequent operations on the enemy's part dictated. His designs were, however, frustrated by the order from the War Office recalling General Loring, and he was compelled, greatly dissatisfied, to go into camp at Winchester, and, instead of initiating the campaign, await the movements of the Federals. He had never deceived himself with the idea that if the enemy had time to collect and organize his force, the Valley could be *defended* by his own little army. He seems to have comprehended clearly that in the strategy afterwards employed by him against General Banks lay the sole prospect of success. That was the *aggressive*, and from the moment when this policy was interdicted, he saw the coming event—retreat.

"Though the troops under my command are inadequate to the defence of this district," he wrote, "yet we must look on the bright side, trusting that a kind Providence will continue to give its protection to this fair portion of our Valley. I regret that . . . . . should not regard the success of the recent expedition as far outweighing the losses sustained."

The winter passed away; the enemy organized his force at leisure, and the first days of March saw heavy columns firmly posted directly in front of Winchester. Of the situation at the moment, Jackson wrote on March 3d:

"My plan is to put on as bold a front as possible, and to use every means in my power to prevent his advance, whilst our re-organization is going on. What I desire is to hold the country, as far as practicable, until we are in a condition to advance; and then, with *God's* blessing, let us make thorough work of it. . . . Banks, who commands about 35,000 men, has his headquarters at Charlestown; Kelly, who has succeeded Lander, has probably 11,000, with his headquarters near Paw Paw. Thus you see two generals, whose united force is near 46,000, of troops already organized for three years or the war, opposed to our little force here. But I do not feel discouraged. Let me have what force you can. . . . I am delighted to hear you say that Virginia is resolved to concentrate all her resources, if necessary, to the defence of *herself*. Now we may look for war in earnest. . . . I have only to say this—that if this Valley is lost, Virginia is lost." The defence of the Valley was the dearest object of Jackson's heart, not only then, but always, and he subsequently alluded to his deep solicitude upon this point, writing: "It is but natural that I should feel a deep and abiding interest in the people of the Valley, where are the homes of so many of my brave soldiers, who have been with me so long, and whose self-sacrificing patriotism has been so thoroughly tested."

This affection of the great soldier for the Shenandoah Valley was more than returned by its inhabitants. Jackson is famous everywhere throughout the world, but the people of that region first saw and hailed the rising sun of his renown. All lovers of purity and goodness now look to him as a noble type of earnest, truthful manhood; but the dwellers on the banks of the Shenandoah cherish his memory with a deeper affection—as that of one whose brain, and heart, and arm, were dedicated to their defence.

The reinforcements—ardently longed for and persistently urged—did not arrive. The march to Romney and consequent suffering of the troops had still further diminished Jackson's little army. It was reduced now to about 4,000 men, and the enemy were advancing with 46,000. Winchester must be evacuated, and Jackson slowly and sullenly falls back, doggedly retiring before the huge columns of the enemy, but striking their advance at every step with his cavalry under Ashby. He has fallen back nearly to Staunton, when suddenly his weary troops are faced about, march down the Valley, and at Kernstown find themselves in front of the Federal army under Shields. Jackson has traversed nearly fifty miles, moving so rapidly that only 2,700 have been able to keep up, but he is in time. Sedgwick has crossed the Blue Ridge through Snicker's Gap, and the head of his column of 15,000 men is at Middleburg, ready to strike General Johnston, who, falling back from Centreville, has reached the Rapidan, when the roar of artillery from the direction of Winchester arrests the Federal general's march. Dispatches quickly come from Shields that Jackson is pressing him hard with a force of unknown size, and General Sedgwick faces about and returns to the assistance of the 11,000 who are threatened at Kernstown by Jackson's 2,700.

Such were the circumstances under which the battle of Kernstown was fought. By assailing Shields, Jackson withdrew a force of 15,000 of the enemy from the projected attack upon Johnston—inflicted a heavy loss upon the foe, and retired with all his baggage and artillery, except two pieces disabled. His enemies declared that his brain was diseased, or he never would have broken down his troops by this tremendous forced march, to attack an enemy nearly five times as strong as himself, and for no considerable object. Jackson did not contradict these statements—he went upon his way.

The following brief notices and details of the battle of Kernstown, from contemporary publications, mayp rove of interest hereafter:

The writer of these pages has not considered it necessary here, or elsewhere, to indicate the particulars in which the letter-writers err in their statements of the main facts. The narratives of the battles already given will point out their discrepancies; and the familiar details will remain for what they are worth.

"The name of Kernstown will shine proudly in our annals. The engagement at that place was the most desperate, and, all things considered, the most successful of the war. It was not a defeat; it was a drawn battle, at the close of which both parties retired, the enemy to a greater distance than our men, who slept almost upon the battle-field. Jackson made the attack in obedience to orders. The blow was struck for a purpose, and that purpose was fully accomplished; it was, therefore, a victory. The marvel is that Jackson's men were able to fight at all, much less a force of five to one in a carefully chosen position. His troops had marched forty-five miles in a day and a half—they had been marching constantly for a week or two before—and when they arrived at the scene of action, part of the small army was far in the rear. Fatigued, worn out, the little band of patriots 'attacked at once and furiously' the huge enemy before them. The 'Shriver Greys,' a gallant handful of exiles from Wheeling, only 30 strong, were thrown out as skirmishers to feel the enemy, and it took three regiments of the Yankees to drive them back. The 21st Virginia regiment, commanded by Col. Patton, and containing our own noble 'Co. F,' from Richmond, made a splendid fight. Gen. Jackson, we hear, complimented them for their bravery, and assigned them hereafter the position of the advance guard—a proud tribute to their pluck and bravery. The Irish battalion fought like tigers—or, which is the same thing, like Irishmen. The 'Stonewall Brigade' came up to the support of the 21st, and did its work heroically, as we all knew it would. The men who held Patterson's whole army at bay, and who won on the field of Manassas a name that will live as long as the English tongue is spoken, gathered new laurels at Kernstown. Five times the intrepid Jackson led his veterans to the charge and drove back the enormous columns of the enemy. Night fell upon the combatants before the reinforcements of either party could come up. Twenty-seven hundred Virginians had attacked 12,000 Yankees—the lowest estimate of the enemy themselves—and when the fight closed, 83 of our men lay dead on the field, with 416 Yankee corpses by their side. Disclaiming any invidiousness, any State vanity, we can but feel proud of our soldiers. We glory in them all, come from what part of the State they may, and in none more than the men of the Valley.

"The knightliest of the knightly race,
Who, since the days of old,
Have kept the lamp of chivalry
Alight in hearts of gold—
The kindliest of the kindly band,
Who, rarely hating ease,
Yet rode with Spotswood round the land
And Raleigh round the seas—

"Who climbed the blue Virginian hills
Against embattled foes,
And planted there in valleys fair,
The lily and the rose—
Whose fragrance lives in many lands,
Whose beauty stars the earth,
And lights the hearths of many homes
With loveliness and worth!

"We thought they slept! the sons who kept
  The names of noble sires,
And slumbered while the darkness crept
  Around their vigil fires!
But still the Golden Horse-shoe Knights
  Their Old Dominion keep,
Whose foes have found enchanted ground,
  But not a knight asleep."

Another writer says:

"The fight was made by the Yankees as they fought at Manassas, first making a demonstration on our right, and then throwing their whole force rapidly to our left. An 'artillery duel' was kept up until about four o'clock, our forces moving gradually to the left, when the enemy's infantry advanced in force. They were met by the 37th and 21st Virginia regiments, and repulsed three times. Three times the Stars and Stripes fell, and three times did our gallant troops drive them headlong down the hill. The 1st brigade, the 'Stonewall,' then came up, and again a fresh column of the enemy was driven back, leaving the side of the hill black with their dead and wounded. * * * *

"No battle has been fought during the war against such odds and under the same trying circumstances. The Yankees fought better than at Manassas, but their officers could be seen riding behind their columns sabring the men on to the work. While the battle lasted, the firing was sharper and more rapid than on the glorious 21st of July. It was equally as hard a fought battle, and against greater odds; and if not so successful on our side, the result leaves no blush of shame behind, and adds new laurels to the desperate bravery of both officers and men of our little army. * * * *

"Letters received from Winchester last night, from reliable persons, state that there is 'no exultation among the Yankees, and that they look upon Jackson's army as a band of heroes.' Our ladies in Winchester gave every attention to our wounded and prisoners. For the first time since the Yankees entered the town, they crowded the streets, and the march of our men to the railroad depot was, as one expresses it, 'a march of triumph rather than of defeat.' The Yankees did not interfere with this patriotic demonstration, or the shouts of our brave boys for Jeff. Davis and the Confederacy.' The same letters represent the Yankees as looking upon Jackson's army, particularly Colonel Ashby's cavalry with fear and trembling. The men claim no victory over us, though the usual noise will be made in their papers. Our people on the border look upon our gallant fight on Sunday in the light of a victory, and seem cheerful and hopeful.

"It is useless to say that General Jackson acted bravely; he was in the thickest of the fight, and exposed to every danger. A braver man God never made. Colonel Allen, of the 2d Virginia distinguished himself. Three times the flag of the 2d Virginia was shot down, and the staff shot away. Colonel Allen, the masses of the enemy close upon him, jumped from his horse and carried the colors from the field. Colonel Taliaferro, of the 21st, had his horse shot under him, and acted his part well. Colonel Echols, of the 27th, had his arm badly broken while leading his men to the field. Colonel Burks, of the 42d, received six shots through his clothing, and his horse was shot four times. Lieutenant Dall, of Delaware, who joined the 5th at Harper's Ferry, was killed, fighting bravely. Captain Austin, of the 5th, was badly wounded, and left on the field. Captain Robertson, of the 27th, going on the field lame, was taken prisoner. Lieut. Junkin, General Jackson's aid-de-camp, was taken prisoner. He mistook a body of Yankees for our men, and was taken. The whole army regrets the loss of the gallant lieutenant. Captain Morrison and Lieutenant Lisle, of the Liberty Hall Volunteers, of Washington College, who fought so gallantly at Manassas, were taken, and his company badly cut up.

"Colonel Ashby held the right, and before the fight was over was completely in the rear of the enemy. He covered our retreat, and by his tireless energy has made himself the terror of the Yankees."

Another writer says;

"Reliable advices from Winchester represent the loss of the enemy in killed at near 1,500, and the wounded at a much larger figure. It is said that about 360 dead bodies were brought to Winchester for transportation Northward. These, as we suppose, were the *élite*, whose friends were able to incur the cost of removal. The mass of course, were buried in the neighborhood of the battle-field.

"Upon inquiring as to the cause of the disparity in the casualties in the two armies, I learn, from some of our men, that the enemy were so thick that it was impossible for our men to miss. Every shot took effect—if it missed the column at which it was aimed, it was sure to hit one in the rear.

"The most deadly strife occurred near the boundary of two fields which were separated by a stone wall. Two of our regiments were in one field, and six Yankee regiments in the other. At first they fired across the wall, but after a while, each party advanced in a run, to get the benefit of the shelter of the wall. Our men reached it first, and the Yankees were then about 40 yards distant. Our men immediately dropped on their knees, and taking deliberate aim, fired deadly volleys into the advancing lines of the enemy. The effect was terrific, and it is said that an Ohio and a Pennsylvania regiment, which were in advance, were almost annihilated. It is said that after this fire not more than 20 men of one of these regiments were left standing.

"We lost two guns in the battle—one from the Rockbridge and one from the Augusta battery. The Rockbridge gun was struck by a cannon-ball and disabled. The loss of the other was caused by the killing of one of the horses, which frightened the others, and caused them to turn suddenly and capsize the carriage. The enemy were close upon us, and left no time to replace it. Our men, however, cut out and secured all the horses but one, and he was cut out by the enemy, and escaped from them, and came galloping to our camp. It would seem as if even the horses were infected with the spirit of rebellion and hatred to the Yankees."

CHAPTER XIII.

ILLUSTRATIONS—M'DOWELL: WINCHESTER.

MAY, 1862, was looked forward to by the Federal authorities as the great month—the hinge of the crisis upon which it would turn.

Their plans were not deficient in ingenuity, and promised favorable results. Upon the Confederate capital four armies were about to converge—Fremont from the West, Banks from the Valley, McDowell from Fredericksburg, and McClellan from the Peninsula. Fremont and Banks, having united their forces, were to cut all the communications, and sweep down upon the devoted capital from the mountains; McClellan was to march to the Chickahominy, and extend his right wing far up that stream; and, at the same time, McDowell was to advance from Fredericksburg and extend his left wing until it formed a junction with McClellan's right. The combined forces were thus to surround Richmond on the east and north with a cordon of fire. Between the army ascending the Peninsula and the army descending from the mountains, the capital of the Confederacy must, in this month of May, be evacuated or destroyed.

To defeat these plans, only two obstacles existed—but they were serious. These obstacles were General Johnston and General Jackson. The forces under their commands were far outnumbered by those of the enemy; but God had endowed these two leaders with a genius for war which more than supplied the lack of numbers.

The purpose of these pages is to exhibit the part enacted in the great drama by General Stonewall Jackson; and the narrative of his battles in the Valley has been given. We proceed now to add, in relation to the great combats which succeeded Kernstown, those illustrations mentioned above.

From Kernstown, Jackson fell back, as we have seen, toward Staunton, pursued by Gen. Banks. Crossing to Swift Run Gap, he took up a strong position there, ready to march in any direction, and confronted the enemy, so long following upon his trail. Many skirmishes took place, but nothing decisive occurred; and Gen. Banks finally fell back, in order to unite his force with that of Fremont, approaching from the West—probably, also, with expected reinforcements from McDowell at Fredericksburg. Jackson took advantage of this movement after his own fashion, and, marching around

Staunton, went to meet Milroy and Schenck, who were approaching that place from Western Virginia. The battle of McDowell followed, as has been seen, and the expected junction between Fremont and Banks was defeated. The following details of this engagement are taken from a letter written on May the 21st, near Franklin, whither the enemy had been pursued:

"About this time, 'Old Stonewall' passed up the road, and had a consultation with Gen. Johnson. Soon after the consultation, Johnson's army pushed up the road in pursuit of the enemy towards Shenandoah mountain, followed by Jackson's. When we arrived at the foot of the mountain, on the east side, we found a regiment of Yankees had been camped there, but had left on hearing of our appearance, leaving behind all their tents, clothing, commissary stores, and a number of small-arms, most of which they broke the stocks of, but several cases were left unopened and in fine order.

"After scouting the mountain thoroughly, we found that three regiments had been camped upon the top, but upon our approach had made a hasty retreat.

"When we arrived upon the summit, we could see the enemy in hasty retreat on the east side of Bull Pasture Mountain, about five miles in advance. It being late in the day, our commander thought it prudent to halt and go into camp for the night.

"At sunrise the next morning, we were again on the line of march in pursuit of the enemy. When we arrived at Bull Pasture Mountain, we ascended to its summit, when Ashby's scouts reported that the Yankees had placed four pieces of artillery on the road leading to McDowell, on the west side of the mountain, where the road passes through a narrow gorge. The heights commanding Monterey were also in possession of the enemy, with artillery planted.

* * * * * * * * *

"We expected to renew the fight the next morning, but the bird had flown, leaving behind, at McDowell, where 3,000 were encamped, all his camp equipage, a large quantity of ammunition, a number of cases of Enfield rifles, together with about 100 head of cattle, which they had stolen, being mostly milch cows.

"At McDowell, Milroy's headquarters, great destruction was done to private property.

"The Yankees had been enjoying themselves finely. They had erected large bake-ovens, and the officers' kitchens were all provided with large cooking-stoves of the most improved pattern.

"On the retreat, our cavalry overtook and captured a number of prisoners. Among them was a colonel, and an able-bodied negro worth at least $1,500.

"We have found a number of dead and many graves along the road, besides abandoned wagons and broken-down horses. I learn this morning that 103 dead Yankees have been found in the mountain hollow, near McDowell, covered with brush.

"People along the road tell us that they pressed all their horses to carry off their artillery, &c.

"We arrived at this place yesterday (Sunday) about three o'clock, P. M. On our approach, the enemy took to the mountains, where they had planted artillery, and set fire to all the works. So dense was the smoke, that we could not find the position until night fell, when it was too dark to shell them. In fact, it is very hard to drive an enemy from the mountain heights, as you can seldom get a position for artillery. This morning our scouts are out in search of a position, and to watch the movements of the Yankees, but I have not yet heard from them.

"Northwestern Virginia is now nearly free from the scoundrels.

"I do not know our destination, as General Jackson never tells any one his plans, not even his brigadiers and aids.

"The Yankees had put up a telegraph wire almost to Monterey; but, on our approach, they abandoned the work, leaving several tons of wire, ladders, &c., behind.

"The fight, I suppose, will be renewed as soon as General Jackson ascertains the enemy's position."

One passage in the above letter will seem a very unnecessary announcement to those who knew the habits of Jackson—"I do not know our destination, as General Jackson never tells any one his plans, not even his brigadiers and aids." This statement will excite the amusement of many persons; for it is made in relation to a man who declared, that "if his coat knew what he intended to do, he would take it off and burn it"—and who said on another occasion, in the low, quiet voice peculiar to him, "Mystery—mystery is the secret of success!"

Jackson returned devout thanks for his victory, and we have in the letter of a correspondent, the following allusion to the scene:

"A significant illustration of the elevated virtues and principles which governed Jackson's public acts was given on Monday last, three miles north of Franklin, in Pendleton county. On the morning of that day, he addressed his troops in a few terse and pointed remarks, thanking them for the courage, endurance, and soldierly conduct displayed at the battle of McDowell, on Thursday, the 8th instant, and closed by appointing 10 o'clock of that day, as an occasion of prayer and thanksgiving throughout the army, for the victory which followed that bloody engagement. There, in the beautiful little valley of the South Branch, with the blue and towering mountains covered with the verdure of Spring, the green sward smiling a welcome to the season of flowers, and the bright sun, unclouded, lending a genial, refreshing warmth, that army, equipped for the stern conflict of war, bent in humble praise and thanksgiving to the God of Battles for the success vouchsafed to our arms in the recent sanguinary encounter of the two armies. While this solemn ceremony was progressing in every regiment, the minds of the soldiery drawn off from the bayonet and sabre, the enemy's artillery was occasionally belching forth its leaden death, yet all unmoved stood that worshipping army, acknowledging the supremacy of the will of Him who controls the destinies of men and nations, and chooses the weaker things of earth to confound the mighty.

"Gen. Jackson is one of the purest men I ever knew. He is far above all political or personal considerations. He is a Christian patriot, deeply impressed with the righteousness of the cause in which he has unsheathed his sword, and, depending upon the aid of a just God, determined to win the freedom of his country, or perish in the holy effort."

The battle of McDowell was fought on the 8th of May; and

was announced by Jackson in his habitual terms of piety and simplicity—"God blessed our arms with victory at McDowell yesterday." Then he went after Banks.

His design now required energy, nerve, rapidity of movement, and all the greatest faculties of the soldier. The design was to defeat or drive Banks before him across the Potomac; to thus divert McDowell from his projected junction with McClellan in front of Richmond; and in the event that success crowned his arms, to cross into Maryland and advance to attack Washington.

The authorities at Washington realized their danger. Lincoln's dispatches teem with allusions to the suspected designs of Jackson. On the 17th of May, he writes to Gen. McClellan:

"In order, therefore, to increase the strength of the attack upon Richmond, at the earliest moment, Gen. McDowell has been ordered to march upon that city by the shortest route. He is ordered—*keeping himself always in a position to cover the Capital from all possible attack*—so to operate as to put his left wing in communication with your right. * * * The specific task assigned to his command, has been to provide against any danger to the Capital of the nation. At your earliest call for reinforcements he is sent forward to co-operate in the reduction of Richmond, *but charged in attempting this, not to uncover the city of Washington; and you will give no orders, either before or after your junction, which can put him out of position to cover this city.*"

On the 21st of May, Lincoln writes to McDowell, at Fredericksburg:

"Gen. Fremont has been ordered by telegraph to move from Franklin on Harrisonburg to relieve Gen. Banks and capture or destroy Jackson's or Ewell's forces.

"You are instructed, laying aside for the present the movement on Richmond, to put twenty thousand men in motion at once for the Shenandoah, moving on the line or in the advance of the Manassas Gap Railroad. Your object will be to capture the forces of Jackson and Ewell, either in co-operation with Gen. Fremont, or in case of a want of supplies or transportation interferes with his movement, it is believed that the force with which you move will be sufficient to accomplish the object alone. The information thus received here makes it probable that if the enemy operate actively against Banks you will not be able to count upon much assistance from him, but may even have to release him. Reports received this moment are that Banks is fighting with Ewell eight miles from Winchester."

General McDowell replies, on May 24th. "The President's order has been received—is in process of execution. This is a crushing blow to us." He adds, on the same day: "I beg to say that co-operation between Fremont and myself, to cut off Jackson or Ewell, is not to be counted upon, even if it is not a practical impossibility. Next, that I am entirely beyond helping distance of General Banks, and no celerity or vigor will avail, so far as he is concerned. Next, that by a glance at the map, it will be seen that the line of retreat of the enemy's forces up the Valley is shorter than mine to go against him. It will take a week or ten days for my force to go to the Valley by this route, which will give it good forage, and by that time the enemy will have retreated. I shall gain nothing for you there, and shall gain much for you here. It is, therefore, not only on personal grounds that I have a heavy heart in the matter, but that I feel it throws us all back, and from Richmond, North, we shall have all our large masses paralyzed, and shall have to repeat what we have just accomplished. I have ordered General Shields to commence a movement by to-morrow morning. A second division will follow in the afternoon."

Such was the position of the pieces on the great chessboard of war at the end of May. McClellan threatening Johnston at Richmond, and clamoring for McDowell—Lincoln, in Washington, telegraphing McDowell to "put 20,000 men in motion" to destroy Jackson, and "cover" his beloved capital. The situation was not without elements of the grotesque—and the complicated movements of the Federal Generals McClellan, Banks, McDowell, Shields, Milroy, and Fremont might have puzzled the brains of the most thorough master of the art of war.

The problem was soon solved, however—the *Deus Ex Machina* appeared in the shape of General Jackson. The battle of Winchester has been narrated; but another account of the affair exists—Gen. Banks'. It is headed: "*Official Report of the March of the First Division, Fifth Corps d'Armée, from Strasburg, Va., to Williamsport, Maryland, on 24th and 25th days of May,* 1862." It is somewhat singular that General Banks should call the movement of his troops a *march*, when, after telling pathetically how "Colonel Kenly's force had been destroyed" at Front Royal, he adds: "It was, therefore, determined to enter the lists with the enemy in *a race* or a battle—as he should choose—for the possession of Winchester, the key of the Valley, and for us the position of safety." The "march" was really a "race," as General Banks inadvertently calls it in his text; and here are some extracts from his account of the affair:

"The strength and purpose of the enemy were to us unknown when we reached Winchester, except upon uncertain reports and unsatisfactory reconnoissances. Our suspicions were strengthened by the vigor with which the enemy had passed our main column, and defeated at every point the efforts of detachments to effect a junction with the main body.

"At Winchester, however, all suspense was relieved on that subject. All classes—Secessionists, Union men, refugees, fugitives and prisoners—agreed that the enemy's force at or near Winchester was overwhelming, ranging from twenty-five to thirty thousand. Rebel officers, who came into our camp with entire unconcern, supposing that their own troops occupied the town, and were captured, confirmed these statements, and added that an attack would be made upon us at daybreak. I determined to test the substance and strength of the enemy by actual collision, and measures were promptly taken to prepare our troops to meet them. They had taken up their positions on entering the town after dark without expectations of a battle, and were at disadvantage as compared with the enemy.

"The rattling of musketry was heard during the latter part of the night, and before the break of day a sharp engagement occurred at the outposts. Soon after four o'clock the artillery opened its fire, which was continued without cessation till the close of the engagement.

"The right of our line was occupied by the Third Brigade, Colonel George H. Gordon commanding. The regiments were strongly posted, and near the centre covered by stone walls from the fire of the enemy.

"Their infantry opened on the right, and soon both lines were under heavy fire.

"The left was occupied by the First Brigade, Col. Dudley Donnelly commanding.

"The line was weak compared with that of the enemy; but the troops were well posted, and patiently awaited, as they nobly improved, their coming opportunity. The earliest movements of the enemy were on our left, two regiments being seen to move as with the purpose of occupying a position in flank or rear. General Williams ordered a detachment of cavalry to intercept this movement, when it was apparently abandoned. The enemy suffered *very serious loss* from the fire of our infantry on the left. One regiment is represented, by persons present during the action, and after the field was evacuated, as nearly destroyed.

"The main body of the enemy was hidden during the early part of the action by the crest of the hill and the woods in the rear.

"Their force was massed apparently upon our right, and their manœuvres indicated a purpose to turn us upon the Berryville road, where, it appeared subsequently, they had placed a considerable force, with a view of preventing reinforcements from Harper's Ferry. But the steady fire of our lines held them in check until a small portion of our troops on the right of our line made a movement to the rear. It is but just to add that this was done under the erroneous impression that an order to withdraw had been given. No sooner was this observed by the enemy than its regiments swarmed upon the crest of the hill, advancing from the woods upon our right, which, still continuing its fire steadily, withdrew toward the town.

"The overwhelming force of the enemy now suddenly showing itself making further resistance unwise, orders were sent to the left by Captain De Hauteville to withdraw the First Brigade, which was done reluctantly, but in order, the enemy having greatly suffered on that wing. A portion of the troops passed through the town in some confusion; but the column was soon reformed, and continued its march in order.

* * * * * * * * *

"Our march was turned in the direction of Martinsburg, hoping there to meet with reinforcements—the troops moving in three parallel columns, each protected by an efficient rear-guard. Pursuit by the enemy was PROMPT AND VIGOROUS; BUT OUR MOVEMENTS WERE RAPID and without loss.

"A few miles from Winchester the sound of the steam-whistle, heard in the direction of Martinsburg, strengthened the hope of reinforcements, and stirred the blood of the men like a trumpet. Soon after two squadrons of cavalry came dashing down the road, with wild hurrahs. They were thought to be the advance of the anticipated support, and were received with deafening cheers. Every man felt like turning back upon the enemy. It proved to be the First Maryland cavalry, Col. Witchky, sent out in the morning as a train guard. Hearing the guns, they had returned to participate in the fight. Advantage was taken of this stirring incident to reorganize our column, and the march was continued with renewed spirit and order. At Martinsburg the column halted two and a half hours—the rear-guard remaining until seven in the evening in rear of the town—and arrived at the river at sundown, forty-eight hours after the first news of the attack on Front Royal. It was a march of fifty-three miles, thirty-five of which were performed in one day. The scene at the river when the rear-guard arrived was of the most animating and exciting description. A thousand camp-fires were burning on the hillside, a thousand carriages of every description were crowded upon the banks, and the broad river rolled between the exhausted troops and their coveted rest.

"The ford was too deep for the teams to cross in regular succession. Only the strongest horses, after a few unsuccessful experiments, were allowed to essay the passage of the river before morning.

"The single ferry was occupied by the ammunition trains, the ford by the wagons.

"The cavalry were secure in its own power of crossing. The troops only had no transportation. Fortunately, the train we had so sedulously guarded, served us in turn. Several boats belonging to the pontoon train, which we had brought from Strasburg, were launched, and devoted exclusively to their service. It is seldom that a river crossing of such magnitude is achieved with greater success, and 'there never were more grateful hearts' in the same number of men than when, at mid-day of the 26th, we stood on the opposite shore.

"My command had not suffered an attack and rout. It had accomplished a 'premeditated' march of nearly sixty miles, in the face of the enemy, defeating his plans and giving him battle wherever he was found. * * *

"Our wagon train consisted of nearly five hundred wagons. Of this number *fifty-five were lost. They were not, with but few exceptions, abandoned to the enemy, but were burned upon the road. Nearly all of our supplies were thus saved.* The stores at Front Royal, of which I had no knowledge until my visit to that post on the 21st instant, and those at Winchester, of which a considerable portion was destroyed by our troops, are not embraced in this statement."

Compare the statement italicized, with Gen. Jackson's official one, which we have presented.

Having given precedence duly to Gen. Banks' official report, let us look at a few statements by eye-witnesses, and participants in the battles, or those who were on the spot soon afterwards. A young officer of the Irish Battalion, writes to his uncle:

"A series of successes have crowned our efforts. We first drove the enemy from Front Royal, defeating and capturing about six hundred prisoners, besides a *very* large quantity of stores of all kinds. Immediately after we got possession of the place a train loaded with coffee came in, which is a perfect God-send to us, as rations of that article have been stopped for some days. We then drove the remaining portion of the army toward Middletown, where we captured a large portion of their wagons, containing a little of most every thing. From thence we wended our way toward Strasburg, where all of their wagons fell into our hands. We left our camp, which was about two miles beyond Luray, and marched twenty-seven miles to reach Front Royal—this was on Friday—we marched all day and night Saturday, and reached Winchester yesterday (Sunday), about five o'clock, or about daybreak. The engagement lasted one hour and a half, but it was a terrific one, short as it was. Their force was repulsed and scattered, and, after once getting on their scent, we did not let them rest. In the three days we have captured about fifteen hundred prisoners. This I can safely say, but I think it will exceed that number, as they are still coming in. A squad of fifty-three has just passed our camp. This does not include the negro women our men bring in with them. Sometimes we see a group of a dozen or more prisoners with three or four negro women. By the way, while here, three of the Yankees *married* negro wenches. We are still pursuing the enemy, but it is the general impression that they will not stop this side of the Potomac. Gen. Shields left Winchester on Wednesday, crossing the mountains, but what course he took I have not learned. The rascals fired all the houses here filled with medical and quartermaster's stores, but the citizens put the fire out; so we save enormous quantities of every thing—stores enough for our army for twelve months. All of our men supplied themselves with clothes, shoes, blankets, and even shirts, socks, drawers, gloves, and every thing a soldier wants or needs.

* * * * * * * * *

"*General Jackson had his war-look on yesterday.* He was so fatigued that, after the fight, he actually went to sleep on his charger. He rode about the battle-field regardless of shot and shell, and looked as if nothing was going on. I was not half so much alarmed as I thought I would be, it being my first appearance on a battle-field. I met with many narrow escapes, as did all of us, for which I am truly thankful. I never felt so proud as when we marched victorious through the town of Winchester in pursuit of a fleet-footed enemy. Thanks to the Most High for his protection to our brave and gallant army. Just think of marching twenty-seven miles and fighting two hours. The men all call themselves Jackson's foot cavalry."

Another writer says:

"The enemy made but a short stand at Front Royal. The 1st Maryland Volunteers, on the Yankee side, was charged by the 1st Regiment of Maryland rebels, who put their old acquaintances to flight in a short time, capturing a stand of colors, killing several, and taking a number of prisoners.

"We took the enemy by surprise, and put them to flight before one-fourth of our forces had entered the town. The cavalry, among which were the Wise Troop and Jack Alexander's company, charged upon the Yankees, in the retreat, killing many, and capturing a large number of prisoners.

"Among the arms captured are about five hundred improved cavalry six-shooters, an article very much needed.

"When we entered Front Royal, the women and children met us with shouts of the liveliest joy. As we passed through the place in double-quick, we could not stop to partake of the hospitality so generously and profusely tendered on all hands.

"Among one of the squads of prisoners, about twenty in number, was a woman, mounted. When we came to the Valley turnpike, we found hosts of prisoners, and the road blockaded with dead and live horses, and wagons heavy laden with subsistence, &c., together with dead and wounded Yankees.

"At early dawn this (Sunday) morning, we advanced and attacked the mighty Banks in front of Winchester. After fighting about one hour, distributing shell and minié balls profusely, our boys made a charge, when the Yankees left at double-quick, after setting fire to the town, and burning their commissary stores.

"The Lee battery of Lynchburg and two others were ordered to pursue in a gallop, and the command was obeyed, they shelling the enemy for five miles.

"When the army passed through the town, men, women, and children were shouting, 'Thank God, we are free—thank God, we are free once more!' Confederate flags and white handkerchiefs were waved from every window, and the happy smiles of lovely women on all sides met the wearied soldier, and cheered him as he hurriedly passed through the place in pursuit of the flying foe.

"After pursuing the enemy for six miles, we were brought

to a halt, and left the finishing stroke to the cavalry, who have captured a large number of prisoners, who have been sent in through the day.

"Prisoners tell me that General Banks has said that he was afraid that he would have to surrender his whole command, and to be relieved of the painful necessity, and to save his own bacon, left before day on an extra car."

The following is from a member of Congress to a friend in Richmond:

"There never was a more successful and more decided and overwhelming victory. When our guns opened on the enemy at Front Royal, they had no idea who was hammering at them, thinking that Jackson was a hundred miles away from them. They were completely surprised and panic-stricken by the suddenness of the attack. They surrendered to us by hundreds, allowing all their stores of every sort, and in the greatest quantities, to be captured, without an effort to defend or destroy them.

"Banks was with the main body of his army at Strasburg when we took Front Royal, and alarmed by our guns, they abandoned their works (which are quite extensive at that point) and fell back towards Winchester; but before they had gotten half-way, old Stonewall was upon them, and their retreat became a rout.

"From Middletown to Winchester, and from thence to Martinsburg, the rush of the retreating wretches is represented to have been more ridiculously terrible than that at Manassas. Our batteries would open upon a wagon in front of a train, knocking it over in the road, and before those behind it could stop their headway, they would come thundering down upon the ruins of the first wagon, whilst other teams would be tumbling in upon them so as to block up the road completely, then Ashby's cavalry would charge upon the more forward of cavalry, or ride down the masses of disorganized infantry, and such a scene of confusion and conflict as they kept up for many miles you possibly may imagine; but I certainly cannot describe.

"Old Banks behaved in a most cruel and cowardly manner on this retreat. He was accompanied by a crowd of negroes whom he was running off to Yankee land, and he preferred to leave his own wounded in our hands than to allow the negro women and children to be turned out of the wagons and have them used for the transportation of the sick and suffering white soldiers of his own army.

"At the first salvo of artillery he puts spurs to his horse and distanced all competitors in the race from the field. At Middletown he stopped for a drink of water, and was blubbering like a baby because reinforcements had not been sent him.

"To give you an idea of the demoralization of the Yankees on their way from Strasburg, I will only mention one fact:

"In the ardor of pursuit, Ashby had separated himself from his men, and had gotten abreast of the Yankee column of cavalry, which was rushing down the turnpike. ALONE *he charged five hundred* of them—dashed through their line, firing his pistols right and left as he did so—then wheeling about, he again charged through them and summoned them to surrender. All who heard his voice at once obeyed, threw down their arms, dismounted, and, at the word, squatted as meekly as so many mice upon the ground, until some of our men came up and took charge of them. In one instance, he took thirty in this way. When our men would charge the Federal cavalry, they would tumble off their horses, roll over, scream and scramble to the road-side in the most amusing manner. But I cannot pretend to jot down a hundredth part of the incidents of this most remarkable victory.

"At Winchester the enemy tried to make a stand in the suburbs, but our boys drove them pell-mell through the streets, and soon beyond Martinsburg.

"Many were killed in the streets, and a remarkable feature of the day was that when the tide of battle rolled toward the town, the glorious women of Winchester turned out to give relief to our wounded and exhausted soldiers, and so regardless were they of danger that they were not deterred from their pious duty by the shot and shell which fell around them. In the streets our men had to advance a guard to clear the women out of the way for our platoons to deliver their fire. This, I am assured, was literally the case in more instances than one."

Another writer says:

"The wild joy with which the inhabitants, especially the ladies, greeted our army in Winchester and Charlestown, can be more readily imagined than described. The 2d Virginia regiment, composed of volunteers from Jefferson, Clarke, and Berkeley, marched through Charlestown with scarcely a halt; such was the pressure of the military discipline in which their brave commander trains them, that they neither asked nor received the privilege of halting to shake hands with their friends and dear ones, though a twelvemonth and more had elapsed since they took the field. The activity of a perpetual '*forward!*' seems to pervade this whole army."

Lincoln's order to McDowell to "put 20,000 men in motion," and go and destroy Jackson, will be recalled by the reader. Here is the manner in which they moved—the paragraph will not be found the least entertaining of those here presented. It is from a Yankee correspondent, whose candor is something unusual.

"Word was flashed over the wires from Washington that the Philistines were upon the Congressional Samsons, and we were summoned to the rescue. The order from the War Department, to send twenty or thirty thousand men to assist Banks and defend Washington, put an entirely new face on matters, and knocked the plans which a month and more of time and *millions of money* had been spent in maturing into that peculiarly chaotic, formless, and void shape popularly known and described as a cocked hat. As McClellan before had been served, so now was McDowell. * * We found the 104th New York at Catlett's Station, with neither tents, arms, nor clothing. They informed us that while innocently encamped at Thoroughfare Gap, undreaming of impending evil, word came to them from the War Department that they were utterly surrounded by the enemy, with an order to destroy every thing and fall back upon the impregnable fortifications and wooden guns of Manassas. So completely did they follow out this edict of destruction, burning tents, arms, equipments, and every thing else, that the only wonder is they didn't blow out their own brains—perhaps they would if they had had any.

"At Markham Station, besides rheumatic pains, I encountered Colonel Ashby's house, a deserted whitewashed tenement, with battered walls and crumbling staircases, and smelling strongly of secession and old cheese. From Markham to Front Royal such a road no intelligent gray mare, of domestic habits and a ruminative and ruminating turn of mind, ever encountered before. It seems as though all the men, women, and children of the country had spent their lazy hours—which, indeed, would include the whole period of their several existences—in rolling huge stones from the mountains down into the roads. If the war ever ends—and there is reason to believe that in the fulness of time it will—let me suggest that the Virginians of this section be punished for their contumacy by being made to pick up the stones, and with them build, in some less inconveniencing grounds, monuments to their own folly. At Front Royal we found Major-general McDowell and several minor generals. They were all determined upon one thing—that thing to bag Jackson and recapture the immense train he took from Banks—for you must know that Banks *lost over two millions of dollars in property, and it is said several thousand prisoners.* Well, then, it had been determined to retake all these national gods and goods.

* * "A word about Blenker's division. With all respect to General Blenker himself, whom I highly esteem as a German and a gentleman, it comprises a lawless set as ever pillaged hen-roosts or robbed dairy-maids of milk and butter. I saw a company of them gutting the cellar of a house, carrying off every thing eatable and drinkable, and only replying to the earnest remonstrance of the proprietary *widow*, and the representation that she had seven children to feed, with a guttural *nix fur stay*. And two infantry captains bathed their yellow beards in the golden cream, and were aiders and abetters, in fact, the overseers and directors of the larceny—not to say brutality.

* * * * * * * * *

"Through the openings between the trees we could see our brave boys surrounded by a cordon of fire, flashing into them from the muzzles of more than a thousand muskets. But not a sign, nor the shadow of a sign of yielding. Their fire met the enemy's, straight and unyielding as the blade of a matador. Oh, for reinforcements! but none came. * * Now our "Bucktails" give back, and anon they break cover and retreat across the fields of waving green between us, firing as they go—but not the hundred and fifty that went in. The rest of them lie under the arching dome of the treacherous forest, and the night dews alone can go to moisten the lips of the wounded ones, for the rebels hold the woods, and we are not now prepared to dislodge them. To send a force to their support would bring on a general engagement, and this, in our present unprepared condition, would be ruin."

We have seen how both Fremont and Shields, advancing from the east and the west to intercept and close in upon the rear of Jackson, entirely failed in their object, and were completely out-generalled. Jackson struck Fremont with his right wing and Shields with his left; stunned both; passed between the two columns, and composedly continued his march up the Valley.

On the 27th of May, at the moment when Banks was defeated and in full retreat—when the heavy column from Fredericksburg was marching toward the mountains, and when Lincoln was trembling for the safety of Washington—Gen. Johnston wrote to Gen. Jackson:

"The most important service you can render the country is the preventing the further strengthening of McClellan's army. * * You compel me to publish orders announcing your success so often, that you must expect repetition of expression."

It will be seen that these instructions were carried out.

We terminate this chapter with the official dispatch of Gen. Jackson, announcing the victory at Winchester:

"WINCHESTER, *May* 26th, 1862.

"GEN. S. COOPER, *Adjutant-general.*

"During the last three days God has blessed our arms with brilliant success. On Friday, the Federals at Front Royal were routed, and one section of artillery, in addition to many prisoners, captured. On Saturday, Banks' main column, while retreating from Strasburg to Winchester, was pierced, the rear part retreating towards Strasburg. On Sunday, the other part was routed at this place. At last accounts, Brigadier-general George H. Stewart was pursuing with cavalry and artillery, and capturing the fugitives. A large amount of medical, ordnance, and other stores have fallen into our hands.

(Signed) T. J. Jackson,
Major-general Commanding."

CHAPTER XIV.

ILLUSTRATIONS—CROSS KEYS: PORT REPUBLIC.

May had passed; June arrived—and the enemy had not succeeded in accomplishing their long-cherished design for the destruction of the rebel armies, and the occupation of the Confederate capital.

McClellan's huge army still confronted Richmond, swinging to and fro on either bank of the Chickahominy—uneasy, dubious, undetermined what course was best for it to pursue. A few days after the battle of Winchester, a portion of the Grand Army was defeated at "Seven Pines," but with that genius for hoping which characterizes these people, the fall of Richmond, distinctly in sight, with its roofs and spires, was looked forward to as an event very soon to take place. A portion of McDowell's force, it is true, was drawn off by Jackson, and he was so weakened that he could no longer hope to effect much by the junction with McClellan's right wing on the Chickahominy—forming the famous "cordon" above mentioned; but then the capital at Washington was safe; President Lincoln's terror dissipated; and the Government there enabled to crowd forward all their spare troops to the Peninsula. Fremont and Shields would soon make short work of the daring Jackson, whose lucky star would speedily be obscured—that general would be driven before them far up the Valley, along which he was then retreating; their combined armies would descend like a thunderbolt upon the rear of the

unfortunate Confederate den; and the rebellion would be "crushed" at a blow.

Such was the situation of affairs early in June—McClellan at "Seven Pines," within four or five miles of Richmond; McDowell on the march to join him; Fremont and Shields pursuing Jackson hotly up the Valley.

We have seen what events occurred at Cross Keys and Port Republic, on the 8th and 9th days of June, at the very moment when McClellan, perched in the top of a tall tree, as some of their writers describe him, was straining his eyes to discern the columns of McDowell on the horizon, and listening for the tramp of Fremont's legions from the mountains. Richmond was directly in his front, with the sunshine on its white spires—"the finest army on this planet" was beneath him, dull, inactive, resting in the trenches dug out from the treacherous mud of the Chickahominy swamp. All things were stagnant.

The news from Port Republic came to break this languid siesta of the Federals—and we have seen how that great battle was fought.

We proceed, as before, to give some of the details which we have collected, for the entertainment of the reader now, and the information of the future historian, who will gather sedulously every circumstance relating to the events of this great period. This book is written in a tent, on the outpost; the enemy yonder, almost in view—but with Jackson, alas! no longer in the front. The real historian of his life will write in a quiet study, in the tranquil days of peace, with no enemy, let us hope, anywhere in view, on all the vast horizon of the Confederate States.

Pardon, therefore, friendly reader, the faults of these pages, which the distant roar of artillery may at any moment interrupt the writer in tracing—and give the author credit for honesty, if not for style.

Fremont was routed at Cross Keys on the 8th of June,

On the morning of the 9th, Jackson turned like a lion upon Shields and hurled his whole column upon that commander, with the results which we have seen. The following details from participants in the battle are interesting:

"On Monday morning, about sunrise, our forces crossed the bridge at the junction of the two streams to attack the enemy, numbering about 12,000, under Gen. Shields, the river here makes a bend or crescent form, circling round a large piece of low grounds, on which there was a heavy crop of wheat. Nearly opposite the bridge and on the other side of this field, the enemy were drawn up in line of battle, and in their front, on a small hill, at the foot of Cole Mountain, commanding the whole position, was the celebrated Clark battery, (consisting of 8 splendid guns, 2 Parrott, 2 mountain howitzers, and 4 rifle pieces,) manned by the artillery corps, under command of —— Clark. From this battery was belched forth one incessant storm of grape, canister, and shell, literally covering the valley, so that the work of attack on our part seemed almost hopeless.

"Jackson, Ewell, and Taylor were all there, and their forces eager for the encounter. But it seemed rash and even desperate to attempt it. General Jackson looked for a while thoughtfully on the scene, and then turning to Taylor, inquired, 'Can you take that battery?—it must be taken or the day be lost.' Taylor replied, 'We can,' and pointing his sword to the battery, called out to his men, 'Louisianians, can you take that battery?' With one universal shout that made the mountains to echo, they declared they could; whereupon, he gave the order in that sonorous voice, 'Forward, charge the battery and take it.' Onward dashed the Louisiana brigade, composed of the 6th, 7th, 8th, and 9th Louisiana regiments, and the Tiger Battalion, assisted by one Virginia regiment, across the low grounds right after the battery. From its mouth now, with renewed violence, poured streams of shell and shot, mowing down our men like grass. The earth seemed covered with the dead and wounded.

"The gallant Colonel Henry Hays, commanding the 9th Louisiana regiment, was badly wounded. His Lieutenant-colonel, De Choine, was shot through the lungs, and after again and again endeavoring to hold his place on the field, was borne off almost insensible. This regiment, one of whose companies was led by Captain D. A. Wilson, of our town, carried into the fight but three hundred and eight effective men, the rest being sick or detailed on other service, of whom one hundred and fifty-eight were killed or wounded. Onward they rushed, sustained by the 6th, 8th, 9th, the Tigers, under Bob Wheat, and the Virginia regiment, all doing their duty like heroes. They dare the battery. Volumes on volumes of shot continue to salute their advance—but they do advance. They strike their bayonets and sabres into the artillerists as they serve the guns, they kill the horses, they seize the guns, they take the battery, and the victory is accomplished. Proud day and proud honor this for those who did this gallant deed! Jackson, Ewell, and Taylor were present cheering on the fight. Every officer, nay, every man, did his duty, the enemy flying in dismay, having no time to spike their guns, and our men seize and direct their fire against themselves. This was one of the most glorious battles of this war, and one of the bloodiest.

"When the bloody scene was over, a moment is spent in thankfulness to God, and another in silent rejoicing at the result. General Jackson now publicly thanked Taylor and the Louisiana brigade for the day's work. 'Take that battery,' said Jackson to Taylor, 'and keep it, for your men have won it—carry it to your native State when you return, and call it the Louisiana battery, and let it be kept as a memento of this day.'"

Another correspondent writes as follows:

* * * "So much for the eventful day of the 8th.

"Like the great Napoleon, General Jackson determined to fight the other column before it could effect a junction with the defeated army. Hence at early dawn on the morning of the 9th (Monday), our brigade was in motion. Having crossed the river, the head of our column was turned down the stream, and then we knew there was bloody work in store for us. About a mile below Port Republic we came in view of the enemy's batteries in position. Then General Jackson, who was at our head, ordered up two of our batteries, the Alleghany Roughs and Rockbridge. But the Yankees had every advantage in position, their left resting on the ridges of the mountain, and their right on the river. Their batteries were placed so as to sweep the ridges on their left and the batteries on their right, so the position of our guns was not as good as desirable. However, the hour for action has come, and the battle of Port Republic commences. The Yankee regiments are moving into line, the old 'Stars and Stripes' can be distinctly seen, but opposite floats proudly and defiantly the 'Sic Semper' of Virginia and the banner of our Confederacy. The 2d and 4th Virginia first moved into position on the enemy's left; the 5th and 27th on his right, next the river. Both of these are exposed to a heavy artillery fire. The Louisiana brigade and part of the 3d Virginia brigade now move into line also, and the bloody tragedy commences. The cannonading is heavy, and the rattle of musketry is sharp, especially on our left. The enemy fight well, for they are Northwestern men. Our left wing act at a great disadvantage, having to move up through dense thickets in the woods; also, the enemy sweep the ridges with canister. A shout comes up from the centre. 'Tis the 7th Louisiana charging one of the enemy's batteries. They take it, but are soon driven back by three regiments and canister from three other pieces. In the mean time the tide of battle rages in the bottom next the river, for there the fighting is desperate. Nothing is now heard save the roar of artillery and the rattle of musketry. A loud and prolonged shout now bursts on the ear. It comes from the 7th and 8th Louisiana, who have again charged and taken the enemy's battery of six guns. They are splendid in a charge! The enemy feel the loss of their guns, and their line wavers. Cheer after cheer bursts from our lines, for the enemy are giving way. Some of them break and run, but others retreat in tolerably good order. The cavalry now charge down the bottoms, making the very ground quake and the Yankees tremble. The Yankees make excellent time, the rout is complete, and the field is ours!

"Those are proud moments for the soldier, when he stands victorious on the bloody field, and sees the columns of the enemy in full retreat. We pursued them about six miles, the cavalry much further, capturing a large number of prisoners. The enemy's loss was heavy, and ours was severe too. Yet the insolent foe was repulsed, and to gain that end some of the best and the bravest blood of the South must be shed."

A trooper writes:

"This has been a week of exhaustion and toil to us—not a moment to write. We have had, indeed, little time even to eat or sleep. When I staggered out of my saddle last night, I had been in it for thirty-six hours, including the whole of the night previous. I slept not a wink, except while coming to camp, and then I dozed a little on my horse. I only dismounted twice during the period stated, and then for short periods.

"Yesterday, we had a terrific battle with one column of the enemy, utterly routing him, capturing 500 prisoners, seven pieces of artillery, four of them splendid brass rifled pieces, and a considerable number of small arms.

"Jackson's retreat, now safely accomplished, has been *even more brilliant* than was his advance, and will be so recorded by historians. With his army encumbered with the spoils of the enemy in vast quantities, with a wagon train probably seven or eight miles long, and with several thousand prisoners, he has retreated before an enemy numbering 20 to 40,000, advancing upon him by different roads, and under the lead of five or six generals of distinction. They threatened, at every road leading into the Valley, to get around him, and sometimes came near doing so, but General Jackson baffled them at every point. Always calm and cool himself, he kept them in perpetual excitement. He would dash like a lion first at one and then at another, always making them feel his fangs in a vital place, till their very caution defeated their object.

"Yesterday the enemy (and our own army agreed with them) thought they had entrapped us. We were in a narrow valley, at one end the enemy as strong as we, and at the other doubly as strong, with only a river between us and them. Jackson whipped the smaller column, and carried off the prisoners, &c., in the very presence of the others, while they were trying to cross the river. To do so, he passed to this point through a trail in the mountain, the mouth of which cannot be noticed from the main road, or, at least, it would never be suspected to be passable for an army, the existence of which neither the enemy nor our army had any suspicion. Until we entered this road, I thought we were gone, for beyond the enemy we whipped there was another overwhelming force, and the road in the direction of Port Republic was entirely commanded by the other large force, whom we could see crowning the heights, and no doubt gnashing their teeth at our escape."

The story of Jackson ordering the removal of one of the enemy's guns from the bridge, and when his order was obeyed by the Federal cannoneers, composedly riding by, has been often repeated, and under many forms. A correspondent of a Northern paper gives what seems to be a truthful version of the affair, and we append his statement:

"Yesterday I met Captain Robinson, of Robinson's battery, on his way home to Portsmouth, Ohio, to recruit. He was at the battle of Port Republic, where his brother lost three guns, and was wounded and made prisoner. Capt. Robinson, who appears to be a very modest and veracious man, relates that while he was working one of his guns, Stonewall Jackson, whose form was familiar to him, came within easy hailing distance, and, standing erect in his stirrups, beckoned with his hand, and actually ordered him to 'bring that gun over here.'

"Captain Robinson replied by eagerly firing three shots at the ubiquitous Presbyterian, but without even the effect of scaring him. 'I might have known,' said he, 'that I could not hit him.'

"Captain Robinson is utterly at a loss to explain this extraordinary personal demonstration of the redoubtable 'Stonewall.' Whether he mistook him for one of his own men, or that some incomprehensible ruse was involved in the act, he does not pretend to guess. But one thing he does know, that Stonewall Jackson is the great man of the war, and that our troops in the Valley believe him to be as humane as he is rapid and daring."

A Southern writer, commenting upon the above, says:

"This story has some truth in it. The fact, as we believe, is that Jackson, finding that this gun commanded the bridge which it was necessary for him to pass, for once in his life played the Yankee, and, riding briskly forward, ordered the gun to be moved to another place, which he designated. The ruse succeeded. The Yankee captain limbered up and commenced moving his piece, when Old Stonewall, putting spurs to his horse, dashed across the bridge. The Yankee discovered the ruse, and let fly with his gun, but it was too late. It was not in the book of fate that the glorious chieftain should fall in that way. We devoutly pray that it may never be his lot to be lost to us by the hand of the enemy."

Sad, prophetic words! "We devoutly pray that it may never be his lot to be lost to us *by the hand of the enemy.*" No enemy's hand struck down the peerless soldier at last. A chance volley from the Confederate lines laid low the pride and glory of the South.

Among the saddest events of those June days in the Valley was the death of Turner Ashby. We find many allusions to this heroic soul in the letters of the time; and the figure of the cavalry leader on his milk-white battle-horse will long remain present to the memory of those who saw him. That historic steed had already received his death wound, in relation to which we find the following paragraph:

"We learn that the gallant Ashby, a few days ago, whilst falling back before the enemy, who pursued along the Valley turnpike, alighted to aid a few men in destroying the bridge across the Shenandoah. The last caisson of his artillery had thundered by, and the Yankee cavalry pursued so closely that a number had crossed the bridge before it could be destroyed. Springing upon his noble gray charger, Ashby sped along the turnpike, followed by eight of the enemy. His pistols were unfortunately empty, and he had no resource but flight. The chase continued for nearly two miles, the Yankees firing at him as they ran. As he neared a place of safety, two of the Yankees, who had outstripped the rest, were nearly abreast of him, when one of them was shot by some of his men, and the other was killed by Ashby with his sabre.

"During the latter part of the chase a shot fired by a long-range gun, at a distance of nearly half a mile, struck his horse in the side. The faithful animal continued with unabated speed, and saved his rider, but the wound was mortal. He was led along the line of a regiment under arms. Our informant says he never imagined so magnificent and spirited an animal. He was white as snow, except where his side and legs were stained with his own blood. His mane and tail were long and flowing; his eye and action evinced distinctly the rage with which he regarded the injury he had received. He trod the earth with the grandeur of a wounded lion, and every soldier looked upon him with sympathy and admiration. He had saved his master at the cost of his own life. He almost seemed conscious of his achievement, and only to regret death because his own injuries were not avenged."

The noble rider was soon to terminate his earthly career, also. This is not the occasion to speak of this brave soul—this noble type of chivalric Southern manhood. The fame of Ashby lives fresh and green in every heart, and the words of Jackson's report will be his epitaph forever.

As before, we append Jackson's dispatch announcing the victory. It is in the following words:

NEAR PORT REPUBLIC, JUNE 9TH,
Via Staunton, June 10th.

Through God's blessing, the enemy near Port Republic was this day routed, with the loss of six pieces of his artillery.

T. J. JACKSON,
Major-general Commanding.

The fall of Ashby had been more than avenged.

CHAPTER XV.

JACKSON IN JUNE, 1862.

AT sunset, on the 9th of June, the campaign of the Valley had terminated.

It had commenced in earnest on the 11th of March, when Winchester was evacuated before the column of nearly 50,000 Federals advancing upon the place. It terminated on the red day of Port Republic, when Jackson routed all his foes, and remained undisputed master of the region.

Thus this great campaign extended over a period of exactly three months.

Those three months will shine forever in our annals, bright with the light of heroism and victory. The astonishing nerve, the almost superhuman endurance, the dash, the skill, the chivalric courage, and the stubborn resolution of the little handful of Confederates and their great leader, will render them and the beautiful region of the Shenandoah famous through all time.

Nothing was expected of Jackson. It is as well to state that fact here. We mean that none but those who had seen and known him well in Mexico believed that he would accomplish any thing. The Romney expedition was regarded as a hair-brained project; and many persons did not hesitate to express their convictions of a want of sanity on the part of the man who devised it. But these cavillers were soon silenced. Kernstown closed some mouths; Winchester and Port Republic quite hushed the foolish babbling about the great leader.

The critics began to understand that war reveals men: falsifying all estimates previously made of them in the quiet days of peace. Jackson was regarded as a common-place, somewhat eccentric "professor," who, by some singular chance, at an early period in his life, had blundered into the arena of arms. A command was intrusted to him by those who knew him better, and the result is before the world. He has surrounded the name of his native land, Virginia, with a halo of glory brighter than all past revolutionary glories;—and to-day is only second to the greatest name of all.

The campaign of the Valley, upon which, as we have said, his fame will chiefly rest, will be studied by military men, through all coming time, as the campaigns of Cæsar and Napoleon are studied—as the recorded work of a master in the art of war. For this class, Jackson will always remain one of the Kings of Battle. Combat was the element in which his great soul breathed freely, and he made war with the air of one "to the manner born." His astounding marches; his rapid advances and masterly retreats; his furious onslaughts before which no enemy could stand, and his sudden disappearance when the enraged foe brought against him overwhelming odds; the manner in which he executed all these movements; the provoking, baffling, incredible strategy which he brought to bear upon the enemy—have made his name and fame as a leader of men immortal in the annals of the South. The children and children's children of the present generation will point out, on the map of Virginia, the positions of Kernstown, and Winchester, and McDowell, and Port Republic—classic names forever now, since Jackson associated them with his glory.

We leave to the historian of the future the task of narrating this great campaign in all its splendid details—to tell in terms which "mount to the height of the great argument" how Jackson marched, and planned, and fought; how he conquered at Bath, Romney, Kernstown, Front Royal, Middletown, Winchester, Charlestown, Strasburg, McDowell, and elsewhere; how he fell upon the enemy finally at Port Republic, whipped him in two battles, and drove Shields and Fremont, as he had driven Milroy and Banks, to ignominious flight. Here we only touch upon the great contests, as upon the man who fought them. In the campaign of March–June, 1862, Jackson displayed all his faculties fully—his far-seeing generalship; his prudent boldness; his indomitable, vice-like resolution and tenacity of purpose, which no storm could shake, no peril affect. Under the calm and simple exterior of the man was a soul that was not born to bend—a will which shrunk from nothing, and broke down every obstacle opposed to it. To say that no braver man ever lived, is to say little. Nothing is better established than the fact that Jackson loved danger for its own sake—a point which we propose to return to—but this common courage which does not recoil from the hissing ball or the bursting shell, was not the courage of Jackson. His stern resolution was deeper and stronger. What marked him as one of the "men of fate" was his astonishing equanimity in the face of perils which would have overwhelmed other men; his cool determination not to "give up;" his refusing to entertain the idea that he could be defeated. At Manassas he surveyed with utter calmness the terrible spectacle of the Confederate lines, reeling back before the Federal hosts, pressing down with their enormous reserves of infantry and artillery; and when Gen. Bee, with uncontrollable anguish in his voice, told Jackson that the day was going against them, his cold reply was—"Sir, we will give them the bayonet." The last words of the brave South Carolinian tell how he fought his old brigade. He stood "like a stone wall"—as stern, stubborn, and immovable. At Kernstown, when a portion of his line gave back before the overwhelming numbers assailing it, he took his stand close to the enemy, amid a storm of bullets—called to a drummer boy—and placing his hand firmly upon the boy's shoulder, said in his brief, curt tones—"*Beat the rally!*" The rally was beaten; Jackson remained by the drummer's side, holding him to his work with the inexorable hand upon the shoulder—the rally continued to roll, and the line was speedily re-formed.

The writer of these lines has seen Gen. Jackson in several great battles, when the "revel of death" was at its height, and the fate of the day hung suspended in the balance—but he never saw the great soldier show the least agitation or doubt of the result. At Fredericksburg, his cheeks glowed and his eyes had the "war-look"—but that was late in the evening, when he had ordered his whole line to advance and attack with the bayonet.

This, however, is not the appropriate place for a characterization of Jackson. We reserve that for the concluding pages of our work. At present, other great events demand attention, for the victor of Winchester and Port Republic, without pausing, enters upon another struggle on a new arena. The Valley is exhausted—every portion of its highways and byways has been trodden by the "Foot Cavalry" until they know, and attach sad or pleasant recollections—memories of fatigue and suffering, or rest and refreshment—to every stone, and bank, and spreading tree upon the road-side; the mountains are left behind, and the old Stonewall Brigade, with their comrades, led by their idolized chief, set out for fresh fields of combat in the lowlands.

Biographies are lame and incomplete affairs when they only contain events and dates. These are the skeleton; but the skeleton expresses no individuality. What is needed, in addition, is the flesh and blood—the flashing eye and the eloquent lip. Events and dates are valuable for reference, but personal details make the picture which impresses the feelings and dwells in the memory, for meditation, example, and instruction.

We have seen what Jackson accomplished. Let us now endeavor to see what manner of man, outwardly, it was who thus overthrew all his enemies, and built himself a name which is the echo of glory and victory. How such men look is interesting—how they dress and appear among their fellowmen. Jackson's costume and deportment were unique, and have doubtless contributed in some degree to that amazing individuality which he has secured in the popular mind. The writer of these lines first saw him soon after the battle of Port Republic, and can thus present an outline of the great athlete, as he appeared, all covered with the dust of the arena, whereon Banks and his compeers had been overthrown by him. Jackson was in his fighting costume at the moment; it was the conqueror of the Valley who moved before us; and, to complete the picture, he had, at the moment when we first encountered him, his "war-look on"—was in his veritable element.

The outward appearance of the famous leader was not imposing. The popular idea of a great general is an individual of stiff and stately bearing, clad in splendid costume, all covered with gold lace and decorations, who prances by upon a mettled charger, and moves on, before admiring crowds, accompanied by his glittering staff, and grand in all the magnificence of high command. The figure of General Stonewall Jackson was singularly different from this popular fancy. He wore an old sun-embrowned coat of gray cloth, originally a very plain one, and now almost out at elbows. To call it sun-embrowned, however, is scarcely to convey an adequate idea of the extent of its discoloration. It had that dingy hue, the result of exposure to rain and snow and scorching sunshine, which is so unmistakable. It was plain that the general had often stretched his weary form upon the bare ground, and slept in the old coat; and it seemed to have brought away with it no little of the dust of the Valley. A holiday soldier would have disdained to wear such a garb; but the men of the Old Stonewall Brigade, with their brave comrades of the corps, loved that coat, and admired it and its owner more than all the holiday uniforms and holiday warriors in the world. The remainder of the general's costume was as much discolored as the coat—he wore cavalry boots reaching to the knee, and his head was surmounted by an old cap, more faded than all: the sun had turned it quite yellow indeed, and it tilted forward so far over the wearer's forehead, that he was compelled to raise his chin in the air, in order to look under the rim. His horse was not a "fiery steed" pawing, and ready to dart forward at "the thunder of the captains and the shouting," but an old raw-boned sorrel, gaunt and grim—a horse of astonishing equanimity, who seemed to give himself no concern on any subject, and calmly moved about, like his master, careless of cannon-ball or bullet, in the hottest moments of battle.

The general rode in a peculiar fashion, leaning forward somewhat, and apparently unconscious that he was in the saddle. His air was singularly abstracted; and, unless aware of his identity, no beholder would have dreamed that this plainly clad and absent-looking soldier was the idolized leader of a great army corps, at that very instant hurling themselves, column after column, upon the foe.

The glittering eye beneath the yellow cap would have altered somewhat the impression that this man was "a nobody"—that wonderful eye, in whose blaze was the evidence of a slumbering volcano beneath; but beyond this, there was absolutely nothing in the appearance of General Jackson to indicate his great rank or genius as a soldier.

Such was the outward man of the famous general, as he appeared soon after the campaign of the Valley—and this plainness of exterior had in no small degree endeared him to his soldiers. His habits were still greater claims on the respect and regard of the best men of his command. He was known to be wholly free from all those vices which are the peculiar temptation of a military life. He lived as plainly as his men, and shared all their hardships, never for a moment acting upon the hypothesis that his rank entitled him to any luxury or comfort which they could not share. His food was plain and simple; his tent, when he had one, which was seldom, no better than those of the men; he would wrap himself in his blankets and lie down under a tree or in a fence corner, with perfect content, and apparently from preference; for to fight hard and live hard seemed to be the theory of war. He was a devout Christian, and rarely allowed passion to conquer him; when he yielded, it was on exciting occasions, and when great designs were thwarted by negligence or incapacity on the part of those to whom their execution was intrusted. Such occasions seldom occurred, and Jackson's habitual temper of mind was a gentle and childlike sweetness; a simplicity and purity of heart, which proved that he had indeed become "as a little child"—walking humbly and devoutly before his God. Prayer was like breathing with him—

the normal condition of his being. Every morning he read his Bible and prayed, and the writer will not soon forget the picture drawn by one of his distinguished associates, who rode to his headquarters at daylight, last November, when the army was falling back to Fredericksburg from the Valley, and found him reading his Testament, quietly in his tent, an occupation which he only interrupted to describe, in tones of quiet simplicity, his intended movements to foil the enemy. Before sitting down to table he raised both hands, and said grace. When he contemplated any movement, his old servant is said to have always known it by his "wrestling in prayer" for many hours of the night; and on the battle-field thousands noticed the singular gestures with the right arm, sometimes both arms, raised aloft. Those who looked closely at him at such moments saw his lips moving in prayer. Like Joshua, he prayed with uplifted hand for victory!

Napoleon trusted in his stars; Jackson in God. In the great scenes through which we shall now see him pass, the hand of the Lord of Hosts will be clearly revealed, according to the true soldier of the Cross, full triumph over all the enemies of his country.

CHAPTER XVI.

COLD HARBOR.

In the latter part of June, the writer of these lines was intrusted, for delivery to a confidential messenger, with a dispatch addressed "Gen. T. J. Jackson, somewhere."

"Somewhere" was, at that moment, as upon many previous occasions, the only known address of the rapidly-moving and reticent commander of the Army of the Valley.

Jackson was on his march to join Gen. Lee. Having

publicly directed his engineer to furnish him, speedily, with maps of the country about *Lexington*, and thus, after a fashion common with him, thrown all speculators, as to his intended movements, off the scent, he had, on the 17th of June, commenced his march toward tide-water. General Robertson's cavalry brigade, with Chew's battery, was left at Harrisonburg, to watch the movements of the enemy in that direction, and check him, if he again advanced upon Staunton; and with the rest of his corps, Col. Munford's cavalry bringing up the rear, Jackson pushed forward, reaching the neighborhood of Ashland, about sixteen miles from Richmond, on the 25th of June.

Jackson's corps at this time consisted of General Whiting's Division, embracing General Hood's 3d Brigade, Colonel Law commanding, with the batteries of Reilly and Balthis; Gen. Ewell's Division, 4th Brigade, General Elzey; 7th Brigade, General Trimble; 8th Brigade, Colonel Seymour; and the Maryland Line, Colonel Johnson, with the batteries of Brockenbrough, Carrington, and Courtney; Jackson's (old) Division, 1st Brigade ("Stonewall"), General Winder; 2d Brigade, Lieutenant-colonel Cunningham; 3d Brigade, Colonel Fulkerson; 4th Brigade, General Lawton; and the batteries of Poague, Carpenter, and Wooding. These veterans, who had met and overthrown the enemy on so many battle-fields of the Valley, were now on their rapid march to join Lee on the banks of the Chickahominy, and try their mettle upon Gen. McClellan.

The position of the opposing armies of Lee and McClellan, at the moment when Jackson was sent for, is familiar to every boy in the Confederate States; for so intense was the interest felt in the movements of these two great gladiators, about to contend, front to front, for the possession of the Southern capital, that even the children of the land knew the position of affairs. McClellan had crossed a portion of his army to the right bank of the Chickahominy, and advanced within four or five miles of Richmond, elaborately fortifying and guarding his flanks. On the left or north bank of the stream, the remainder of his army was strongly posted on the heights from Meadow Bridge, nearly due north of the city, to Bottom's Bridge, nearly due east. The Federal position thus resembled a crescent, some twenty miles in extent, which the Chickahominy intersected near the lower extremity.

General Johnston had struck at the Federal left, near Seven Pines, and driven him back on the last day of May. Wounded in the action, this accomplished soldier had yielded the command to General Lee; and the design of again assailing the enemy without delay, was speedily adopted by that general. A flank movement against McClellan's right, beyond the Chickahominy, was determined upon; and as Jackson, with his invincible corps, had just disembarrassed himself of Shields and Fremont, he was ordered by the commander-in-chief to hasten forward from the Valley, and passing by way of Ashland toward Cold Harbor, attack the enemy in flank and reverse, while the main body of the army assailed him in front.

On the morning of the 26th, the great plans of Lee began to unfold themselves, and the immense drama commenced. The enemy were driven off at the point where the Brooke turnpike crosses the Chickahominy, and Brigadier-general Branch crossed, directing his march to form a junction with General A. P. Hill, who had crossed at Meadow Bridge. Hill engaged the enemy at Mechanicsville, and stubbornly held his ground until night, when the enemy retired from his position there, and fell back upon the main body at Gaines' Mill. The way having thus been cleared, General Longstreet's corps, consisting of his veteran division, the Old Guard of the Army of the Potomac, and General D. H. Hill's division, debouched from the woods on the south side of the stream, crossed, and took position on the left bank.

Meanwhile Jackson had steadily advanced, preceded and

guarded on his left by Stuart's cavalry, toward Cold Harbor, on the enemy's right and rear. General Whiting's division held the advance, and the Federal forces retired before him. At Tottapotomoi creek, a sluggish stream, with abrupt banks, heavily wooded, the enemy's picket felled trees across the road, and destroyed the bridges. Hood threw forward some of his Texas skirmishers, however, Capt. Reilly opened with his guns, and the enemy disappeared. Whiting quickly repaired the bridges, the army resumed its march, and still skirmishing and driving the Federals, bivouacked for the night at Hundley's Corner. Jackson, following the orders of General Lee, had thus borne away from the Chickahominy, where the reverberating roar of artillery indicated the progress of a great battle—had gained ground toward the Pamunkey, driving all before him—and was now in a position to descend, next day, like a thunderbolt on the enemy at Cold Harbor, attacking with his fresh troops, and deciding the fate of the day.

The great day arrived, clear and cloudless. Jackson gradually converging toward the Chickahominy again, and advancing steadily, with Ewell in front, drove the enemy before him, surmounted every obstacle which they had placed upon the roads to bar his progress, and about five in the afternoon reached Cold Harbor.

Not a moment was lost in making his dispositions for battle. Stuart, with his cavalry, was posted on the left to charge and intercept the enemy if they attempted to retreat in the direction of the Pamunkey; and hardly had line-of-battle been formed, when heavy firing on the right indicated that Gen. A. P. Hill, who had gone in that direction, was hard pressed. Jackson immediately ordered a general advance of his entire corps, which hastened forward, Whiting's division on the right of the line, and Jackson's, Ewell's, and D. H. Hill's, in the order named, from right to left.

The welcome sound of Jackson's guns came to Lee and

Longstreet as they were hastening forward from Gaines' Mill, and the entire Confederate force on the left bank of the Chickahominy, which had only awaited the arrival of Jackson, advanced in one wild charge, and the battle began to rage with a fury, until then unknown.

We do not attempt a general account of this mighty contest—that is left to the historian of the war. We confine our notices of events to the part taken in the battle by Gen. Jackson's corps.

The position of the enemy in his front was a powerful one, and nothing but hard, stubborn fighting could carry it. The Federals were posted on a ridge nearly parallel to the Chickahominy—their right resting near McGee's house, their left on a bluff, bristling with artillery, and protected by a deep ravine, and double line of breastworks. In their front a swamp and sluggish stream, a wood of tangled undergrowth, and heavy masses of felled timber, made successful attack almost hopeless. Jackson ordered Gen. D. H. Hill to make the assault on the left, and it was done with great gallantry and success. The men rushed through the swamp, tangled underwood, and felled trees, in face of a heavy fire; and after a fierce and bloody contest, drove the enemy back on their reserve. They took position behind a fence and ditch; and Hill determined to press on, when his attention was called to a battery which was so posted as to pour a destructive enfilading fire upon his advancing line. It was necessary first to silence this battery; and Col. Iverson, with the 1st, 3d, and 20th North Carolina, charged and captured it. The enemy immediately attacked him in force, and succeeded in recapturing the guns, but not until Gen. Hill had advanced over the dangerous ground, and, supported by the "Old Stonewall Brigade," under Gen. Winder, was engaged in an obstinate contest with the entire Federal force in front of him.

Meanwhile, Gen. Ewell had a hard fight upon Gen. Hill's right. The same obstacles barred his advance upon the enemy's position, but he charged through the swamp, up the hill in face of a terrible fire, and fought with that daring which had so often excited the admiration of his commander. Reinforced by Lawton and Trimble, Gen. Ewell continued the struggle until dusk, when his ammunition being completely exhausted, he fell back.

Jackson's old division was the third in the line, counting from left to right, and was held as a species of reserve, to be sent to the support of any part of the line which was hard pressed. The 1st "Stonewall" Brigade moved on the enemy's front through the swamp, so frequently mentioned, and did some of the hardest fighting of the whole day. The enemy contended with especial obstinacy for the possession of the ground at this point, which was the key of his position; and the roar of his artillery and musketry, as his fire converged upon it, was appalling. Jackson said that night, in the hearing of the writer, that it was "the most terrible fire of musketry he ever heard," and all who heard it will recognize the truth of the description. The old brigade did not flinch from the ordeal. Under its brave leader, Gen. Charles Winder, it moved steadily on, amid the tempest of projectiles, and driving the enemy from point to point, stormed his last position, three hundred yards beyond McGee's, with the bayonet. The 2d Brigade was sent to reinforce Gen. Wilcox, at his own request, but arrived too late to take part in the engagement. The 3d Brigade, sent to support Whiting, also came too late. The 4th Brigade took part in the general charge late in the evening.

Gen. Whiting's division, which held the right of Jackson's line, advanced through the wood and swamp, in face of a murderous fire. Hood's 4th (Texas) Brigade charged with a loud yell, and rushing down the precipitous ravine, leaping ditch and stream, pressed forward over the enemy's abatis, and every obstruction, driving all before them. They lost 1,000 men, but they took 14 pieces of cannon, nearly a regiment of prisoners, and strewed the ground with the Federal dead. It was of the Texans that Jackson, on the next day, said, as he surveyed the ditch and abatis over which they had charged: "The men who carried this position were soldiers indeed."

The movements which we have thus related in sequence, took place together, all along the line. It was a close, almost hand-to-hand encounter on our part, with small-arms only—but with one striking exception. The only artillery used was that of Capt. John Pelham, of the Stuart Horse Artillery. Pelham was sent forward with two guns, a Blakely and Napoleon, to a position in advance of the old Cold Harbor House, and ordered to engage the enemy's batteries on the eminence in front, diverting their fire from Hill, and the Stonewall Brigade. Capt. Pelham performed this important duty with a gallantry and nerve which extorted the admiration of all who witnessed the affair. He opened upon the heavy batteries of the enemy at close range with unfaltering resolution; and though his Blakely gun was soon disabled and obliged to be withdrawn, he continued to fight the batteries in front with his one Napoleon, directing the management of the gun in person, and holding his ground with that stubborn courage which afterwards immortalized the young artillerist at Fredericksburg. The diversion produced by the galling and persistent fire of the Napoleon was exceedingly important in its effect upon the fortunes of the day; and other batteries having been brought up and put in action at the same point, the enemy's fire began sensibly to slacken.

It was at this moment, and just as night was descending, that the general and decisive charge was made all along the line, in obedience to Jackson's brief, stern order—"Press them with the bayonet," Hill's, Ewell's, Whiting's, and Jackson's divisions all charged. Hood's Texans and the Stonewall Brigade, in advance of all the rest, pressed forward with cheers of defiance, over every obstacle—and before this terrible charge in front, and the storm of artillery on their right, the enemy wavered, broke, and were put to rout. Posted in advance of his batteries, his figure clearly revealed by the fires which the enemy had kindled to draw the artillery fire from their guns—Jackson heard the wild cheers of his men as they pursued the flying enemy in the direction of Grapevine Bridge.

The foe was routed, and as Jackson's brigade decided the fate of the first battle of Manassas, so Jackson's corps decided the day at Cold Harbor. The heroic troops who had driven the enemy from their powerful positions on the Chickahominy, back to the point where they fell into the stern clutch of Jackson, were nearly exhausted by the enormous struggle; and when the roll of musketry at Cold Harbor announced the presence of Jackson with his veteran troops, fresh for the encounter, a thrill ran through the Confederate host, and the hearts of the Federals sunk.

Jackson's appearance decided all.

CHAPTER XVII.

THE RETREAT OF M'CLELLAN TO MALVERN HILL.

When night fell on Friday, June 27, 1862, Gen. McClellan was routed.

Thenceforward the only question was, how could he withdraw his shattered and disheartened forces to a place of safety. Two lines of retreat were left—both perilous. One down the Peninsula, with the vengeful Confederates assailing him at every step; forcing him to turn and give battle day by day, if, indeed, the first encounter did not terminate in the destruction of his command. The other toward James river, on the right bank of the Chickahominy, right through the Confederate lines—through swamps and streams—over treacherous roads—with Lee on his rear and flank, ready to destroy him.

Neither prospect was inviting, but rapid decision was necessary; and Gen. McClellan determined to retreat toward Harrison's Landing, on James river.

The following paragraphs from the army correspondence of the *New York Tribune*, exhibits the condition of affairs at the moment when the retreat commenced; and the first sentences contain a statement of the effect produced upon the minds of the enemy by Jackson's flank attack at Cold Harbor:

"My note book says that, at 6 o'clock, the enemy commenced a determined attack on our extreme right, evidently with a design of flanking us. It was an awful firing that resounded from that smoke-clouded valley—not heavier than some in the earlier part of the engagement, but more steady and determined. It was only by overbearing exhausted men with fresh ones that the enemy succeeded in turning that flank, as, at length, he did succeed, only too well; and he accomplished it in three-quarters of an hour. At the expiration of that time, our officers judiciously ordered their men to fall back; the order was not obeyed so judiciously, for they ran back, *broken*, *disordered*, *routed*. (Italics those of the correspondent.) Simultaneously the wounded and skulkers about the buildings used as hospitals, caught a panic, whether from a few riderless horses plunging madly across the field, or from instantaneously scenting the rout, does not appear. A motley mob started pell-mell for the bridges. They were overtaken by many just from the woods, and it seemed as if Bull Run were to be repeated.

"Meanwhile, the panic extended. Scores of gallant officers endeavored to rally and re-form the stragglers, but in vain, while many officers forgot the pride of their shoulder straps, and the honor of their manhood, and herded with the sneaks and cowards. Oh, that I had known the names of those officers I saw, the brave and the cowardly, that here, now, I might reward and punish by directing upon each individual the respect or the contempt of a whole people!

"That scene was not one to be forgotten. Scores of riderless, terrified horses, dashing in every direction; thick flying bullets singing by, admonishing of danger; every minute a man struck down; wagons, and ambulances, and cannon, blockading the way; wounded men limping, and groaning, and bleeding, amid the throng; officers and civilians denouncing, and reasoning, and entreating, and being insensibly borne along with the mass; the sublime cannonading, the clouds of battle-smoke, and the sun just disappearing, large and blood-red—I cannot picture it, but I see it, and always shall."

It is only justice to the fallen leader to say that he conducted the movement towards Harrison's Landing with great military skill; and although he had the benefit of some terrible negligence, incapacity, misunderstanding, misconception,—call it what you will,—on the part of his enemies on the right bank of the Chickahominy, yet he achieved the movement successfully, and got under cover of his gunboats, broken down and shattered, but not cut to pieces and annihilated.

The battles which took place every day during this retreat will long be memorable for the obstinate courage of the Confederate assaults, and the heavy losses inflicted upon both combatants. Otherwise, the battles are not important. They were terrible, bloody, full of the darkest tragedy, but not decisive. McClellan massed his artillery finally at Malvern Hill, and maintained his ground until night, when he evacuated his position and retreated to Harrison's Landing, under cover o. his gunboats.

We shall only touch upon the movements of Gen. Jackson during these days. He had his part in the stirring events of the time, but we shall not dwell upon this portion of his career —simply adverting to the operations of his corps in the various battles.

On the morning of the 28th, Jackson sent Gen. Ewell forward to Dispatch Station, on the York River Railroad, Gen. Stuart being in advance with his cavalry. The cavalry attacked and routed a party of the enemy, and Ewell tore up and destroyed the railroad at that point. Finding from cavalry reconnoissances toward the White House that the enemy had not retreated in that direction, Gen. Ewell proceeded toward Bottom's Bridge, on the next day, returning thence and rejoining the main corps.

On the night of the 29th, Jackson, who had remained, up to that time, upon the battle-field, put his corps in motion, and crossed to the right bank of the Chickahominy, at Grapevine Bridge. This bridge had furnished an avenue of escape to McClellan on the night of the 27th, when his army gave way; and, having passed over the rolling and uncertain structure of loose logs, half buried in the slushy soil, he had destroyed it behind him. Jackson hastily reconstructed it, and pushing forward, arrived at Savage's Station, on the York River Railroad, where he gathered up about 1,000 stragglers from the Federal army, and found immense stores abandoned.

From Savage's Station he proceeded to White Oak Swamp, and came upon the enemy strongly posted with artillery and sharpshooters in advance, behind the stream; the bridge over which they had passed having been destroyed. Here a hot artillery fight took place, but the enemy continued to fall back, and Jackson pressed forward to Frazier's farm, where he met Generals Lee and Longstreet, and was assigned to the front. His presence infused new ardor into the pursuit of the retreating enemy, and, advancing under an incessant fire, he found his corps confronted by the entire army of McClellan, drawn up on Malvern Hill.

The Federal commander had thus escaped to an almost impregnable position, but, in doing so, had passed through scenes the description of which, in army letters, harrowed for many months the blood of the whole Northern people. In that retreat of the defeated army, the depths of tragic horror were fathomed—human endurance seemed to have been exhausted. The following sentence from the *New York Tribune's* correspondent will convey some idea of the scene:

"Huddled among the wagons were 10,000 stragglers—for the credit of the nation be it said that four-fifths of them were wounded, sick, or utterly exhausted, and could not have stirred but for dread of the tobacco warehouses of the South. The confusion of this herd of men and mules, wagons and wounded, men on horses, men on foot, men by the road-side, men perched on wagons, men searching for water, men famishing for food, men lame and bleeding, men with ghostly eyes, looking out between bloody bandages, that hid the face—turn to some vivid account of the most pitiful part of Napoleon's retreat from Russia, and fill out the picture—the grim, gaunt, bloody picture of war in its most terrible features.

"It was determined to move on during the night. The distance to Turkey Island Bridge, the point on James river which was to be reached, by the direct road was six miles. But those vast numbers could not move over one narrow road in days; hence every by-road, no matter how circuitous, had been searched out by questioning prisoners and by cavalry excursions. Every one was filled by one of the advancing columns. The whole front was in motion by seven P. M., General Keyes in command of the advance.

"I rode with General Howe's brigade of Couch's division. taking a wagon track through dense woods and precipitous ravines winding sinuously far around to the left, and striking the river some distance below Turkey Island. Commencing at dusk, the march continued until daylight. The night was dark and fearful. Heavy thunder rolled in turn along each point of the heavens, and dark clouds spread the entire canopy. We were forbidden to speak aloud; or, lest the light of a cigar should present a target for an ambushed rifle, we were cautioned not to smoke.. Ten miles of weary marching, with frequent halts, as some one of the hundred vehicles of the artillery train, in our centre, by a slight deviation crashed against a tree, wore away the hours to dawn, when we debouched into a magnificent wheat field, and the smoke stack of the Galena was in sight. Xenophon's remnant of ten thousand, shouting, 'The sea! the sea!' were not more glad than we."

It is certain that the whole Federal army shared this feeling.

Another writer in the *New York Times*, who strives to conceal the extent of the enemy's discomfiture, says:

"When an aid of General McClellan rode back and reported that the way was all open to James river, a thrill of relief ran through the whole line, and a sight of the green fields skirting its banks was indeed an oasis in the terrible desert of suspense and apprehension through which they had passed. The teams were now put upon a lively trot, in order to relieve the pressure upon that portion still in the rear.

"General McClellan and staff rode ahead and took possession of the old estate known as Malvern Hill, one mile back from Turkey Island Bend. It is a large, old-fashioned estate, originally built by the French, and has near it, in front, an old earthwork, constructed by General Washington during the Revolutionary War. It has a spacious yard, shaded by venerable elms and other trees. A fine view of the river can be had from this elevated position. General McClellan expressed the opinion that, with a brief time to prepare, the position could be held against any force the enemy can bring against us.

"Exhausted by long watching and fatigue, and covered thickly with the dust of the road over which we had passed, many officers threw themselves upon the shady and grassy lawn to rest. The soldiers also, attracted by the shady trees, surrounded the house, or bivouacked in the fields near by.

"General McClellan immediately addressed himself to the task of preparing dispatches for the government."

From the composition of his dispatches, announcing the successful occupation of a new and more favorable position for his projected advance upon Richmond, Gen. McClellan was diverted by the intelligence that the enemy were approaching to attack him in his last stronghold.

In speaking of the hard-fought battle of Malvern Hill, we shall confine ourselves to a brief notice of the part taken in the contest by Gen. Jackson's corps. The command lost here some of its best men—sleeping now amid the dim pines of Charles City.

Jackson formed his line in the following order: Whiting's division on the left, at Poindexter's farm; D. H. Hill more to the right; Taylor's brigade of Ewell's division, forward between Hill and Whiting, the rest of that division, in rear of the first line. Jackson's division was halted near Willis's Church, and held in reserve, concealed amid the dense woods.

Hill hearing, as he supposed, the signal from Gen. Lee for a general advance, put his lines in motion, and advanced to attack the tremendous position before him. He was met by overwhelming numbers, and so hard pressed that he was compelled to call urgently for reinforcements. Jackson promptly sent forward Ewell's reserve and his own old division, but owing to the swampy nature of the ground, the thick undergrowth and gathering darkness, their march was so much retarded that they did not arrive in time to enable Hill to maintain his position. He was forced to fall back with heavy loss, at nightfall.

On the left, Gen. Whiting with his batteries drove back an advance of the enemy upon Jackson's centre; but this was decisive of no results; Jackson's corps slept on the field in front of the enemy—but in the morning the Federal army had retreated.

Such was the part borne by Gen. Jackson in the battle of Malvern Hill one of the most hotly contested of the war. It has not been necessary to the design of this work, to describe the great combat in all its details, any more than the battle of Cold Harbor. We add, however, the following animated sentences of a writer soon after the event, which convey a very truthful idea of the fury of the contest, and the conditions upon which it was fought.

"Gen. McClellan," says this writer, "prepared, in the language of one of his officers, to 'clothe the hill in sheets of flame.' Every ravine swarmed with his thousands, and along the crest of every hill flashed forth his numerous artillery, having for the most part an unbroken play over the ascending slope, and across cleared fields of twelve hundred yards in length.

"Notwithstanding the formidable nature of this position, it was determined to attack him. It was not in the plan of our skillful and able general-in-chief, whose genius had conceived the whole of the strategy which crushed McClellan, to permit the enemy to stand at bay, and arrest our terrible pursuit merely by a show of battle-array—and so, late in the afternoon of Tuesday, 1st July, this tremendous contest commenced. Soon Malvern Hill was sheeted with ascending and descending flame of fire. Thirty-seven pieces of artillery, supported at a greater distance by heavy and more numerous batteries, and by his gunboats, kept faithful ward over the enemy's position, and ploughed through our columns even before they could see the enemy or deploy into line of battle. Undismayed by the most terrible cannonading of the war, the terrible advance of Magruder's forces commenced. Onward, in the face of a storm of shot and shell, they pressed forward, until in musket range of the enemy, and then they opened their terrific fire. Whole lines of the enemy fell as they stood, or, attempting retreat, were overtaken by the fatal bullets of our troops, who never veered in their aim or recoiled, while the enemy's infantry remained in range, and when forced back for a time by the avalanche of converging artillery, yet when the infantry of the enemy ventured again beyond their batteries, our heroic lines advanced with shout and bayonet, and drove them back among the reserves and behind the wall of fire which flamed along the mouths of the circling cannon. Thus the contest ebbed and flowed until night spread its mantle on the battle-field.

"The batteries of the enemy were not captured by assault, because no line of men could live in their converging fires, sweeping unobstructed the attacking forces for twelve hundred yards, but his line of infantry was repeatedly broken with frightful slaughter by the fierce charges of our troops, who held their position and slept on the field, within one hundred yards of the enemy's guns. The extent of the carnage of the enemy no one imagined until daylight revealed it in the horrors of the battle-field. Our dead lay close together, producing thus upon the beholder an exaggerated impression of the number; but an examination showed that the loss of the enemy much exceeded ours. His dead lay everywhere—

here in line of battle, there in wild confusion of rout and retreat—not a ravine, not a glade, not a hill that was not dotted by their mangled forms, while every dwelling, out-house, barn, and stable for miles around was crowded with their dead and dying. In many places groups of dead were found distant from the battle-field, where it was evident they were carried with the intent of bearing them to the river, and where they were roughly and rudely tossed on the wayside when the panic overtook their escort. Every indication showed the wildest flight of the enemy. Cannon and caissons were abandoned, and for miles the road was filled with knapsacks, rifles, muskets, &c., &c. Loaded wagons were left in the road, with vast quantities of ammunition unexploded. Caisson drivers opened their ammunition chests and threw out their powder and round shot to lighten their loads, to enable them to keep up with the rapid flight. It is hazarding but little to say, that when night put an end to the battle, the whole army of McClellan, with the exception of the artillery, and its diminished infantry guard near Crew's and Turner's houses, was utterly disorganized, and had become a mob of stragglers. At daylight next morning nothing could be seen of his army except some cavalry pickets, that in the distance observed our advance. We do not believe that fifteen thousand of the Grand Army of the Potomac retreated from the bloody heights of Malvern Hill as soldiery. If nature had scooped out the bed of James river twenty miles distant from Malvern Hill, the Grand Army of the Potomac would have ceased to exist."

McClellan had been enabled, by massing his artillery upon strong positions, to repulse a portion of the Confederate assault, and hold the ground until the welcome shades of night put an end to the contest. But the battle of Malvern Hill, indecisive as it appeared, had a conclusive effect upon the Federal army. The frightful carnage which took place in their ranks bore heavily upon the spirits of men who were completely exhausted by the prostrating fatigue and excitement of six days of marching and fighting, almost without rest or food. From the 26th of June, the Federal troops had had no breathing space. They were either engaged in desperate combat with the foe during all that time, or retreating, hotly pursued. That foe, like a vengeful Nemesis, still hovered over them, as fresh and vigorous, to all appearances, as ever, and under these combined influences of fatigue, famine, disaster, and hopelessness, the hearts of the enemy sunk. They gave up all further idea of victory; many threw down their arms, and *sauve qui peut* was now the order of the day throughout almost the entire Federal army. They no longer looked forward toward the Confederate lines, but backward toward Harrison's Landing, where, under the shelter of the gunboats, they saw their only hope of extrication from the horrors which surrounded them. Broken in spirit, prostrated physically, and seeing in further contests additional disaster only, they gave up the struggle, straggled away, and arrived at the haven of safety a confused and disorderly mob, rather than a disciplined and effective army.

Let the following paragraph, from the correspondent of the *New York Tribune*, at Harrison's Landing, on the 2d of July, describe the demeanor of General McClellan, and the condition of his troops:

"General McClellan came on board the mail boat, greatly perturbed. He met General Patterson as he stepped on board, laid his hand on his shoulder, and took him in a hurried manner into the aft cabin, or ladies' saloon. As he went in he beat the air with his right hand clenched, from which all present inferred there was bad news. To the astonishment of the writer, it was subsequently explained 'that the whole army of the Potomac lay stretched along the banks of the river where we lay, having fought their way all through from Fair Oaks, a distance of thirty miles.' General McClellan, however, claimed that his troops 'had fought the Confederates in superior numbers every day for a week, and whipped them every time.' To a question as to the location of certain divisions and their generals, the answer was, 'They are scattered everywhere, but are, nevertheless, in a solid, compact body.' And in reply to another remark, it was said, 'What we want is fresh men; they (the troops) are worked to death.' The description of the troops, on a dead level on the banks of the river, covered from head to foot, and up to their knees in mud in the soft, moist alluvial soil, is painfully graphic. 'Under some trees which lay in clusters, the men were crouched. They looked,' says the writer, 'as if they were more dead than alive. They were covered to the crown of the head with mud; their faces and clothes were literally coated, while their shoes and boots had several pounds of the nasty yellow stuff into and all around them.'"

Such was the termination of the long agony of invasion—defeat, disaster, ruin. The boasted plans for taking the Confederate capital had all failed. The splendid army, which, by General McClellan's sworn statement on his trial, amounted to more than 150,000 men, of whom 112,000 were hale, hearty and effective, had been routed and overwhelmed; beaten in battle after battle; driven ignominiously from its positions, and huddled together—a shrinking, trembling, broken-spirited flock of sheep—under the bristling portholes of the gunboats on James river. That tragic end of all its hopes was patent to the great world of America and Europe. Glozing dispatches could not smooth over the disaster; the pretence of a premeditated "change of base," to a more favorable position for advancing upon Richmond, deceived nobody. The Old World and the New—England, France, New York, Lincoln and Seward, and their compeers—saw that this was *defeat;* for the time, final, irrevocable defeat. McClellan had played for a great stake; brought all his skill, strategy, brain and strength and nerve to bear upon the contest. The game went against him; he was bankrupt; and the world would not believe that he rose the winner.

We have presented a rapid narrative of these great battles, so far as Jackson's corps took part in them. The statements of fact are all that is needed: comment is unnecessary. The plans of General Lee were those of a great commander, and the best proof of their eminent wisdom lies in the fact, that McClellan speedily discovered, but could not counteract them.

The hand of Fate was on him, in the person of Lee; he had been outgeneralled; and, though prompt intelligence reached the Federal commander, as he stated on his trial, that Jackson was approaching—though he wrote to Lincoln, on the 25th of June, that he would "probably be attacked to-morrow"—the position of his forces was such that he could not guard against the assault, and his fate was already decided. The hand upon the dial pointed to the fated moment; the hour struck; and the star of McClellan, the "Young Napoleon" of popular fancy, went down in blood.

Lee had thus outgeneralled, and soon outfought and triumphed over his opponent. He had proved himself the greatest captain of the age, but with what magnificent lieutenants! Longstreet, the hard, stubborn, unyielding fighter, who, like the "War Horse," a name given him by Lee, snuffed the coming battle, and fought with a skill, a courage, a resolution, so admirable! Stuart, the prince of cavalry leaders, with his native genius for the career of arms, his nerve, his daring, his *élan* in a charge, and that coolness which never deserted him, whatever peril menaced, or disaster seemed imminent. A. P. Hill, of the "Light Division," the chivalric, dashing, steady, indomitable leader. Ewell, the blunt, stern, abrupt, thoroughly reliable soldier, who never yielded, and compelled victory to his standard. Hood, the immovable rock, which dashed back every wave that struck it. The generals of divisions and brigades; the colonels of regiments; the commanders of squadrons and battalions; the captains of companies—all cooperated in this grand result, upholding the hands of their great commander-in-chief, and insuring the success of the Confederate arms.

Among those lieutenants of the great captain one name shines with unsurpassed lustre—the name of Jackson. It was Jackson who came with his fresh troops to decide the fate of the obstinate contest; to hurl his trained legions upon the enemy, and to drive them from the hard-fought field.

With what skill, courage, and perfect success this was done, the reports of General Lee will show. These two men had now met for the first time in the war; had seen each other at work; and there sprung up at once between the two eminent soldiers, that profound respect, confidence, and regard, which thenceforth knew no diminution, no shadow of turning. Jackson said of Lee, "He is *a phenomenon.* I would follow him blindfolded." And when the former was struck at Chancellorsville by the fatal bullet which forced him to quit the field, Lee wrote:

"I have just received your note informing me that you were wounded. I cannot express my regret at the occurrence. Could I have dictated events, I should have chosen, for the good of the country, to have been disabled in your stead. I congratulate you upon the victory which is due to your skill and energy."

It was on the field of Cold Harbor that this great and noble friendship had its beginning. The men measured each other, face to face, saw each the other's stature; and thenceforth knew what they had to rely on. This utter confidence was the crowning glory of both; and the note of Lee at Chancellorsville will remain forever the glorious epitaph of Jackson; the declaration of the latter, above recorded, is a noble authority for the historian of the future, in delineating the great form of Lee.

Jackson fought at Cold Harbor and Malvern Hill, as everywhere, with the science of a great soldier; but the arduous toil and anxiety of earlier days in the Valley was spared him. His troops no longer required watching, and careful manœuvring, to make them victorious. The raw levies had become veteran legions; the inexperienced volunteer officers had grown to be masters of the art of fighting. Like bloodhounds, they had only to be loosed, to follow with unerring accuracy the trail of victory. The writer of this page saw Gen. Jackson in those days, and he was utterly calm. He had the air of one who knew upon what he relied, and foresaw the event. His troops and the skilful leaders who commanded them, had been placed in position; the lines of the enemy pointed out; thenceforth, the affair lay with them; and once unleashed, these dogs of war never paused until the prey was run down, and in their clutch.

Malvern Hill was the end of the struggle around Richmond. It is true that Gen. Lee sent Jackson forward on the next day, toward Harrison's Landing, and that, on the day after, there was a desultory skirmish between the opposing forces. But the roll of great events was exhausted; the curtain had fallen upon the bloody drama.

The Confederate army remained in front of the enemy until the 8th of July. Jackson was strongly in favor of an advance, and subsequent revelations, by Gen. McClellan, of the strength and condition of his army at that time, afford ample grounds for believing that such an advance would have terminated in his destruction.

Upon grounds, however, which seemed to them at that time conclusive, the Confederate authorities determined to retire; and on the 8th of July, our forces were accordingly withdrawn. Jackson's corps fell into line, left the hot pine woods in which they had lain, sweltering, in front of the enemy, and took up the line of march for the neighborhood of Richmond.

Jackson had lost at the battle of Cold Harbor, 589 killed, and 2,671 wounded. At the battle of Malvern Hill, 377 killed, and 1,746 wounded.

The famous corps had sustained, in the fullest degree, its noble reputation, won in the hard combats beyond the mountains; had left its mark all along the road from Ashland, by Cold Harbor, to Malvern Hill; but, alas! had left, too, some of its most precious blood, poured out in the lowlands, as other precious blood had been, in the Virginia Valley. Those brave hearts sleep now under the green sod of the Hanover slopes; in the silent and mysterious swamps of the Chickahominy; and beneath the dim pines of Charles City, sighing over their unknown graves. But they are not forgotten. Their names are linked with the name and fame of Jackson, and will live forever.

CHAPTER XVIII.

POPE.

THE disastrous termination of the battles around Richmond only aroused the Northern government to new efforts. Hard fighting had failed to secure their object; brutality and frenzied rage against the "rebels" were now to be the controlling elements of the Federal policy.

All restraints of decency were to be laid aside; the rules of civilized warfare ignored; the gentlemen of the South contending in open and honorable conflict for their homes and liberties were to be treated as slaves in revolt against their masters.

The radical party had finally gained the ascendency, and the signal was given for new and more extensive preparations for carrying on the war. The object now was to overwhelm, by every means, honorable or dishonorable, the strength oi the "rebellion."

A bill was passed confiscating the slaves of all persons loyal to the South. Another act directed slaves to be armed and enrolled as troops. Military commanders were authorized to seize and make use of any property, real or personal, belonging to citizens of the Confederacy, necessary or convenient for their commands, without compensation to the owners.

The war was thus to be conducted in future upon the *radical* programme; upon the fundamental principle that rebellion against the "best government the world ever saw" was a crime of so deep a dye, that those guilty of it, should be treated without mercy, and as enemies beyond the pale of civilized warfare. Napoleon, when it was necessary, subsisted his armies on the country through which he passed, but honestly paid for every thing. It was reserved for the Federal government to seize every species of property without compensation; to ransack clothes-presses and china closets, and rob the very hen-roosts and dairies.

The new campaign was to be inaugurated in that beautiful region of Virginia lying north of the Rappahannock and Rapidan. During the month of July, while McClellan was still lying on the hot shores of James river, with a portion of his defeated army, fresh levies were rapidly hurried forward to Washington. That city became one great camp: and under the inspiring influences of the new radical *régime*, a large force was soon ready to take the field. This body of men was known as the "Army of Virginia"—and was speedily sent forward to Warrenton, Little Washington, and Fredericksburg, with a view to advance upon Gordonsville, and cut the communications between Richmond and Staunton.

The command of the "Army of Virginia" was intrusted to Major-general John Pope; a personage chiefly renowned for having been cowhided without resistance by a Southern gentleman, for embezzling large sums of public money, and for having been guilty, while commanding in Missouri, of outrages which "challenge a comparison with the most infernal record, ever bequeathed by the licensed murderer to the abhorrence of mankind."

The career of Pope in Virginia is one of the most grotesque chapters in the annals of war. Let us not speak of him with indignation, or in terms of labored insult. Opprobrious epithets cannot reach him; and the present writer would derive no satisfaction from dwelling on the fact that Gen. Pope, as all now concede, was a braggart, a poltroon; guilty of systematic falsehood; and proved to have perpetrated in his own person, outrages which mark the low-born and low-bred wretch. He has been called a "Yankee compound of Bobadil and Munchausen." But unfortunately this Bobadil commanded a large army; this Munchausen signed "Major-general" beneath his name.

Before following the further movements of General Jackson, let us notice some of the proceedings of the Federal troops, under the leader whom he was soon to overthrow. The subject, as we have said is grotesque: and suppressing our indignation at the outrages which laid waste one of the fairest portions of the State, we may contemplate with a species of curious interest, the doings of these vermin; their robbery of hen-roosts; their predatory excursions in search of eggs; their guttural reply to all questions, "*I vites mit Ziegel;*" and their amusing confidence in their resistless prowess, up to the very moment when they fled, affrighted before Jackson—their great commander Pope, for once *not* bringing up the rear.

One of the few pieces of light literature read in the latter days of his life, by General Jackson, was an article in a number of the *Cornhill Magazine*, styled "Campaigning with General Pope." This article gave the experiences of a roving Englishman from Washington to Cedar Run, and presented a curious picture of the state of things at the moment. Some of these incidents, derived from various sources, will furnish, as we have said, an appropriate introduction to the battle of Cedar Run, in which the outrages perpetrated upon the defenceless inhabitants were fully avenged.

General Pope, the willing instrument of the brutal party now in the ascendant, was tall of stature, vulgar in feature, and full of "brag and bluster." He had secured his command by boasting and braggadocia—by the declaration, that he "had seen nothing of his enemies but their backs;" and he now prepared to sustain himself by still more magnificent rodomontades.

He knew the character of his countrymen, and arrived at his headquarters in a special car, decked out with flags and streamers, floating in the wind. He then proceeded to pen his "order" to the army.

"I desire you to dismiss from your minds certain phrases, which I am sorry to find much in vogue among you. I hear constantly of taking strong positions and holding them: of lines of retreat, and bases of supplies. Let us discard such ideas. The strongest position which a soldiea should desire to occupy, is the one from which he can most easily advance upon the enemy. Let us study the probable line of retreat of our opponents, and leave our own to take care of itself. Let us look before and not behind. Disaster and shame lurk in the rear."

Such was the order issued by General Pope on taking command, and the last sentence had something prophetic in it. "Disaster and shame lurked in his rear" as he advanced, and as he fled. His next order was, that all disloyal male citizens should be immediately arrested; the oath of allegiance offered them; and if they took it, and "furnished sufficient security for its observance," they should be released. If they refused it, they should be sent beyond the extreme pickets, and if found again within his lines treated as spies—that is, shot. "If any person having taken the oath of allegiance as above specified, be found to have violated it, he shall be shot, and his property seized and applied to the public use." Lastly, "all communication with any person whatever living within the lines of the enemy" was prohibited; "any person concerned in writing, or in carrying letters or messages, will be considered and treated as *a spy*." Such was the infamous "Expatriation Order" which General Pope fulminated at the peaceful inhabitants of Culpepper. It was followed by another more execrable still, issued by Steinwehr, one of Pope's subordinates, to the effect that the prominent citizens in every district should be arrested, and held as hostages for the good behavior of the population. If any of the Federal troops were "bushwhacked"—that is, shot by guerillas or irregular troops, the citizens should suffer death.

It is obvious to what all this tended—complete subjugation of the people, soul and body. But it ludicrously failed. Pope has only the historic infamy of his atrocious "orders"—they utterly failed to attain their purpose. The brave women and children of Culpepper laughed at him: the old men swore at him to his face; and the great Yankee Bombastes Furioso, by the enormities which he committed, only hastened the steps of the inexorable fate which approached in the form of Jackson.

A few details of the manner in which searches and "subsisting on the country" were accomplished will appropriately introduce, as we have said, the great events which followed.

We present these details just as they were given by eye-witnesses of both parties, and leave the reader to make his own comments.

A gentleman of Culpepper writes:

"One peculiarity in the army of the '*greatest of our generals*,' ought to be recorded as a matter of some possible interest in the future. There were two regiments, forming a corps of lictors and executioners, who usually went in advance—yet in different squads—for the purpose of gathering the first spoils, and of striking terror to the hearts of the people. They were stated (by their comrades of a more decent complexion) to consist almost exclusively of public malefactors (the only exceptions being young men who were induced to take commissions), selected and hunted up amongst all the most notorious dens of infamy and crime in the United States.

* * * * * * *

"An elderly gentleman was sitting in his porch, and of a sudden a large body of cavalry galloped up into his yard and surrounded his house. The officer who had, as a rider or officer, the appearance of an overgrown cobbler or weaver, dismounted and entered his porch. The gentleman rose and addressed him: 'Will you take a seat, sir?' 'No, sir,' said

the colonel; 'I have come to make a search of this house.' Gentleman—'Well, sir, I hope you will make a thorough examination, and I will assist you, with a hope that I may be spared any future visitations of this sort.' (Calling to a servant.) 'Boy, bring me all the keys of the house.' He proceeded, followed by the colonel. 'We will first explore this room; it is the parlor; there, sir, are some presses.' Colonel—'What's in them, sir?' Gentleman—'Books, sir, I believe, exclusively; but I desire that you examine them all for yourself,' at the same time throwing open the upper part. All were books. Yankee—"There's a lower part. What's in that?' 'Open it, sir, and look for yourself.' All books again. Yankee—'There's a box, sir. What's in that?' 'I think, sir, it's a box packed by my family; but I desire you to make a thorough exploration of it. I will open it if I can find the key.' The box was opened, in dived the Yankee colonel, and stirred and rummaged every thing inside; but finding nothing but towels, baby clothes, and such trumpery, he emerged, to pursue his search elsewhere; and as he did so he saw the hilt of a sword of the last century, so hanging as for the blade to be hidden by one of the presses. He was immediately animated with the idea that he had probably made an important capture. 'Why, sir,' said he, '*here's a sword;* what's that doing there?'—at the same time taking it down. Gentleman—drawing himself up to his full height, and looking with a most withering scorn upon the low-bred brute, replied calmly and deliberately—'Yes, sir, that is a sword. It has a little story which gives it a value in my eyes. It would be of very little use to the Federal army. It was buckled on by a young officer, who was in the first company formed in the State of Virginia for the war of the Revolution. He fought with it in the first battle South, and afterwards at Yorktown. He was never absent from the army during the entire Revolution. He fought with it at Saratoga, and Trenton, and Monmouth, and Germantown, and Brandywine, and on many other fields. He returned home aud continued a warm friend of Washington, and well known to Washington. He lived for a great number of years the intimate friend of John Marshall, who was also his companion in arms; and when he died he left me that sword. That portrait hanging near is his, and I am his son! The gentleman was *Daniel F. Slaughter*—perhaps as generally, certainly as favorably known as any man in the State of Virginia.'"

The same gentleman gives the following account of the treatment of the Rev. Mr. George, near Culpepper Courthouse. This clergyman, on the appearance of the enemy, applied for a guard, which was furnished, in the person of one soldier. Mr. George then says:

" 'But before the guard arrived some twenty or more men collected in the garden and yard, went at once to work in destroying my bees, broke into my study through the back window, broke open my desks and a trunk, stealing a variety of things, and tumbled all my papers into confusion and disorder.' The guard that came first, Mr. George said, seemed to try to protect him, but it was impossible. 'The work of housebreaking and plundering proceeded until nearly every locked place on my plantation had been forcibly entered—not excepting the basement rooms of my dwelling-house—some of them several times.'

" His crop of wheat was wasted or taken off, his corn-house repeatedly broken open and the corn carried off, spring-house broken open, every thing, such as vessels, &c., stolen and taken away. Then came fresh regiments, 28th New York and 46th Pennsylvania. Depredations proceeded. 'My study was again broken open, and robbery was the order of the day. General Crawford soon after came and established his headquarters in my yard, and although he continued the guard granted by Colonel Donelly, and appointed others, it seemed impossible to arrest the work of housebreaking and plunder, which was increased by the well-known order of General Pope.'

* * * * *

" 'Gen. Pope and his staff arrived, and my yard became *his* headquarters also. No sooner had his train arrived than my garden inclosure, in different places, was thrown down, a blacksmith shop set up in the garden, and various horses tethered in it also. * * * Almost all the fencing on my plantation was now burnt up. * * * I addressed a note to Gen. Crawford's A. A. G. upon the subject, and the next day received a verbal reply to the effect, that although *sorry for me, they could do nothing for my relief, and that I had better prepare to submit to my fate.*

" 'During the time of their occupancy of my premises, my beautiful farm was laid waste, the meadow, which would have yielded not less than fifty tons of hay, a clover field, which would have produced as much more, one hundred and twenty acres of fine sod land, two thousand bushels of wheat, forty bushels of oats, not less than fifty barrels of corn, the field of growing corn, from which I expected a yield of four hundred barrels, almost destroyed by government men and horses; every gate on my farm cut up or broken, carriage curtains torn off, and much of the carriage houses and doors burnt up, fifteen hundred dollars' worth of horses and colts, one hundred dollars' worth of cattle, one hundred and fifty dollars' worth of sheep, one hundred dollars' worth of hogs, together with my saddles and bridles, wagon harness, &c. * * * In consideration for which, I have, up to this time, a quartermaster's receipt for five or six barrels of corn and twelve tons of hay. * * * I became acquainted with a number of *privates*, who seemed to understand that citizens here had rights that ought to be respected. But the great body of them, as they appeared to me, delighted in that interpretation of Gen. Pope's order, which gives a license for robbing all who may belong to "*Secesh Land.*" I know not how often bitter curses were heaped upon me, my life and the destruction of my property threatened for kindly remonstrating against their robbery. In some instances, when asked if they had authority from a quartermaster or commissioned officer to appropriate my property to their uses, they referred me to Gen. Pope. I may mention, that within so many weeks my study was five times broken open, and my corn house and barn not less than one dozen times, each. This brief review sickens me. I feel thankful to officers and men who showed me kindness, and refer the cases of those of a contrary character to the decision of him who judgeth righteously.'"

From the same series of records we take the following description of the Northern soldiers:

"Of the rank and file I know but little. Some companies seemed to be of a decent agricultural or mechanical complexion; but by far the greater part were the most unsavory-looking wretches I ever beheld. The Irish were the next best; then came the genuine Dutch, about as cleanly and intellectual as the overgrown sows of 'der Vaterland.' Meeting a greasy-looking beast of that brood, I asked him, 'What do you want here? Are you fighting for Fraternity and Union?' Perfectly incapable of comprehending me, he drawled out, '*Yah! Vat you mean!*' I repeated the question in an explanatory way, but in vain. As I turned from him, he said: '*Ve vites mit Ziegel!*' Next came the selected assassins and thieves, who were probably received upon certificates of their actual convictions and service in the penitentiaries. And last, and worst of all, the Puritans and psalm-singers of pious New England—their care to look after the little niggers' morals, and to attend to the general business of the Underground Railroad. These are the people who have been sent with 'the greatest of our generals,' as a Northern paper calls Major-general John Pope—a commander suited to the force, a force worthy such a commander.

"When the celebrated proclamation, embodying the facts that *he came from the West, never looked but at the backs of the enemy*, and had established his headquarters in his saddle, was published, he was not yet in the field! It was from his arrival, or a few days afterwards, that I propose to take him up, and to proceed to recount his deeds and record his end."

The most detailed accounts of the depredation of Pope's troops are, however, derived from the enemy themselves. So shocking were these permitted, if not ordered transgressions of all the laws of decency and common honesty, that even some of their own men had the grace to exclaim against them, and demand, for the honor of their people, that these enormities should be checked.

One of these Federal correspondents from the army writes:

"A great evil exists to a great extent in the army of Virginia. I allude to the practice of procuring (through itinerant traders and city hucksters) every denomination of spurious paper and broken bank-notes, as well as *fac-simile* notes of the Confederacy, and passing them indiscriminately upon the unsuspecting inhabitants, poor as well as rich, old and young, male and female. Your correspondent is cognizant of several instances where this has been perpetrated, in return for kind nursing by poor aged women. Unless this system is checked, will not the whole country be overrun by the hordes of counterfeiters and swindlers on the close of the war?

"The country is flooded with bogus Secesh money; it is impossible, in many cases, to tell the good from the bad. We went into a small store at 'Orleans' one day, where they were selling 'fip calico' at thirty-five cents per yard, and the whole contents of the store you could carry in a bushel basket, and found the proprietor was taking all the paper offered. On looking over his 'pile,' we found four different kinds of Richmond ones, and two of fives. Many were the most worthless imitations. He was very indignant at 'Banks's men,' whom he alleges passed it upon him.

"Meeting an aged contraband this morning, who had been into camp selling eggs, butter, &c., we found he had 'pay for massa' in Secesh paper, nearly all bogus. He said he did not care what kind it was; he took whatever was offered."

Another, writing from Culpepper Court-house, draws the full-length picture as follows:

"The army of Virginia has undergone a marked change in a very important particular. The new usage which has been instituted in regard to the protection of Confederate property, and the purpose of the Government to subsist the army, as far as practicable, upon the enemy's country, has produced a decided revolution in the feelings and practices of the soldiery, and one which seems to me very much to be regretted.

"Unless these innovations are guarded by far more stringent safeguards against irregular and unauthorized plundering, we shall let loose upon the country, at the close of the war, a torrent of unbridled and unscrupulous robbers. Rapid strides toward villany have been made during the last few weeks. Men who at home would have shuddered at the suggestion of touching another's property, now appropriate remorselessly whatever comes in their reach. Thieving, they imagine, has now become an authorized practice, and under the show of subsisting themselves, chickens, turkeys, hams, and corn have become a lawful plunder, with little discrimination as to the character or circumstances of the original owner.

"It is to me a very serious and unfortunate state of facts, when soldiers will rush in crowds upon the smoke-house of a farmer, and each quarrel with the other to get the best and greatest share. I blush when I state that on the march through a section of country, every spring-house is broken open, and butter, milk, eggs, and cream are engulfed, almost before the place is reached by the men. Calves and sheep, and, in fact, any thing and every thing serviceable for meat, or drink, or apparel, are not safe a moment after the approach of the army. Even things apparently useless are snatched up, because, it would seem, many men love to steal.

"At a place where I not long ago spent a night, scarcely an article to which the fertility of a soldier could suggest the slightest use remained to the owner upon the following morning. There had been soldiers there, you might wager. Pans, kettles, dish-cloths, pork, poultry, provisions, and every thing desirable, had disappeared. The place was stripped, and without any process of commissary or quartermaster. So it has been in innumerable instances. Many a family, incapable of sustaining the slightest loss, has actually been deprived of all.

"I not long ago saw a dozen soldiers rushing headlong through a field, each anxious to get the first choice of three horses shading themselves quietly under a tree. The animals made their best time into the farthest corner of the field, with the men close upon them; and the foremost ones caught their prizes and bridled them as if they had a perfect immunity in such things. A scene followed. A young lady came out, and besought the soldiers not to take her favorite pony. The soldiers were remorseless and unyielding, and the pony is now in the army.

"I know a case where a family were just seating themselves to dinner, when some of the soldiers being that way, they went in and swallowed every thing. That was not all; but whatever in doors and out of doors the soldiers wanted was readily appropriated, and the proprietor of the place told me sorrowfully that they had ruined him—he never could now get out of debt. I hardly regretted his misfortune so much on his account as for the influence of this thieving upon the soldiers. I was really gratified to hear his little boy say, 'Pap says he wouldn't vote the secession ticket again if he had the chance.' His patriotism was evidently drawing too heavily upon his fortunes, and I was rejoiced to find him in an inquiring state of mind. But unless a check is given to this promiscuous and unauthorized plundering, the discipline and value of the army will be destroyed; and when the enlistments have expired, we shall let loose a den of thieves upon the country.

"One favorite form in which this will exhibit itself is the passing of Philadelphia Confederate notes. Whenever we advance into a new section, the floodgates are immediately opened, and the *fac simile* Confederate notes are poured out upon the land. They pass readily, and seem to be taken gladly for whatever is held for sale. Bank-notes and shinplasters are given for change. Horses and other valuable property are often purchased with this currency. A party of soldiers entered a store, not long since, fortified with exhaustless quantities of V's and X's, and commenced buying. Forty pounds of sugar was first ordered, when the storekeeper, pleased with the sudden increase of business, called in his wife to assist him in putting up the sugar in small parcels. Seventy-five cents a pound was the cost. That was a small matter. Matches were purchased. Twenty-five cents per box was the charge. Tobacco also found a ready market. Each man provided himself with a straw hat. But the crowning act of all was the abstraction from the till of money already paid to the dealer for his goods, and the purchase of more goods with the same spurious medium."

Such were the outrages practised on the unarmed inhabitants of Culpepper by this band of brigands—this motley crew of jail-birds, malefactors, released convicts, and Dutch-Yankee vermin, from the cellars and rookeries of Europe and the North. Their unbridled license was known and permitted by Pope; and though he subsequently issued an order declaring that such proceedings were unauthorized, and must cease, he only did so, when even the Northern people—venomous as was their hatred of the rebels—began to murmur at such incredible villanies.

The plague, as of *obscene vermin*, had, however, been let loose, and had done its work. The Federal horde had passed over the land, and left a desert behind them. The fences had disappeared; the forests were felled; the farm lands were turned into common; and so thorough had been the work of pillage and rapine that heads of families began seriously to dread that their little children would soon be without bread. When the writer of these lines passed through Culpepper in August, a few days after Pope's disappearance, it was as much as he could do to procure food for himself and forage for his horse.

Pope advanced toward the Rapidan, and had, as yet, encountered no foes. His right extended to the foot of the Blue Ridge, his left toward the confluence of the Rappahannock and Rapidan. The vast horde advanced, sweeping all before it; and the people of the North hailed with noisy triumph, the successful march, to this central position, of the "greatest of our generals."

This was the state of things in the last days of July; and Gen. Pope looked with longing eyes toward Gordonsville, where he had already, in fancy, established his headquarters, and whence he would descend, like an avalanche, upon the metropolis of the South.

Man proposes; God disposes. That destiny which would so soon crush him like an egg-shell, in an iron hand, was already on the march.

CHAPTER XIX.

CEDAR RUN.

When Gen. Pope thus advanced toward the Rapidan, seriously threatening, with his large force, the Central Railroad at Gordonsville, Gen. McClellan was still with a considerable portion of his army at Harrison's Landing, and professed to design another attack upon Richmond. It was thus rendered necessary for the Confederate government to retain a sufficient number of troops at the capital to repulse any movement from that direction.

It was equally important, however, to check Gen. Pope; and to that end, Gen. Jackson, who had gone into camp on the Mechanicsville road, not far from Richmond, was directed to proceed toward Gordonsville, and guard that point against the threatened assault upon it.

His own "old division," and Gen. Ewell's, were accordingly moved in that direction, and reached Gordonsville on the 19th of July.

Receiving reliable information that the Federal army in his front greatly outnumbered his own forces, Jackson sent back to Gen. Lee for additional troops, and was reinforced by Gen. A. P. Hill's division.

It was not long before the advanced forces of cavalry, on both sides, came into collision. On the 2d of August, whilst Col. Jones, by direction of Brig-gen. Robertson, was moving with the 7th Virginia cavalry, to take charge of picket posts on the Rapidan, he received intelligence, before reaching Orange Court-house, that the enemy were in possession of that town. Continuing to advance, Col. Jones found the main street full of Federal cavalry, and charged the head of the enemy's column—another portion of the regiment, under Major Marshall, attacking them in flank. Both attacks were successful, and the enemy were driven from the place. But our forces were still greatly outnumbered; and, in consequence of the large body of the enemy in front, together with the fire of their flanking parties, Jones was compelled to fall back. He made another stand, however, not far from the town, and the Federal cavalry retired. In this brief contest Col. Jones, while gallantly charging, at the head of his men, received a sabre wound, and Major Marshall was captured.

Having received information that only a portion of Gen. Pope's army was at Culpepper Court-house, Gen. Jackson determined to advance and attack it before reinforcements arrived; and accordingly, on the 7th of August, moved with his entire force from Gordonsville in the direction of the enemy. On the morning of the 8th, Gen. Robertson's cavalry, which had advanced beyond the Rapidan, drove back that of the enemy, and pursued them on the road leading from Barnett's Ford to Culpepper Court-house, the rest of the troops following, with Ewell's division in front. The enemy's cavalry continued, however, to display unusual activity, and to guard his trains, which were seriously endangered, Jackson detached Gen. Lawton's brigade, which was thus prevented from taking part in the battle of the next day.

On the 9th of August, Jackson reached a point about eight miles from Culpepper Court-house, and found the enemy posted in heavy force, in his front, near Cedar Run, and a short distance west and north of Slaughter Mountain. A large body of Federal cavalry occupied a ridge on the right of the road, but retired when a battery, under Lieut. Terry, opened upon it. The fire was responded to by a battery of the enemy beyond the ridge; and his cavalry subsequently returned, and reoccupied its former position.

General Early was now ordered to advance, keeping near the Culpepper road; and General Ewell, with his two remaining brigades—Trimble's and Hays's, the latter commanded by Colonel Ferns—was directed to diverge to the right, and pass along the slope of Slaughter's Mountain. Early, forming in line of battle, moved into the open field, and pushed forward to the right of the road, driving the enemy's cavalry before him to the crest of a hill which overlooked the ground between his troops and the opposite hill. Along this hill the enemy's batteries were posted, ready to open as soon as he appeared. In his front the country was, for some distance, open and broken. A corn-field, and to the left of it a wheat-field, upon which the shocks were yet standing, extended to the opposite hill, which was covered with timber. As soon as Early reached the eminence described, the Federal batteries opened upon him, large bodies of cavalry appearing in the wheat-field to the left. Gen. Early having retired his troops under the protection of the hill, Captain Brown, with one piece, and Captain Dement, with three pieces, planted their guns in advance of his right, and opened a rapid and well-directed fire upon the Federal batteries.

By this time General Winder, with Jackson's division, had arrived. Having disposed Campbell's brigade, Lieut.-colonel Garnett commanding, to the left, under cover of the wood near the wheat-field: Taliaferro's brigade parallel to the road, in rear of the batteries of Poague, Carpenter, and Caskie, then being placed near the road, under the direction of Major Andrews, chief of artillery of the division; and Winder's brigade, Colonel Ronald commanding, as a reserve—he was proceeding to direct, with his usual skill and coolness, the movements of those batteries, when he was struck by a shell, from which he expired in a few hours. "It is difficult," says General Jackson, "in the proper reserve of an official report, to do justice to the merits of this accomplished officer. Urged by the Medical Director to take no part in the movements of the day, because of the then enfeebled state of his health, his ardent patriotism and military pride could bear no such restraint. Richly endowed with those qualities of mind and person which fit an officer for command, and which attract the admiration and excite the enthusiasm of troops, he was rapidly rising to the front rank of his profession. His loss has been severely felt." The command of Jackson's division now devolved upon Brig.-general W. B. Taliaferro, whose brigade during the remainder of the action was commanded by Colonel A. G. Taliaferro.

In the mean time, General Ewell, with the brigades of Trimble and Hays, reached the northwest termination of Slaughter's Mountain, and upon an elevated spot about two hundred feet above the valley below, had planted Latimer's guns, which opened with marked effect upon the enemy's batteries. For some two hours a rapid and continuous fire of artillery was kept up on both sides, our own batteries being admirably served, and damaging the enemy seriously. Major Andrews handled his guns with great gallantry and success, until he was severely wounded and taken from the field. About five o'clock, the enemy threw forward his skirmishers through the corn-field, and advanced his infantry, until then concealed in the wood, to the rear and left of his batteries. Another body of infantry, apparently debouching from one of those valleys, hidden from view by the undulating character of the country, moved at the same time upon Early's right, which rested near a clump of cedars, where the guns of Brown and Dement were posted. The infantry fight soon extended to the left and centre, Early being warmly engaged with the enemy on his right and front. As Gen. Hill had arrived with his division, one of his brigades, Gen. Thomas', was sent to Early, and joined him in time to render efficient service.

Whilst the attack upon Early was in progress, the main body of the Federal infantry moved down from the wood, through the corn and wheat fields, fell with great vigor upon our extreme left, and, by the force of superior numbers, bearing down all opposition, turned it, and poured a destructive fire into its rear. The enemy pushing forward, and the left flank of Taliaferro's brigade being, by these movements, exposed to a flank fire, fell back, as did also the left of Early's line, the remainder of his command holding its position with great firmness.

During the advance of the enemy, the rear of the guns of Jackson's division becoming exposed, they were withdrawn. At this critical moment, Branch's brigade of Hill's division, with Winder's brigade further to the left, met the Federal forces flushed with their temporary triumph, and drove them back with terrible slaughter through the woods. The fight was still maintained with obstinacy between the enemy and the two brigades just named, when Archer and Pender coming up, a general charge was made, which drove the enemy across the field into the opposite wood, strewing the narrow valley with their dead. To retrieve this serious disaster they had recourse to their cavalry. An impetuous charge was made upon Taliaferro's brigade; but the enemy were met with such determined resistance by Taliaferro in front, and by so galling a fire from Branch's brigade in flank, that their cavalry was driven from the field in disorder, and with heavy loss.

On the right, Ewell had been forced to remain inactive. The incessant fire of our batteries in the valley, sweeping his only approach to the enemy's left, had prevented him from advancing. This difficulty now no longer existing, he moved forward with his two brigades, Trimble in the advance, and pressed on under a heavy fire from the enemy's artillery—his front covered by skirmishers from the 15th Alabama, and the brigades advancing in echelon of regiments. Thus repulsed from our left and centre, and now pressed by our right, centre, and left, the enemy fell back at every point of his line, and retreated, leaving his dead and wounded on the field of battle.

The bloody contest had thus terminated in the complete rout of the Federal forces, and the piles of dead which met the eye upon every hand, bore witness to the fury with which the conflict had raged. Engaging a force outnumbering him two to one, with heavy reinforcements hurrying forward to overwhelm him, Jackson had held his ground with that stubborn nerve which had never yet failed to compel unwilling victory to his standard. The enemy had fought hard, but had fought in vain. They had advanced with jests and triumphant laughter; with the assured expectation of utterly annihilating their opponents; with "Booty and Beauty" awaiting them in the fresh fields of Central Virginia. But in their path they had found the inexorable *Stonewall*. Contact with that fatal obstacle had shattered them; and at nightfall they retreated, broken, and in confusion, through the woods full of dead and dying.

As night fell, the full-orbed moon soared aloft, and poured

its mellow light upon the field of carnage. Jackson had again triumphed over his enemies—the boasted power of Pope was broken in his grasp, and all was well.

Over the beautiful slopes of Culpepper covered with the wounded and dying; the battle-flag of the South floated proudly in the light of the calm August moon.

CHAPTER XX.

DETAILS.

THUS commenced the great movement of the Confederate forces northward, which drove the enemy from Virginia and obliged him finally to concentrate his entire available strength in Maryland for the defence of his own soil.

In the midst of their dreams of triumph they had received a staggering blow; their further progress was summarily checked; and the imposing array which had advanced in all the pomp and pride of war, was a disorderly mob, rather than an army, flying to that "rear" where their general had perpetually declared "lurked disaster and shame."

The hand which struck them thus heavily was Jackson's—that ubiquitous fate of Northern leaders, meeting and overthrowing them at every turn. Two months before he had defeated Fremont and Shields at Port Republic; less than three weeks afterwards his troops had suddenly appeared near Richmond, and hurling themselves upon McClellan's right, decided the event of the hard-fought field of Cold Harbor. Now, those same unresisting men, under the same indefatigable commander, had emerged from the woods of Culpepper and formed line-of battle in front of Pope, and struck and overthrew him.

Nothing could have astonished the enemy more than the

presence, there, of the invincible, mysterious "Stonewall Jackson," as they universally called him. But a short time before the battle he was supposed by the enemy to be rapidly advancing down the Valley upon Winchester. The Federal camps there were in tumult; the drums beat to arms; and the affrighted enemy, we are told by one of their own writers, reminded each other of the brief blunt words of Jackson when he fell back last, that "he would return again shortly, and as certainly as now."

While the enemy at Winchester were thus beating the long roll in expectation of his coming, he was near Gordonsville; before their fears had subsided, he had passed the Rapidan, and defeated the "greatest of our generals." The Northern people began to experience toward Jackson the sentiment of the Scottish mothers of the middle age, when they quieted their crying children with the threat, "Hush! or the Black Douglas will get you!"

It is more than probable that General Pope and his followers shared this feeling. When the guns began to roar at Cedar Run, the "greatest of our generals" penned a dispatch in which he announced the fact, and concluded with the announcement—"I go to the front to see." But he never reached it. He passed through Culpepper Court-house, the citizens assert, with the haughty bearing of one who had never experienced the emotion of fear, and had no doubt of the result; but he stopped before reaching the battle-field. He allowed his troops to be defeated within sight of him; and made no attempt to rally them. He saw them rushing in a disordered crowd toward the Rappahannock, and did not interpose in their path. These facts are completely established; and this general, like his predecessors, seemed to have come under the spell of Jackson; to lose all his brain and courage when brought in contact with that "avenging Nemesis" of the South.

The battle of Cedar Run was planned and executed with that skill and nerve which characterized all the military movements of General Jackson. He had opposed to him, according to Pope's official report, Banks and Siegel's corps, and a division from that of McDowell, amounting in all to 32,000 troops. To meet these 32,000 men, fresh, thoroughly equipped, and flushed with anticipated triumph, he had only two divisions, and a portion of a third. These statements are made from official papers.

The conflict, which resulted in a Confederate victory against such great odds, was hard and desperate. At one period of the battle, a portion of the Southern troops were pressed by numbers so overwhelming that they were forced back, thrown into disorder, and the day seemed about to be decided in favor of the Federals. It was at this moment that Jackson, ordinarily so cool, silent, and deliberate, was mastered by the genius of battle—and exhibited, as he had rarely done, before that *gaudium certaminis*, and passionate excitement which Murat displayed in his cavalry charges. Galloping to the front, amid the "fire of hell" hurled against his broken and disordered lines, now rapidly giving way before the onset of the enemy, with his eyes flashing fire, his face flushed, his voice rising to loud and strident tones, he rallied the confused troops, and brought them again into line. Having thus re-formed them under the terrible fire of the foe, he did not lose a moment, and gave his stern order to charge with the bayonet. His presence; the magic of his eye, and voice; the sight of their great leader in the front, cheering them on, produced an irresistible effect upon the men. They advanced with shouts which struck terror to the hearts of the foe; the ground which they had lost was regained; and the enemy, in their turn, driven back, and finally put to rout.

Those who saw Jackson, at the moment when he passed like a thunderbolt to the front, and thus rallied his men, in the very jaws of destruction, declare that he resembled the genius of battle incarnate.

The conflict continued, as we have seen, until night. The

Southern troops were greatly exhausted by the arduous struggle, and the hours of darkness were not propitious for a forward movement: but so anxious was Jackson to reach the enemy's stronghold at Culpepper Court-house before morning, that he determined to pursue. An advance was accordingly ordered, Hill's division in front; and after proceeding cautiously for about a mile and a half, they came on the enemy. Pegram's battery, supported by Fields' brigade, took position just beyond the wood, through which Jackson had passed, and suddenly opened upon the enemy before they suspected its presence. The result was gratifying. The Federal forces were thrown into complete confusion and scattered in every direction, to escape the shell rained down on them. A desperate effort was made to cover their further retreat, however, and it proved successful. Three of their batteries were soon worked into position; a heavy cannonade commenced; and although the single battery of the Confederates fought the three opposed to it with unflinching nerve, it was finally silenced and forced to retire with severe loss.

This terminated the fighting for that day. Colonel Jones having made a reconnoissance with his cavalry, in front and to the right of the Confederate lines, and ascertained that Federal reinforcements had arrived, Jackson considered it imprudent to continue to move forward during the darkness, and ordered a halt for the night. On the following morning, the 10th, having reason to believe that the Federal army had been so largely reinforced as to render it unadvisable to attempt a further advance, Jackson gave directions for his wounded to be sent to the rear, the dead to be buried, and for the collection of arms from the battle-field. In the course of the morning, General J. E. B. Stuart arrived, on a tour of inspection, and at Jackson's request took command of the cavalry, and proceeded to reconnoitre. Convinced by the report of General Stuart, and information derived from other sources, that the enemy's force concentrated in his front was so heavy as to render it unwise for him to renew the action, General Jackson determined not to advance upon them —but posted his troops in such a manner as to receive any attack of the enemy. On the 11th, a flag of truce was received from the Federal commander, who requested permission until 2 o'clock to remove and bury his dead, not already interred by our troops. This was granted; and the time subsequently extended, by request of the enemy, to 5 o'clock in the evening.

Jackson remained in position until night—August 11th—when he fell back toward Gordonsville, with the hope of drawing Pope on, procuring reinforcements, and meeting the vast columns of the enemy upon more equal terms.

Jackson had thus encountered and defeated a greatly superior force of the enemy; driven them nearly two miles; remained in possession of the battle-field, forcing them to ask permission to bury their dead, and, only when they received overpowering reinforcements, fallen back. He had captured 400 prisoners, among them a brigadier-general, 5,302 small-arms, one Napoleon gun and caisson, with two other caissons and a limber, and three stands of colors. His loss was 223 killed and 1,060 wounded; but this he said, in his guarded phrase, was only "probably about one-half of that sustained by the enemy."

The victory had been dearly purchased. Some of the most valuable officers and men had fallen; among the former, Gen. Charles Winder and Col. Richard H. Cunningham. Gen. Winder had long been in command of the "Old Stonewall Brigade," and had fought it with a skill and courage which extorted the warmest commendation from Jackson. Colonel Cunningham, commanding the 21st Virginia, had proved himself a most accomplished soldier, and enjoyed the full confidence of his superiors and his men. These two noble soldiers were, at the time, prostrated by sickness, and on the night before the battle occupied the same tent. Their physical weakness would have simply excused them for remaining absent from their commands; but the high soldierly pride which animated their hearts would not permit them to be idle lookers-on, while their comrades were contending so desperately against the heavy columns of the enemy. They took command of their troops in the battle, gave their small remaining strength to the cause which they loved so deeply, and fell, at the post of honor, noble martyrs in the great cause of Southern independence.

Jackson fell back behind the Rapidan, and on the 14th of August—"to render thanks to God for the victory at Cedar Run, and other past victories, and to implore his continual favor in the future—Divine service was held in the army." On the plains of Orange, as amid the blue ranges of the mountains after McDowell, the followers of Jackson bent their bronzed faces in prayer to the Giver of Victory.

Jackson's dispatch announcing the result of the battle was as follows:

"HEADQUARTERS VALLEY DISTRICT,
August 11th, 6½ A. M.

COLONEL:—On the evening of the 9th instant, God blessed our arms with another victory. The battle was near Cedar Run, about six miles from Culpepper Court-house. The enemy, according to statements of prisoners, consisted of Banks', McDowell's, and Siegel's commands. We have over four hundred prisoners, including Brigadier-general Prince. Whilst our list of killed is less than that of the enemy, yet we have to mourn the loss of some of our best officers and men. Brigadier-general Charles S. Winder was mortally wounded whilst ably discharging his duty at the head of his command, which was the advance of the left wing of the army. We have collected about 1,500 small-arms and other ordnance stores.

I am, Colonel,
Your obedient servant,
T. J. JACKSON,
Major-general Commanding.

Col. R. H. CHILTON, A. A. G."

General Pope's was in these words;

"HEADQUARTERS ARMY OF VIRGINIA,
Cedar Mountain, 7:30 *A. M.*, *Aug.* 12.

To Major-gen. HALLECK:

The enemy has retreated under cover of the night.

His rear is now crossing the Rapidan, toward Orange Court-house.

Our cavalry and artillery are in pursuit.

JOHN POPE,
Major-general, &c."

CHAPTER XXI.

THE MARCH TO MANASSAS.

JACKSON thus retired before the enemy toward Orange. The foe, who knew his mode of warfare, seldom pressed him hard, and General Pope's "cavalry and artillery in pursuit" did not make very zealous efforts to come up with the Confederates.

The enemy seemed, indeed, to have a presentiment of the truth; to comprehend that this retrograde movement was, in reality, the drawing back of the arm to strike a heavier blow; the crouch of the tiger that he may spring with greater force and certainty upon his prey.

The special pleading of General Pope, in regard to the battle of Cedar Run, deceived none of the astute authorities at Washington, and they speedily arrived at the conviction that, to make headway in the new field of operations, it would be necessary to concentrate there all the troops which were operating in Virginia. A brief period only had, therefore, elapsed before a fleet of transports appeared in James river, proceeded to Harrison's Landing, and took on board the entire remnant of McClellan's army, which had lain there cowering under the gunboats since their defeat on the Chickahominy. The plan of the Federal authorities was to unite McClellan's forces with those of Pope; to hurry forward from Fredericksburg the troops under General Burnside, and forming one great army of these three distinct bodies, concentrate them between the Rappahannock and the Rapidan, with a view to penetrate the heart of Virginia, cut the communications of the Confederate capital, and either drive the rebel government from the State, or reduce it to submission.

This design was energetically undertaken, and the Confederates were promptly called on to decide whether they would stand on the defensive, for the protection of Richmond against this new attack, or advance upon the enemy, and "carry the war into Africa."

The latter determination was speedily arrived at; offensive operations were decided upon; and no sooner had General Lee satisfied himself that McClellan was evacuating his position on James river, than he hastened to put his troops in motion to attack General Pope before the expected reinforcements reached him.

The main army moved rapidly to Orange Court-house, and General Lee lost no time in commencing operations. He decided, it would appear, to attack General Pope's right flank and front at the same time, and the movement against the enemy's right was intrusted to General Jackson.

A portion of Jackson's corps accordingly moved from its camp near Gordonsville, and bearing well to the left, crossed the Rapidan, and proceeded in the direction of Madison Court-house. From that point the force could descend upon the enemy's right flank and rear, while General Lee assailed him in front; and thus, hemmed in between the Rappahannock and the Rapidan, the Federal army would be destroyed or forced to surrender.

This design was frustrated by the unexpected movements of the enemy. Gen. Pope had no intention of again attempting a trial of strength with Jackson, who had already handled him so roughly at Cedar Run, and, doubtless, the presence of General Lee in his front did not diminish his inclination to retire. With a prudence which ill-assorted with his publicly-expressed determination to take no steps toward that "rear" where "lurked disaster and shame," he no sooner suspected the projected attack than he fell back promptly to the north bank of the Rappahannock, and crowning every hill with his batteries, prepared to dispute its passage. This movement produced a corresponding change in the plans of General Lee. He advanced across the Rapidan, and the whole army was united in the neighborhood of Culpepper Court-house.

We shall insert here a paragraph or two, relating to the movements of the Southern troops, written by "Personne," the excellent correspondent of the *Charleston Mercury*, and interesting as furnishing those familiar details, which will hereafter be read with so much interest. We quote the following sentences from the writer's diary:

"*August* 19, *near Orange Court-house.*—Orders issued from headquarters for the army to move forward in light marching order. At daylight, every thing in motion toward the Rapidan, which is ten miles distant. The enemy in front and on this side of the river. Longstreet at the head of his column. The Federals back rapidly as we advance, our front and their rear-guard having one or two slight skirmishes. Jackson is moving toward the left, probably with a view to flank the enemy in case of a stand.

"*August* 20.—Army crossed the Rapidan, the water thigh deep. Scene exciting and amusing. Nearly whole day thus occupied.

"*August* 21.—The enemy in close proximity, and we have to move cautiously. Longstreet's corps is in front. From a hill on the other side of the Rapidan we have a magnificent view for miles. Three columns—long, black winding lines of men, their muskets gleaming in the sunshine like silver spears—are in sight, moving in the direction of Fredericksburg, or down the opposite bank of the river. More skirmishing in front. Good many stragglers by the wayside, but they are generally broken-down soldiers, and trudge slowly along in the tracks of their comrades. An attractive part of the procession is the baggage trains, wending their way in the rear of the army. Thousands of wagons are in sight, and between the stalling of trains, the shouting of drivers, and the chaotic confusion which emanates from the motley mass, no man can complain of the *ennui* of the march.

"Nothing can be more picturesquely beautiful than the bivouac at night. Thousands of troops line the woods on both sides of the road for miles. Camp fires are glimmering in the trees, muskets are stacked along the edge of the forest, and the men are disposed in every conceivable manner. Some are rolled up in their blankets, and already dreaming away the fatigues of the day; some are sitting around the camp fires watching the roasting ears, and discussing the 'coming events which cast their shadows before,' and some are among the trees, moving to and fro in the gray film of smoke that has arisen from the myriad fires and rests upon the earth. We live on what we can get—now and then an ear of corn, fried green apples, or a bit of ham broiled on a stick, but quite as frequently do without either from morning until night. We sleep on the ground without any other covering than a blanket, and consider ourselves fortunate if we are not frozen stiff before morning. The nights are both damp and cold.

"*August* 22.—To-day another busy scene. The army resumed its march at daylight. Longstreet's twelve brigades moving toward the Potomac on the right and Jackson on the left. The latter has passed the Rapidan Station on the Virginia Central Railroad, and is pressing on northeast of Culpepper. Several small skirmishes have taken place on the front, and eighty or ninety prisoners went by on their way to the rear. Among the Yankees captured by Jackson were two men, who, as soon as they fell into our hands, commenced to ask after their old comrades in the artillery company. An inquiry being instituted, they confessed that eight months ago they were soldiers in our army, but that, being tired of service, had deserted and joined the ranks of the enemy. Without further ado, the general ordered them to be hung to a tree, which was done in the presence of a large portion of his army."

A portion of this extract paints with great accuracy the

commissariat of the Southern army. "A bit of ham broiled on a stick" was a luxury with the men, and the time was soon to come when it would be unattainable: when the entire force would be called on to subsist upon green corn roasted on the embers—sole bill of fare of the tired and hungry soldier. General Lee had thus massed his army between the Rapidan and Rappahannock; his designs were speedily to take shape, and become "clothed in act."

Jackson bivouacked opposite Warrenton Springs, on the evening of August 22d, and immediately threw two brigades of Gen. Ewell's division across the river. On the next day a fresh in the river destroyed the bridge, and as Jackson had determined to withdraw the force, he rebuilt the bridge, which they then repassed, after a brief but warm engagement with the enemy.

At the very moment when Jackson was thus feeling the enemy on the Rappahannock, General Stuart, at the head of his cavalry, had, by one of those bold dashes which characterized him, penetrated to their rear, and, in the midst of night and storm, struck them at Catlett's, a station on the Orange and Alexandria Railroad, where General Pope then was in person. Pope escaped; but with the loss of his coat and hat, and some members of his staff. The most valuable part of the captured property, however, was a box of official papers, which is said to have clearly exhibited the strength of his army; his anxious desire for reinforcements; his expectation that they would soon arrive; and the small hope he had of success, if, meanwhile, he was assailed by the Confederates in force. These documents were laid before Gen. Lee; and the revelations which they contained of the enemy's designs, probably led to the great movement which speedily commenced.

General Lee determined to send an expedition against the enemy's rear, in order to cut his communications, and force him to fall back from the Rappahannock. The movement would necessarily be attended with great peril; would demand on the part of the officer in charge of it, great energy, judgment, and decision; and it was necessary to intrust the execution of the project to one of the most competent generals of the Southern army. The antecedents of General Jackson pointed him out as a person eminently fitted to undertake this great movement; and to him it was accordingly assigned.

Jackson lost no time in preparing to move forward. *Delay* was a word not found in the vocabulary of the leader who had swooped from the heights of McDowell upon Front Royal and Winchester; pushed on to the Potomac; passed back by forced marches between the converging columns of the enemy; defeated them at Port Republic; and as suddenly fallen upon McClellan's right at Richmond.

On Monday, August 25th, he moved his command, consisting of Ewell's, A. P. Hill's, and Jackson's old division, toward Jeffersontown, producing upon the enemy the impression that the Southern forces were falling back. But at Jeffersontown his route was suddenly changed. Facing to the right, he ascended the banks of the Rappahannock, passed through the small village of Amosville, and crossed the river at Hinson's Ford, dragging his artillery with difficulty up the narrow and rock-ribbed road beyond. From that moment rapidity of movement was essential to success. The presence of Jackson in that region could not long be concealed, and it was vitally important that the Confederate forces should push on, and pass through Thoroughfare Gap—their proposed line of advance—before the enemy could occupy that strong fortress, and bar their passage.

The famous "Foot Cavalry" were now called upon to put forth their utmost strength. A long and exhausting march was before them; every moment was precious; Thoroughfare Gap must be reached before the enemy arrived; and the ordinary rules of marching must be changed. As though recognizing the truth of the maxim, that wherever two men can place their feet an army can move, Jackson pushed on beneath the very shadow of the Blue Ridge, "across open fields, by strange country roads and comfortable homesteads, by a little town in Fauquier, called Orleans, on and on, as if he would never cease," declares one of his men. The troops were scarcely permitted to pause for an instant; weary, footsore, almost without food, they were still marched steadily forward; and the result exhibited the sound judgment and foresight of their leader. Reaching Salem, on the Manassas Gap Railroad, at midnight, they were put in motion again at dawn of day; and, passing "crowds, all welcoming, cheering, staring with blank amazement" at the sight of Confederate troops in that Yankee-ridden land, pressed on through the Plains to Thoroughfare Gap.

The mountain gorge was undefended—the enemy had been completely "headed off"—and passing rapidly between the frowning ramparts, Jackson, with his little army, hungry and exhausted, but resolute as ever, descended like a hawk upon Manassas. Gen. Pope, in his official report, declares that he knew of Jackson's movement. He makes this statement to relieve himself from the charge of a want of generalship, in having been surprised; but his declaration has rather the opposite effect. The truth doubtless is, that scouts brought him word of *some* movement of the enemy in that direction; but it seems plain, from all the testimony, that General Pope considered it only a raid by a small body, probably of cavalry. General Stuart was between him and Jackson with a cordon of pickets, and a perfect net-work of scouting parties; and we are thus justified in declaring that the movement was a complete surprise. Had General Pope suspected for an instant that the rumored force advancing to turn his right flank, and strike his rear, was the army of Jackson, led by that general in person, his operations on the Rappahannock would have terminated two days earlier than they did;

Thoroughfare Gap would have been defended; and the conditions under which the great battles at Manassas were fought would have been changed.

Gen. Stuart had pushed in advance with his cavalry, ascended the Bull Run Mountain by a winding and rocky road, to the right of the Gap, and descending the eastern acclivity, taken his post again in front and on the flanks of the army, which on the afternoon of Tuesday, the 26th, reached the neighborhood of Manassas.

This march will always remain famous in history. It was the achievement of a leader, fertile in resource; close in his calculations of time and material; unerring in decision and execution. It had completely surprised the enemy, who, fancying that the main attack would be made by Lee, upon the Rappahannock, had paid no attention to the threatening rumors of an intended assault upon their rear, attributing it to a few wandering guerillas, who could be repulsed by the garrison at Manassas; and persistently kept their eyes upon the main body of the Confederates in their front, up to the moment when the intelligence reached them that they were completely cut off from Washington, and must fight upon terms dictated by their adversaries.

The illustrious leader had thus stolen a march upon his enemies, and won new laurels; but in contemplating the splendid success of the chief, let us not lose sight of the credit which belongs to his men. The troops who executed that great movement displayed a soldiership and devotion to the great cause of the South—an endurance, a heroism, a cheerfulness under privation and hardship, which would do honor to the most celebrated nations of history. In two days they had marched nearly fifty miles, almost without food or rest, to attack. Had they passed over the ground, pursued by a triumphant enemy, it would have been different; but they made this steady and rapid advance to attain a position in which they expected to be immediately assailed by overwhelming masses of the enemy, and bear the brunt of Pope's huge horde, hurled, in mad and desperate rage, against their weary lines. They were, many of them, barefooted, limping, "weary unto death," fainting from want of food and rest; but they did not lag behind on that account. "Close up!" was the word all along the line; and they marched on, broken down in strength, but with spirits that no privations or fatigue could overcome. The correspondent of the "Mercury" has described their food; but only those who saw the Southern troops, in those days, can realize the sufferings which they were called upon to undergo—and did undergo with the cheerfulness of the true soldier, fighting, not for pay or rations, like the hired mercenary, but for a cause which they dearly loved, and were willing to make all sacrifices for, without a murmur. The phenomenon was then and there presented of an army living for days upon nothing but green corn and unripe apples; of exhausting marches, incessant combats, and unresting movements, almost without food or sleep. And, as we have said, there was not a murmur heard in all the corps; the flower of the Southern youth, reared in homes of affluence and luxury, were toiling on over the dusty ways, or lying, weak and exhausted, by the roadside, or fighting while so feeble that they could scarcely handle their muskets—but they did not permit one word of complaint to escape them, one thought of despair to enter their hearts. Their feet were on their native Southern soil, the foe in front of them; the fixed resolve of every soul in Jackson's army was to drive that insolent enemy from our borders, or perish.

The writer of these pages saw the men of the South, in that great crisis of our history; and his pulse still throbs, as he recalls the grand and noble spectacle which they presented.

Jackson approached Manassas, as we have said, on Tuesday, the 26th of August. At Bristoe, a station on the Orange and Alexandria Railroad, about four miles from the Junction,

Stuart's cavalry fired into a train of cars, which, however, got by to Manassas; and the infantry succeeded in stopping and capturing two or three other trains, which were speedily burned. Jackson was thus completely in the enemy's rear; held possession of the railroad which supplied their army and the first act of the great drama had been played. When the curtain descended, this was the position of affairs. Lee was in Pope's front; Jackson in his rear; the Federal reinforcements from Washington and Fredericksburg had not arrived; Gen. Pope must fight on ground and conditions selected by his enemy. A cool and determined spirit would not, however, have regarded the situation as desperate. Lee, with his main body, was still a long way off; Burnside was approaching from below; reinforcements were being hurried forward from Alexandria; and Jackson was playing a game which might, with good hopes of success, be retorted against himself. *He* might be the "cut off" party; his command attacked before Lee could arrive; and, indeed, the Northern journals, which had speedily gained intelligence of his presence in Pope's rear, congratulated their readers that the famous "Stonewall," who had given them so much trouble, was now completely flanked, and about to fall into the clutches of his enemies.

Proceeding upon this view of the subject, Gen. Pope put his columns in motion, and advanced to protect his communications, and attack Jackson before he could be reinforced by Lee.

Let us follow the movements of the personage who was thus threatened. The first thing necessary was to gain possession of Manassas; and this work was intrusted to General Stuart. Jackson sent him Trimble's brigade, to co-operate with the cavalry; and notified Stuart to take charge of the movement. The force at Manassas did not make a very stout resistance. Gen. Stuart advanced with his cavalry, until challenged by the enemy's interior sentinels, and fired on with canister, and finding the ground impracticable for cavalry, by night, sent for the infantry. When it arrived, he directed Gen. Trimble to rest his centre on the railroad and advance, which was immediately done; and, after a brief contest, the place was captured, Colonel Wickham, with a portion of the cavalry, cutting off the enemy's retreat.

The amount of stores captured at Manassas was very large. Five or six pieces of artillery, ten locomotives, two railroad trains of enormous size, loaded with many millions' worth of quartermaster and commissary stores; 50,000 pounds of bacon, 1,000 barrels of beef, 20,000 barrels of pork, several thousand barrels of flour, and a large quantity of forage. In addition to these public stores, were the contents of the sutler's shops, containing, says an eye-witness, "an amount and variety of property, such as I had never conceived of." The same writer says: "'Twas a curious sight to see our ragged and famished men helping themselves to every imaginable article of luxury or necessity, whether of clothing, food, or what not. For my part I got a tooth-brush, a box of candles, a quantity of lobster salad, a barrel of coffee, and other things which I forget. The scene utterly beggared description. Our men had been living on roasted corn since crossing the Rappahannock, and we had brought no wagons, so we could carry little away of the riches before us. But the men could eat one meal at least. So they were marched up, and as much of every thing eatable served out as they could carry. To see a starving man eating lobster salad and drinking Rhine wine, barefooted and in tatters, was curious; the whole thing was indescribable."

This vast mass of public and private stores, with the exception of what the men consumed or carried away with them, a bakery, furnishing daily 15,000 loaves of bread, and all the public buildings of the place, were, on the evening of Wednesday, consigned to the flames, and utterly destroyed.

When the army evacuated the place, on that night, the last building was in flames, and the ruin was complete.

But we anticipate events. The attack upon Manassas was made about daylight on the 27th, and when Gen. Jackson arrived, the place was in our possession. We were not to hold it without a further struggle, however, on the part of the enemy.

Intelligence of the danger to which this great magazine ot stores was exposed, having reached Washington, a brigade of New Jersey troops, under Gen. Taylor, was promptly ordered forward by railroad, to defend it. The train reached the bridge over Bull Run about seven in the morning; the troops were disembarked; and the entire command hurried forward as rapidly as possible toward Manassas. Our skirmishers, who had been posted along the crest of hills overlooking Bull Run, fell back before the enemy, and they were thus drawn on towards the fortifications, where the infantry and dismounted cavalry awaited them in silence. They had advanced, in line-of-battle, within close and deadly range, when suddenly the artillery in the breastworks opened their iron mouths, and a storm of shot and shell greeted them. They fell back immediately in great confusion, behind a sheltering crest, and were at once attacked by our infantry, who drove them, "like scattered partridges," says an eye-witness, completely routed, through Blackburn's Ford, to the opposite side of Bull Run. Here they were fired into by the guns of the Stuart Horse Artillery, under Major Pelham, who poured round after round of canister into the broken and flying ranks, covering the ground with dead, and driving the enemy to ignominious flight. General Taylor was killed, his son, nephew, and at least one-half of his officers wounded, and the road over which the enemy fled, pursued by the merciless Horse Artillery of Pelham, was marked at every step by their dead.

Later in the day, an attack was made by General Ewell upon Bristoe, a station, as we have said, about four miles from the Junction. General Hooker commanded the Federal force—the advance guard of Pope's army then pressing forward—and outnumbered Ewell so largely, that after an obstinate struggle, the latter, in accordance with previous orders, fell back across Muddy Run to the main body of the army at Manassas. This incident of the day, which in no degree affected the general result, was claimed by the enemy, after the fashion peculiar to them, as a great Federal success; and in view of the events which soon followed on the plains of Manassas, we can afford to concede all which they claim in reference to this affair of advance guards. Ewell had certainly felt them very roughly; fell back coolly; and preparations were speedily made for greater events.

During the entire day, the cavalry were engaged in observing the enemy, reporting his movements, and capturing detached parties in all directions. General Fitz Lee was sent on an expedition toward Fairfax Court-house, to still further damage the Federal communications, and, if possible, cut off the retreat of Taylor's brigade; and the entire region was scoured by efficient officers of cavalry, who notified General Jackson of every movement.

At nightfall, Manassas, which had been set on fire, was evacuated; and when the enemy took possession on the following morning, Stuart's few remaining cavalry falling back before them, they found only smoking ruins, and the burnt and blackened remains of their great masses of stores.

The destruction of these stores was of vital, inestimable importance to General Jackson. It doubtless seemed hard to his hungry soldiers, that after a march of fifty miles, almost without food, they should be called upon to destroy the tempting commissary stores, and innumerable luxuries of the sutlers' shops, almost before they had satisfied the cravings of nature. But the personal comfort of the army was at that moment a very small item in the account. The destruction of these stores was one of the great objects of the expedition; Pope depended upon them for the subsistence of his army; and the success or failure of the grand operations about to commence was involved in depriving the enemy of their benefit.

General Pope's official report shows how thoroughly he was crippled by the capture of Manassas. He rests his apology for the defeat which followed solely upon the want of rations for his men and forage for his horses. Describing his starving condition, and inveighing against General McClellan for refusing to dispatch trains of supplies without an escort of cavalry, he attributes all to the destruction at Manassas. There were some grounds for his statement. Even if General Fitz Lee's cavalry had permitted a convoy to pass, it could not have arrived in time; and General Pope declares in his report, that whether defeating Jackson, or defeated by him, it was a simple question of time whether he should fall back behind Bull Run, toward his supplies, or "starve." He adds that the battle of Saturday was fought because he had no option in the matter, and could not delay an engagement. "Starvation" for men and horses stared him in the face, and drove him to renew the action.

Such were the excellent results immediately achieved by General Jackson in the capture of the enemy's magazines at Manassas. That historic place had thus been twice destroyed by the Confederate commanders—first by Johnston, and then by Jackson.

It had twice been occupied by the enemy, on the next day, but under different circumstances. The troops which took possession of it when Johnston evacuated and destroyed it in March, were the advance guard of an army thoroughly provisioned, and in high spirits. Those who entered it on the 28th of August were hungry, and with spirits already darkened by the shadow of Jackson.

CHAPTER XXII.

JACKSON AT BAY.

JACKSON turned his back on the burning houses of Manassas at nightfall.

His position was now perilous in the extreme. The main body of Lee's army was in motion, and marching by the same route which he had followed, to his assistance; but Pope was moving to attack him, and the head of the Federal column had already come in collision with General Ewell. Lee had the arc of the circle to follow, while his adversary moved over the chord; and all now depended upon the former's celerity, and Jackson's strategy in meanwhile keeping the enemy at bay. If General Pope could once come up with, and strike Jackson before Lee and Longstreet arrived, the contest would be desperate, as the Confederates did not number 20,000 men; and to ward off the threatened blow until the main body came to his succor, was now the aim of Gen. Jackson.

The movement brought into play all his great resources of energy, nerve, prudence, and generalship. He might have retired without difficulty before the enemy, in the direction of Aldie, and turning the Bull Run Mountain at its northern extremity, formed a junction with Longstreet, and defied the foe; but this withdrawal of the advance force was no part of the plan of General Lee. The design of that commander was to engage the enemy with his whole force in the neighborhood of Manassas, while they were laboring under the embarrassments occasioned by the destruction of their stores and communications—while the men and horses were hungry and exhausted—and before supplies could reach them from Alexandria. The retreat toward Aldie, on Jackson's part, would have lost to him half the fruits of the great movement—thwarted Gen. Lee's plans—and reversed the whole programme of operations. General Jackson accordingly banished all thoughts of such a retrograde movement, and with that stubborn nerve which characterized him, determined to fall back slowly to a position within supporting distance o Longstreet, contest every inch of the ground, and only retire when the existence of his army made it necessary.

Accordingly, just after sunset, he put his troops in motion, and begun the movement which was to effect his object. His corps was divided, and took different routes. Hill's division, with a detachment of cavalry, set out on the road to Centreville, crossing at Blackburn's Ford, and thus drawing the attention of the enemy in a false direction. Hill did not proceed beyond Centreville, however. Having reached that point, he faced to the left, took the Warrenton road, and re turned, recrossing Bull Run at Stone Bridge. Near this point, he rejoined Jackson, who had fallen back, with Ewell's division, his own and the rest of the cavalry, and taken up a position on the battle-field of Manassas; his left resting near Sudley Ford; his right at a point a little above the small village of Groveton. The crest which he occupied was part protected in front by a railroad cut—that of a projected road branching from the main Manassas railroad near Gainesville, and running toward Alexandria. Here he was in a position to repulse the enemy unless they advanced in overpowering force; to form a junction with Longstreet as soon as he arrived, and, if hard pressed, retire up the right bank of Bull Run toward Aldie.

Deceived by the movements of A. P. Hill toward Centreville, a force of the enemy had followed him in that direction, and pursued hotly until his rear-guard passed Stone Bridge. This was in the afternoon. But meanwhile the cavalry force of the two armies had not been idle. General Stuart disposed his cavalry so as to cover Jackson's front in the direction of

LT. GEN. R. S. EWELL.

Engraved for the Life of Jackson.

C. B. Richardson Publisher.

Warrentown and Manassas; and having intercepted a dispatch from the enemy, directing cavalry to report to General Bayard at Haymarket, near Thoroughfare, Stuart proceeded in that direction, with his two fragments of brigades, to attack it, and establish communication with Longstreet, whose arrival was looked for with intense anxiety. On the way, Stuart captured a party of the enemy, and, having sent his dispatch through by a trusty messenger, engaged the enemy's cavalry, while Longstreet was fighting at Thoroughfare Gap. The skirmish was still going on, when the sound of artillery from Stone Bridge indicated a battle there, and quietly withdrawing from the action, General Stuart hastened to place his command upon Jackson's right flank.

As the cavalry approached, the dust which they raised induced the apprehension on General Stuart's part that his command, coming as it did from the direction of the enemy, would be taken for a part of the Federal force. A staff officer was accordingly dispatched with the intelligence of his approach, and Jackson promptly informed that the supposed enemies were friends. He was reconnoitring at the moment with General Ewell and others in front of his troops, drawn up in line of battle, and no sooner knew that his flank was not threatened, than, pointing to the enemy in his front, he said, briefly, "Ewell, advance!"

Ewell immediately threw forward his own division and Jackson's, and attacked the enemy, who were seen advancing along the Warrenton turnpike, with the apparent intention of crossing Bull Run at Sudley Ford and Stone Bridge. A fierce engagement, in the last two hours of daylight, followed; the enemy finally gave way, and at nightfall were entirely repulsed. General Ewell had been badly wounded in the knee, and his valuable services were lost in the subsequent battles, but the enemy had suffered heavy loss and yielded the field—the opposing armies remaining in front of each other in line of battle, waiting for daylight.

The mild hours of the August evening which witnessed this contest on the historic plains of Manassas, were marked also by a sharp engagement between Longstreet and the enemy in the gorge of Thoroughfare Gap. This wild and romantic pass in the mountains, with its frowning, fir-clad battlements on either side—its narrow and winding road, and its rugged walls rising rock above rock to the summit, right and left—was defended by a considerable force of the enemy, with powerful batteries judiciously posted to take the eastern debouchment with shell and canister. General Lee, who had pressed forward over the same road followed by Jackson, and reached the lofty hill upon the western opening of the pass late in the afternoon, determined not to delay the attack. A brigade was accordingly sent forward, and bravely rushed into the gap in face of a hot fire of musketry and a storm of shell from the enemy's artillery beyond. The conflict was kept up with great spirit for some time; but Lee having sent a force by Hopewell Gap, a little north of Thoroughfare, to take the enemy in flank and rear, they hastily withdrew their batteries, and left the way open to Longstreet, who passed through about nine o'clock at night.

When a courier brought to Jackson the intelligence that Longstreet had passed Thoroughfare, and was rapidly pressing forward to join him, he drew a long breath and uttered a sigh of relief. The long agony was over—the great movement which would remain among his proudest glories had terminated in complete success.

Longstreet—nay, Lee himself—was near, and all was well.

CHAPTER XXIII.

MANASSAS: AUGUST 29, 1862.

On the morning of Friday, August 29th, Jackson's corps was drawn up to receive the anticipated assault of the enemy, posted directly in his front. His position was a strong one. His left rested near Sudley Ford, and his right a little above the small village of Groveton, on the Warrenton turnpike—a portion of the line being protected by the deep cut for the projected railroad, already mentioned. Thus posted, General Jackson was in a condition to repel any assault of the enemy, unless it was made in overpowering force; and confident of his ability to hold his ground until reinforcements arrived, he presented a dauntless front, ready to accept battle at any moment.

The fatal error of General Pope was his delay in making this attack. Confusion seems to have reigned in the Federal counsels, and the plainest dictates of common sense, much more of military science, were utterly disregarded. It was known that Lee was advancing with Longstreet's corps—that great reserve whose blows were so heavy, and told for so much in every contest. The route of this corps was also well known; there could be no doubt that they would advance through Thoroughfare Gap; and yet Thoroughfare Gap, the key of the whole position, the Thermopylæ pass which ten men could have held against a thousand, was inadequately guarded, and suffered to be cleared. The veriest tyro in arms would have understood that all depended upon hurling the entire Federal column upon Jackson before Longstreet arrived; but General Pope either did not see the importance of doing so, or was unable to accomplish it. In his defence, he presents an elaborate array of charges against General Porter, and other officers, for delay, inefficiency, and actual treason, in not coming up in time; but the rejoinders of these officers are fatal in the extreme to General Pope's character for generalship, and the fact remains clearly proved that he was out-generalled, as he was out-fought by General Jackson.

The hour for the execution of the movement referred to above had now passed. The golden moment upon which the hinges of destiny turned had slipped away. That most terrible of phrases, "too late," applied in all its force to the movements of the Federal army.

A cloud of dust from the direction of Thoroughfare Gap, on that eventful morning, told the tale of despair to General Pope, of succor and good hope to Gen. Jackson. The great corps which had turned the tide of victory upon so many hard-fought fields was steadily pressing onward, and the advance was now on the Warrenton turnpike, beyond Gainesville, not far from Jackson's right.

All the morning Gen. Longstreet was coming into position. The far-seeing eyes of the great soldier who commanded the Southern army had embraced at a glance the whole situation of things, and his plans were formed with consummate skill. The design was to envelop the enemy, as it were, and occupy a position from which he could be struck in front, flank, and rear at the same moment, if he made a single error; and this design dictated an order of battle not dissimilar from that which was crowned with such success on the banks of the Chickahominy.

Jackson fronted, as we have said, directly toward the Warrenton road, his right resting near Groveton. When Longstreet arrived, his troops were steadily advanced in a line *crossing* the Warrenton road, his left resting upon a range not far from Jackson's right—the two lines forming an obtuse angle, and resembling somewhat an open V. The village of Groveton was in the angle thus formed, about a mile distant;

and the fields in its vicinity were completely commanded by heavy batteries. These were placed upon a ridge at the angle mentioned, where Longstreet's left and Jackson's right approached each other, and were commanded by that accomplished soldier and admirable artillerist, Colonel (now Brigadier-general) Stephen D. Lee, of South Carolina.

The advantage of this order of battle is apparent at a glance. If the enemy advanced, as it was probable they would do, upon Gen. Jackson, to crush him before Longstreet was in fighting trim to assist him, they would expose their left flank to the latter, and be placed in a most perilous position. If they succeeded in driving Gen. Jackson back, and followed up their success by a general advance all along the line, that success would only expose them still more to the heavy arm of Longstreet ready to fall upon their unprotected flank. Their very victory would be the signal of their ruin. Triumph would insure destruction. The rapidly closing sides of the great V would strike them in flank and rear, huddle them together in a disorderly mob, and end by crushing them with its inexorable vice-like pressure.

Their only hope in advancing upon Jackson was to penetrate between him and Longstreet, thereby dividing the line-of-battle. But Stephen Lee was there, with his batteries crowning the crest, and the design was hopeless.

Such was Gen. Lee's order of battle. The enemy were as yet unaware of it. They adhered to their design of overwhelming Jackson before succor reached him; and during the whole forenoon were moving their troops to the left, and massing them in his front. Skirmishing and cannonading, rather desultory in their character, and not important, went on during this movement of the enemy; but it was not until three or four o'clock that the battle commenced in earnest.

At that time the enemy rapidly advanced with a force, consisting, it is said, of Banks', Siegel's, and Pope's divisions, and supported by a heavy fire of artillery, threw themselves with great fury upon Jackson's right. Their design was to divide our line, and the assault was made with great spirit. Ewell's division, however, concealed behind the embankment of the railroad received them with a fire so galling that they were repulsed with heavy loss. The bold stroke to cut our line thus failed at its very inception; and the Federal forces did not seem to relish the idea of immediately renewing the attack.

As they fell back in disorder before the hot fire of the Southern infantry, they were saluted by a shower of shot and shell from the batteries posted on the high ground in our rear; and so accurate and effective was this fire that scarcely a shot failed to strike some portion of the surging, panic-stricken mass of Federals. They fell by hundreds, and the line which had advanced in all the pomp and splendor of martial strength, scattered and slunk away, completely routed and disheartened, to the shelter of the woods. The mortality was so great that of one of the enemy's regiments only three men, it is said, remained unhurt.

A pause in the conflict was speedily followed by another attack—this time very generally directed all along the line. The enemy brought up their best troops; spared no exertions; and fought with a fury which indicated the importance they attached to some measure at least of success in that portion of the field. Their batteries hurled a storm of iron missiles upon our lines; and protected by this heavy fire, their infantry advanced at a double-quick, bent apparently upon breaking through the bristling hedge of bayonets or leaving their dead bodies on the field. The conflict continued hour after hour, and was really terrific. Jackson's brave troops never wavered, however; and the great leader was everywhere among his men, cheering them on, and holding them steady amid the hottest fire of infantry and artillery. They thus continued to hold their own obstinately without a thought of yielding—but the strength which had borne them through such exhausting marches and hard conflicts within the preceding four or five days began to flag. Other causes conspired to render assistance necessary. Heavy reinforcements were being rapidly pushed forward by the enemy, and our troops had shot away all their cartridges. "We got out of ammunition," writes a young soldier of A. P. Hill's division to his mother, "we collected more from cartridge-boxes of fallen friend and foe. That gave out, and we charged with never-failing yell and steel. All day long they threw their masses on us; all day they fell back shattered and shrieking. When the sun went down, their dead were heaped in front of that incomplete railway, and we sighed with relief, for Longstreet could be seen coming into position on our right. The crisis was over; Longstreet never failed yet; but the sun went down so slowly." Without ammunition, the men of Jackson seized whatever they could lay their hands on to use against the enemy. The piles of stones in the vicinity of the railroad cut were used—and it is well established that many of the enemy were killed by having their skulls broken with fragments of rock.

The conflict went on in this way all the afternoon, and was exceedingly obstinate. The enemy had not succeeded in driving Gen. Jackson from his position; but his brave men were beginning to grow weary in the unequal struggle with a foe who threw against them incessantly heavy reinforcements of fresh and trained troops, constantly arriving from the rear and hurried to the front, to take the place of those who had been repulsed.

Gen. Lee saw that the moment had arrived for a demonstration on the enemy's left, and this was made about nightfall, when Jackson's right began to yield ground slowly and sullenly before the masses brought to bear upon it. Hood's division was ordered forward; and no sooner had these splendid troops thrown themselves with ardor into the contest, than the whole appearance of the field suddenly changed. Up to that moment the conflict had been obstinate, but the firing upon both sides had perceptibly decreased in intensity—the Federals, like their opponents, appearing fatigued by the persistent conflict. The enemy, as we have said, had gained ground upon Jackson's right, and were pushing forward their sharpshooters in advance of their main line, further and further, as our men sullenly retired inch by inch. It was just at this dispiriting moment that Hood's division advanced; and the quick tongues of flame leaped from the muzzles of his muskets, lighting up the gathering gloom with their crimson light. These "fires of death" were followed by the sharp crack of the guns from end to end of the great field between the opposing lines—and then dusky figures were seen advancing rapidly from the *Confederate* side. The next jets of flame spurted into the darkness were near the edge of the wood where the enemy were drawn up; then with one long roar of musketry and a maze of quick flashes everywhere, Hood's men charged forward with wild cheers, driving the enemy before them into the depths of the forest.

The impetuous charge had instantly changed the fortunes of the day. Jackson's brave men were inspired with new ardor, and pressed forward with cheers, all along the line. The enemy were unable to withstand the shock, and when the deep darkness of night, lit up now only by a few flashes of artillery, put an end to the conflict, the Federal lines had been forced back more than half a mile from the position which they had held before Hood charged.

By order of Gen. Lee, the troops, however, fell back to their former strong position, for the real struggle on the next day, and bivouacked for the night—a circumstance which possibly induced Gen. Pope to telegraph that, although he had sustained a loss of 8,000 men, he had driven back the entire Southern army.

What remained after the long and obstinate conflict—above the smoke, the dust, the blood—was this: Jackson had held his ground against the vast masses thrown upon his lines—had sustained the shock everywhere without flinching—and night and Longstreet had come.

He had foiled the enemy at every turn; had obstinately held his ground against every attempt to dislodge him; had fought with that dogged determination which compels the eagles of victory to perch upon the standards of the leader who possesses it; had triumphed over his foes, and was safe.

Longstreet was there upon his right, with his strong and veteran corps; Lee was by his side to take from his shoulders a portion of that burden of care and anxiety which would have crushed most men, and oppressed even the iron strength of Jackson; the enemy were repulsed; their men and horses were, by *his* exertions, cut off from all supplies; victory, on the morrow, was, humanly speaking, a certainty.

The stern soul of Jackson, the soldier, must have rejoiced within him, when night came, and all was well. But the childlike heart of Jackson, the humble Christian, was full of pity for his brave followers, and of prayer to the God in whom he trusted, for their welfare, and his country's success.

CHAPTER XXIV.

MANASSAS: AUGUST 30, 1862

SATURDAY, the great day which was to terminate the long conflict, dawned, clear and beautiful.

With the first dawn of day, the Southern troops were under arms, and prepared for the contest which was to ensue. All of our force had now arrived, with the exception of Gen. R. H. Anderson's division of Longstreet's corps, which was only a few miles from the field; and line-of-battle was formed immediately.

The order of battle remained unchanged. Jackson still

occupied his former position, with his left near Sudley, his right above Groveton; and Longstreet's line, as before, stretched away obliquely, the interval between the two being protected by the eight batteries of Col. Lee. Gen. Stuart's cavalry was posted on the right and left wings, and batteries were so disposed as to serve as supports to the advancing columns, or repulse the onset of the enemy.

The Federal army adapted its line, in some measure, to our own. It curved backward from the centre, following the conformation of our two wings, and is said to have embraced Gen. Heintzelman on the right; Gen. McDowell on the left; and Porter, Siegel, and Reno in the centre. Their batteries were disposed in a manner similar to our own, and their cavalry held well in hand to take an active part in the battle.

It was in this attitude that the two armies remained in face of each other for many hours—neither advancing to the attack. Gen. Lee's policy was plainly to await the assault in his strong position behind the railroad, and on the high ground of the Groveton heights—thus forcing the enemy either to attack him, or retire across Bull Run, for supplies, pursued by the Southern troops. Gen. Lee could hold his position indefinitely, having uninterrupted communication with his rear; but the Federal general was forced to fight or retreat—and the obvious policy was to await his advance.

The strength of our position was evidently appreciated, and persistent attempts were made to draw the Southern troops from it. About one o'clock a feint was made upon our right, and a brisk encounter took place between the advance forces; but the enemy were speedily driven back with artillery, and our troops retained their position. Heavy masses then moved in the direction of our left, and Gen. Jackson prepared for an instant renewal of the fierce conflict of the preceding day. Several demonstrations were made, but the failure here was as marked as it had been on the right—and the Federal forces withdrew, apparently designing to fall back in the direction of Manassas.

These movements, during the whole forenoon, and up to four in the evening, were vigilantly watched by our generals. The great drama evidently absorbed all their attention, and, though outwardly calm, the latent fire of the eye showed that the design of the enemy was fully understood, and every thing ready for the earnest work which would speedily succeed all this manœuvring, these elaborate ruses and feints. The enemy had completely failed in achieving their object—they had attempted in vain to deceive the wary eyes of Lee and Jackson and Longstreet—and they now prepared to abandon their useless movements, and trust the event of the day to superior numbers and stubborn fighting.

The Southern troops had witnessed the complicated evolutions of the enemy across the wide fields and through the forest, with little anxiety. The conflict of the preceding day had given them confidence, and the men lay down in line-of-battle, laughing and jesting. Virginians, Georgians, Alabamians, Mississippians, Texans, Floridians, Carolinians—all awaited the development of the enemy's designs with entire calmness, and a species of indifference which was very striking. They were in this careless mood—some talking, others jesting, others again sleeping beneath the warm August sky, when suddenly the roar of thirty pieces of artillery shook the ground, and filled the air with their tremendous reverberations. Every man started to his feet—and the cause of the heavy cannonade was plain.

The enemy, entirely foiled in their attempt to draw us from the heights, had suddenly advanced at a double quick, as before, against our centre, where Jackson's right and Longstreet's left came together. The attack was made upon Jackson's line first, by a dense column of infantry, which had been massed in a strip of woods, in close vicinity to Groveton. Three heavy lines had been formed for the charge, and as the first of these lines emerged at a double quick from the woods, they were greeted with the murderous fire above described. Col. Lee had opened upon them with all his war-dogs at once, and the writer of these lines has never, during his whole experience, witnessed such handling of artillery. The fiery storm was directed with astonishing accuracy, and the brigades which led the charge were almost annihilated by the shot and shell which burst before, behind, above, to the right, to the left—raking and tearing them to pieces. They were swept away before this horrible fire, like leaves in the wind, and disappeared, broken and flying in the woods—to be immediately succeeded, however, by another brigade charging as before. Again the iron storm crashed through the ranks; and again they broke and ran. A third force, heavier than before, now advanced with mad rapidity, and in the midst of the awful fire of our batteries, threw themselves upon Jackson, and engaged him with desperation. Reserves followed; and the fight became furious—Jackson's troops mowing down their opponents, but suffering heavily themselves.

We shall continue our description now in the graphic words of "Personne," the writer formerly quoted from, who after speaking of the three lines pushed against our troops by the Federals, says:

"Jackson's infantry raked these three columns terribly. Repeatedly did they break and run, and rally again under the energetic appeals of their officers, for it was a crack corps of the Federal army—that of General Sykes and Morrell; but it was not in human nature to stand unflinchingly before that hurricane of fire. As the fight progressed Lee moved his batteries to the left, until reaching a position only four hundred yards distant from the enemy's lines, he opened again. The spectacle was now magnificent. As shell after shell burst in the wavering ranks, and round shot ploughed broad gaps among them, you could distinctly see through the rifts of smoke the Federal soldiers falling and flying on every side.

With the explosion of every bomb, it seemed as if scores dropped dead or writhed in agony upon the field. Some were crawling on their hands and knees, some were piled up together, and some were lying scattered around in every attitude that imagination can conceive.

"With the dispersion of the enemy's reserve, the whole mass broke and ran like a flock of wild sheep. Jackson's men, yelling like devils, now charged upon the scattered crowd; but you could notice that they themselves had severely suffered, and were but a handful compared with the overwhelming forces of the enemy. The flags of two or three regiments did not appear to be more than fifty yards apart. The brilliant affair did not occupy more than half an hour; but in that brief time over three hundred and fifty Yankee souls had been launched into eternity, and five times that number left mangled on the ground. It was like the waves rolling against a solid rock, and dashing back in showers of spray. A golden opportunity was now at hand for Longstreet to attack the exposed left flank of the enemy in front of him; and he accordingly ordered the advance of Hood's division, which moved obliquely to the right and forward of the position it had occupied. Kemper next followed, with the brigade of General Jenkins on the right of that of Pickett, and Jones' division completed our line of battle. The brigade of Evans acted as a support to Hood.

"Not many minutes elapsed after the order to attack, before the volleys of platoons, and finally the rolling reports of long lines of musketry, indicated that the battle was in full progress. The whole army was now in motion. The woods were full of troops, and the order for the supports to forward at a quick step was received with enthusiastic cheers by the elated men. The din was almost deafening. The heavy notes of the artillery, at first deliberate, but gradually increasing in rapidity, mingled with the sharp treble of the small-arms, gave one an idea of some diabolical concert in which all the furies of hell were at work. Through the woods, over gently rolling hills, now and then through an open field, we travel toward the front. From an elevation we obtain a view of a considerable portion of the field. Hood and Kemper are now hard at it, and as they press forward, never yielding an inch, sometimes at a double-quick, you hear those unmistakable yells which tell of a Southern charge or a Southern success.

"The troops they encounter are the best disciplined in the Yankee army, and for a little while most obstinately do they contest every inch of ground over which we advance. Nothing, however, can withstand the impetuosity of our boys. Every line of the enemy has been broken and dispersed, but rallies again upon some other position behind. Hood has already advanced his division nearly half a mile at a double quick—the Texans, Georgians, and Hampton Legion loading and firing as they run, yelling all the while like madmen. They have captured one or two batteries and various stands of colors, and are still pushing the enemy before them. Evans, at the head of his brigade, is following on the right, as their support, and pouring in his effective volleys. Jenkins has come in on the right of the Quinn House, and, like an avalanche, sweeps down upon the legions before him with resistless force. Still further to the right is Longstreet's old brigade, composed of Virginians, veterans of every battlefield, all of whom are fighting like furies. The First Virginia, which opened the ball at Bull Run on the 17th of July, 1861, with over six hundred men, now reduced to less than eighty members, is winning new laurels; but out of the little handful more than a third have already bit the dust. Toombs and Anderson, with the Georgians, together with Kemper and Jenkins, are swooping around on the right, flanking the Federals, and driving them toward their centre and rear. Eschelman, with his company of the Washington Artillery, Major Garnett, with his battalion of Virginia batteries, and others of our big guns, are likewise working around upon the enemy's left, and pouring an enfilading fire into both their infantry and artillery.

"We do nothing but charge! charge!! charge!!! If the enemy make a bold effort to retrieve the fortunes of the day (and they made many), and we are repulsed, it is but for the moment, and the regiments rallying upon their supports, plunge back again into the tempest of fire that before swept them down.

"Some of the positions of the enemy were strong as Nature could make them, and were charged five or six times, but each time our soldiers were turned back by sheer physical inability to surmount the obstacles before them. It was then grand to witness the moral heroism with which, though their comrades went down like swaths of grass under the mower's scythe, other men continued to step into the path of death with cheerful alacrity, and still to fall with the battle-shout upon their lips, and the proud smile of conscious valor on their faces."

Such are the animated paragraphs of "Personne."

Gradually as the fierce struggle progressed, the sides of the open V, which our order of battle resembled, closed upon the flanks of the enemy. Colonel Lee's artillery still continued to play with destructive effect upon their front, and the batteries were regularly advanced from position to position, raking from every hillock, with a merciless storm of shot and shell, the lines of the enemy.

The battle has now become terrific. The ruses and manœuvres of the morning had long yielded to desperate, stubborn fighting, and the day depended not so much upon any military skill of the generals, as upon the character of the troops engaged. The Northern man was pitted against the Southerner, and from the first the result was not doubtful. The enemy fought hard, but that "heart of hope," which adds so much to the efficiency of the soldier, had deserted them, and they contended doggedly, but without the dash and fervor which compel victory. Gradually the great Southern lines closed in upon them, Longstreet's right pressed down upon their left, and Jackson's column swung round, steady, heavy, resistless, upon their right, huddling the disordered regiments and brigades upon their centre.

This was the situation of affairs as the sun sank slowly toward the west, and the Confederate leaders now concentrated all their forces for a last charge, which should carry every thing before it. The batteries redoubled their exertions, the air was hot and sulphurous with exploding missiles, whole ranks went down before the whirlwind of iron, and the continuous streaming roar of musketry was frightful in its intensity. The enemy continued to give ground; our reserves were hurried forward to the front, and just as the sun sank, a general bayonet charge was made all along our lines. From the dust and smoke of battle there appeared all at once before the eyes of the disheartened Federals a rapidly advancing line with gleaming bayonets, and this line swept forward at a run, with the resistless power of a torrent. "They came on," says the correspondent of a Northern journal, "like demons emerging from the earth." There was no pause, no hesitation. The Federal volleys tore through the line, but could not check it. The men pressed on with deafening cheers over the dead and dying—the ranks closing up where gaps were made—the fury of battle burning in every soul; and before this resistless charge the last remnant of hope deserted the Federal troops. They no longer came up to the struggle. They broke, ran, and, pursued by the pitiless fire and gleaming bayonets of the Confederates, disappeared, shattered and overwhelmed, in the rapidly gathering darkness.

The field was ours. The long contest was ended; victory assured; the great army which had advanced to the assault with colors flying and certain of victory was a routed and decimated multitude, which now thought of nothing but its safety behind the sheltering heights of Centreville.

Jackson's veterans had taken their full part in the desperate combat, and sweeping down upon the wavering lines, had led the wild charge which put them to final rout. The fighting of the old corps had been obstinate, dogged, fatal, as always. They had sustained every assault with undaunted firmness; repulsed every attempt to force them from their ground; and then advancing in their turn, had pushed the enemy from position after position, and swept onward to victory.

"It was a task of almost superhuman labor," says the correspondent from whom we have already quoted, "to drive the enemy from those strong points, defended, as they were, by the best artillery and infantry in the Federal army; but in less than four hours from the commencement of the battle our indomitable energy had accomplished every thing. The arrival of R. H. Anderson, with his reserves, soon after the engagement was fully opened, proved a timely acquisition, and the handsome manner in which he brought his troops into position, showed the cool and skilful general. Our generals—Lee, Longstreet, Jackson, Hood, Kemper, Evans, Jones, Jenkins, and others—all shared the dangers to which they exposed their men. How well their colonels and subordinate officers performed their duty is best testified by the list of killed and wounded.

"The battle raged in the manner described until after dark, and when it was impossible to use fire-arms, the heavens were lit up by the still continued flashes of the artillery, and the meteor flight of shells scattering their iron spray. By this time the enemy had been forced across Bull Run, and their dead covered every acre from the starting point of the fight to the Stone Bridge. Had we been favored with another hour of daylight, their rout would have been as great as that which followed the original battle of Manassas. As it was, they retreated in haste and disorder to the heights of Centreville. We had driven them up hill and down a distance of two and a half miles, captured between twenty and thirty pieces of artillery, several hundred prisoners (though few soldiers cared to be troubled with the latter), and some six or eight thousand stand of arms.

"The field after the battle is a portion of the history of the day which pen cannot fully describe. But if the reader can imagine himself standing on the heights around the old Henry House, and looking across the country in the direction in which we advanced, over the gullies, ravines, and valleys which divided the opposite hills, he will see dead and wounded lying by thousands as far as the eye can reach. The woods are likewise full of them. It has been remarked by every one that the enemy on this vast hecatomb outnumbered us five or six to one. They lie thickest upon the slopes and summits where their batteries were planted, and the infantry were drawn up as supporters, in many instances as many as eighty or ninety dead marking the place where fought a single regiment. It is one of the singular coincidences of this strange battle, that Hood's brigade encountered on Saturday precisely the same troops whom they met at Gaines' Mill in the battles before Richmond—the Duryea Zouaves, fierce fellows in red baggy breeches, red skull caps, and blue embroidered jackets—and as on that occasion literally mowed them down.

"In front of the Chinn House, which is now a hospital, the havoc has been terrible. The ground is strewn not only with men, but arms, ammunition, provisions, haversacks, canteens, and whatever else the affrighted Federals could throw away to facilitate their flight before our onsets at that point. Several cannon, broken caissons, wheels, and numbers of dead horses were also to be seen here.

"In front of the position occupied by Jackson's men, the killed are even more plentiful. In many places you cannot walk three steps without being compelled to step over or around a corpse."

Such was the great second battle of Manassas. The description of "Personne" is vivid and accurate, though it omits many facts. The part taken by Major-general Stuart in the events of the day was important. He commanded the division of infantry which toward nightfall made the vigorous and successful attack upon the enemy's left; and his cavalry were engaged on the flanks of the army throughout the day. As the enemy were giving way on our right an impetuous charge was made by a body of cavalry under Col. Munford, of the 2d Virginia, which terminated, after a close hand-to-hand conflict, in the complete rout of the largely superior force brought against him. This ended the conflict in that part of the field, and the enemy broke and fled, pursued by our artillery and cavalry to the banks of Bull Run, over which their confused column hastened on its way to Centreville.

The gallant young soldier of A. P. Hill's division, from whose letter to his mother we have already quoted, has the following sentences specially relating to our subject:

"Saturday morning — day ever memorable! for it broke the back of the great lying nation—our corps still held that ridge, and Longstreet formed on our right, obtuse-angled to us, so that, if they attacked, upon forcing us back, their flank would be exposed to Longstreet; and, if they forced him back their flank would be exposed to us. This arrangement was concealed from them, so far, that they suspected our strength to lie to our left. Skirmishing and distant cannonading lasted till one, P. M., when the action commenced, and soon grew infinitely furious. But they were out-generalled and beaten from the start, and, at half-past four or five, P. M., it was plain that they were terribly whipped. The fight was by far the most horrible and deadly that I have seen. Just at sunset, our wings swept round in pursuit; Jackson swinging his left on the right, as a pivot, and Longstreet in the reverse method. Their dead on the field were in such numbers as to sicken even the veterans of Richmond and the Shenandoah Valley; they left 2,000 dead—rotting clay—and almost innumerable wounded. Their discipline and the night saved them from a rout. They retreated in tolerable order to Centreville. 'Twas decisive; their whole army engaged—only two corps of ours; and their loss, I think, ten to one on our side."

Thus ended the bitter contest upon the weird plains, already so deeply crimsoned with Southern blood. Strange Providence which rolled the tide of battle there again! which made the huge wave break in foam again in the melancholy fields around Stone Bridge. It was a veritable repetition of the fierce drama of July, 1861. "Batteries were planted and captured yesterday," says a writer, "where they were planted and captured last year. The pine thicket, where the Fourth Alabama and Eighth Georgia suffered so terribly in the first battle, is now strewn with the slain of the invader. We charged through the same woods yesterday, though from a different point, where Kirby Smith, the Blucher of the day, entered the fight before."

The strength of the invader of our soil was broken again, as it had been in the battle of the 21st July. Again he fled ignominiously across Bull Run, pursued by our victorious troops, leaving behind him the *debris* of a panic-stricken retreat. In August of 1862, as in July of 1861, the writer of these lines saw, as he followed the retreating horde, the rubbish of knapsacks, oil-cloths, swords, guns, bayonets, artillery.

broken-down vehicles, and—worse rubbish still—dirty Federal stragglers in blue coats, with coarse, low-browed faces, full of deceit and vulgarity—that vulgarity of the soul which is in these people, and can no more be rooted out than the spots of the leopard can be changed, or the skin of the Ethiopian made white. All this crowded upon the right, along the same road to Centreville over which Pope retreated, as McDowell had retreated before him, routed and broken.

A few words will terminate our sketch of these great events.

On Sunday, Jackson's corps was again in motion, and pressed the enemy toward Centreville. General Stuart pursued with his cavalry, and fought their rear-guard at Cub Run Bridge, which they burned behind them. The cavalry moved to the left, struck into the Little River turnpike, toward Chantilly, and, getting into the enemy's rear, fired into their trains; then—Sunday evening—rapidly retreating toward Fairfax Court-house. On Monday morning, the advance of Jackson, who had changed his line of march and followed the cavalry, appeared on the Little River road, and on the afternoon of that day—September 1st—a brief but severe encounter took place at Ox Hill, just above the little village of Germantown. The Federal force engaged was a portion of Franklin's corps, which had taken no part in the battles of the preceding days, and the contest was, for a time, exceeding obstinate—the Federals losing General Kearney, and other prominent officers. The battle was, however, interrupted by a severe thunder-storm, and, darkness coming on soon afterwards, the enemy took advantage of that circumstance, and withdrew from our front.

On the same night they retreated from Fairfax Court-house, and the Confederates, on the next day, entered in triumph, amid the joyful exclamations of the loyal inhabitants, so long subjected to the insults and oppression of their enemies.

Pope—like Banks, Fremont, Shields, and Milroy—had passed away; his lurid star obscured by the clouds of disaster and defeat. The star of Jackson mounted toward the zenith—it was the star of Victory.

CHAPTER XXV.

INVASION OF MARYLAND.

Thus ended the great summer campaign, which was to have "crushed the rebellion" before the forest leaves were touched by the finger of autumn.

It had commenced with boasts and braggadocio; it ended in ignominious defeat. General Pope had advanced with the air of a world-conqueror about to exterminate a foe whom he despised. He slunk away with his shattered columns behind the defences of Washington, like a dog who has been met by the lash, and driven howling from the field.

The battle-flag of the South floated proudly where the standards of the enemy had flouted the air, and new fields were open to the Southern army. Maryland was now undefended; and the smoke of battle had scarcely lifted from the plains of Manassas, when our victorious columns were in motion toward the upper Potomac.

Long before, Jackson had written to a friend, who was the recipient of his most private feelings:

"I am cordially with you in favor of carrying the war north of the Potomac."

It would appear, that from the beginning of his military career, he had looked forward to an invasion of the enemy's territory as the only certain means of bringing the war to an end; and if his abruptly terminated campaign toward Romney in January be attentively studied, it will leave the impression that even then, with the great force in front of him, he believed that greater results would be achieved by a forward movement, and a transfer of hostilities to the region beyond the Potomac, than by falling back, and yielding possession of the Valley, to be overrun and plundered by the enemy.

To advance seems, indeed, to have been the prime maxim of this great man's military philosophy—to strike the foe, without waiting to be struck by him—to make him feel the horrors of war, amid his own homes, and thus impressing upon *the people* of the North the atrocious nature of the contest, compel an early peace.

The signal of the long-wished-for advance now came. "On to Maryland!" was the watchword; and the old veterans of Jackson moved forward at the signal, joyous, elated, confident of victory, and burning with ardor at the thought that the fair fields of Virginia, the homes of their loved ones, would be relieved of the horrors of war.

No time was lost by Gen. Lee in commencing his movement. It was necessary to gain a foothold in Maryland before the disorganized forces of the Federal government were again put in fighting condition, and the campaign began with energy and rapidity.

Gen. Jackson having, after his custom, inquired with great interest what roads led to the Potomac, in the direction of Arlington Heights, and ordered maps to be prepared of the region for his use, put his troops in motion toward Leesburg. Marching by Dranesville, which he reached on September 3d, the second day after the battle at Ox Hill, he arrived at Leesburg on the 4th, and was there joined by the other corps of the army.

On the 5th the passage of the Potomac was effected without resistance. It is said to have been an inspiring spectacle. Says a correspondent:

"When our army reached the middle of the river, which they were wading, the troops were halted, General Jackson pulled off his hat, and the splendid bands of music struck up the inspiring air of 'Maryland, my Maryland,' which was responded to and sung with 'the spirit and with the understanding' by all who could sing, and the name of all who could then and there sing was legion."

No pause was permitted now; and the army pushed forward rapidly toward Frederick City, which the advance reached on the same day. We shall quote again from "Personne," the intelligent writer whose letters have already supplied us with particulars of the movements and contests of the army. The paragraphs extracted are valuable as presenting the impressions of an eye-witness, and thus affording a life-like picture of events at the moment when the pages were written. The letter is dated at Frederick City, September 7th, two days after the arrival of the Southern army:

"Thus far," says "Personne," "we have everywhere met with hearty hospitality. Along the road the farmers have welcomed the presence of our men with a sincerity that cannot be misunderstood, opened their houses and spread their boards with the fat of the land. One Marylander, with whom I met, has fed in twenty-four hours six hundred hungry men, free of charge. Others have been proportionately liberal.

"Our reception up to this point has been all that we could desire. With a few, the enthusiasm has been highly demonstrative, but the majority content themselves with quiet manifestations of the warm sympathy they feel. Nearly all the houses along the route of march were open, and invitations were freely extended to the officers to spend the day and night. A slight indication of the grateful outbursts of the people was in the presentation of a magnificent horse to Gen. Jackson, by the farmers, within an hour after he touched Maryland soil.

"The advance of our army arrived on Friday night, and we are now encamped around the town. Martial law has been proclaimed, a provost marshal appointed, and a strong guard of our men patrols the streets to preserve order.

"In the sentiment of the people we are not much disappointed. It is apparently about equally divided, and there is yet little openly expressed enthusiasm. As Jackson's army marched through, the houses were mostly closed, and from between the window blinds the citizens could be seen anxiously peering, as if they expected to see a crowd of bugaboos intent upon nothing but rapine and slaughter. A few of the residences were open, however, and in those ladies and gentlemen were waving their handkerchiefs, and displaying the Confederate flag. From one, the residence of a Mr Ross, a lawyer of high standing, his family were distributing to the soldiers as they passed eatables and clothing to such as seemed most needy.

"Afterwards the family invited many officers to the house, where they were handsomely entertained with wines, cigars, and other luxuries. Mr. Ross himself has been confined in Fortress McHenry for the bold stand he took at an early hour in favor of the South.

"As soon as the troops were encamped, many were permitted to enter the town, and in a short time it was thronged. Confederate money was taken without a murmur by all who opened their stores, and for the first time during the campaign we enjoyed the privilege of purchasing at peace prices the articles we most required. Coffee could be had in abundance at twenty-five cents per pound, sugar at eleven and twelve cents, salt fifty cents a sack, boots five and seven dollars a pair, shoes three dollars, flannel forty cents a yard, and every thing else in proportion. Lager beer, ice cream, dates, confections, preserves, all found ready sale, and were liberally dispensed and disposed of.

"There are three or four churches in the town, and to-day they are filled with our officers and men, attending divine service."

"Personne" thus continues his letter on Monday, September 8th:

"Frederick to-day presents a busy scene, more like that of a Fourth of July festival than a gathering of armed invaders. A majority of the stores are closed to general admission, because of the crowds eager to press and buy, but a little diplomacy secures an entrance at the back door, or past the sentinel wisely stationed, to protect the proprietor from the rush of anxious customers. Prices are going up rapidly. Every thing is so cheap that our men frequently lay down a five dollar bill to pay for a three-dollar article, and rush out without waiting for the change. The good people here don't understand it. Bitter complaints are uttered against those who refuse Confederate money, and it is understood that the authorities will insist upon its general circulation.

"The people are beginning to recover from their surprise at our sudden appearance, and to realize the magnitude of our preparations to advance through and relieve Maryland from her thraldom. Some are still moody, and evidently hate us heartily, but we are more than compensated by the warm welcome of others, who now begin to greet us from every quarter. Only a few moments ago I met a lady who confessed that although she had Confederate flags ready to expose in her windows as we passed, she was afraid to wave them, lest being discovered by her Union neighbors she should be reported to the Federals in case of our retreat, and be thereby subjected to insult if not imprisonment at their hands. To assure me how true were her sentiments, she introduced me to a large room in her house, where there were fourteen ladies, young and old, busy as bees, making shirts, drawers, and other clothing for the soldiers.

"She was also distributing money and tobacco to the soldiers. Judging probably from my rags that I too was in a destitute condition, she benevolently desired to take me in hand and replenish my entity throughout, but of course I declined, and though I could not help smiling at the ingenuous oddity of the proposition, a tear at the same time stole down my cheek at the thought of the sufferings which these noble-hearted ladies must have endured to prompt the unselfish generosity by which they endeavored to express their delight in our presence.

"Though thousands of soldiers are now roaming through the town, there has not been a solitary instance of misdemeanor. I have heard no shouting, no clamor of any kind, and seen but a single case of intoxication—a one-legged Yankee prisoner.

"All who visit the city are required to have passes, and the only persons arrested are those who are here without leave. This quiet behavior of our men contrasts so strongly with that of the Federals when here as to excite the favorable comment of the Unionists. None of the latter have, to my knowledge, been interfered with, and, as far as I can learn, it is not the policy of our commander to retaliate. We shall, on the contrary, pursue a conciliatory course, and by kindness endeavor to show these misguided people that our home should be their home, and our God their God.

"One of these Union men frankly confessed to me that he feared his own neighbors more than he did our troops, and he should regret to see us depart.

"The only outrage, if outrage it can be called, which has taken place, was committed by the citizen Secessionists, who entered the office of the Frederick *Examiner*, a Black Republican newspaper of the darkest dye, and tore it to pieces, the editor himself fleeing on the first symptoms of our advance.

"We pay for every thing as we go, the farmers being compensated for all damage by the burning of rails, use of forage, or destruction of crops, before we break up camp.

"We are told by Marylanders that we shall have an accession to our ranks in this State of over forty thousand men, and that when we arrive within striking distance of Baltimore, twenty thousand men will rise in arms and join our standard. A gentleman from that city informs me that the excitement there is intense, the streets being blocked up by the crowds, and an armed force of cavalry and infantry constantly patrolling the city to keep down the increasing signs of a revolution.

"Recruiting here goes on rapidly. Within two days five companies have been formed, and it is stated that from the surrounding country over seven hundred entered our ranks while *en route*.

"Pennsylvania, the border line of which is only some twenty-five or twenty-eight miles distant, has sent us nearly a hundred recruits, who prefer service in the Confederate army to being drafted in that of the North.

"Altogether, our movement has been thus far marked by the most gratifying success. Every detail has been successfully carried out, the troops are in good health, and full of enthusiasm, the commissariat is improving, and we wait for nothing more anxiously than the order to resume our march onward."

On the same day General Lee issued his expected address to the people of Maryland, which the citizens and the army equally looked for with the deepest interest. Up to this moment no indications of the intended policy of the invading general had been given, and the paper was seized upon and perused with avidity as soon as it appeared.

It was in the following words:

"HEADQUARTERS ARMY OF NORTHERN VIRGINIA,
Near Frederick Town, September 8th, 1862.

"TO THE PEOPLE OF MARYLAND:

"It is right that you should know the purpose that has brought the army under my command within the limits of your State, so far as that purpose concerns yourselves.

"The people of the Confederate States have long watched, with the deepest sympathy, the wrongs and outrages that have been inflicted upon the citizens of a commonwealth allied to the States of the South by the strongest social, political, and commercial ties.

"They have seen, with profound indignation, their sister State deprived of every right, and reduced to the condition of a conquered province.

"Under the pretence of supporting the Constitution, but in violation of its most valuable provisions, your citizens have been arrested and imprisoned upon no charge, and contrary to all forms of law. The faithful and manly protest against this outrage, made by the venerable and illustrious Marylanders, to whom, in better days, no citizen appealed for right in vain, was treated with scorn and contempt. The government of your chief city has been usurped by armed strangers; your Legislature has been dissolved by the unlawful arrest of its members; freedom of the press and of speech have been suppressed; words have been declared offences by an arbitrary decree of the Federal Executive, and citizens ordered to be tried by a military commission for what they may dare to speak.

"Believing that the people of Maryland possessed a spirit too lofty to submit to such a government, the people of the South have long wished to aid you in throwing off this foreign yoke, to enable you again to enjoy the inalienable rights of freemen, and restore independence and sovereignty to your State.

"In obedience to this wish our army has come among you,

9*

and is prepared to assist you with the power of its arms in regaining the rights of which you have been despoiled.

"This, citizens of Maryland, is our mission, so far as you are concerned.

"No constraint upon your free will is intended—no intimidation will be allowed.

"Within the limits of this army, at least, Marylanders shall once more enjoy their ancient freedom of thought and speech.

"We know no enemies among you, and will protect all, of every opinion.

"It is for you to decide your destiny, freely and without constraint.

"This army will respect your choice, whatever it may be; and while the Southern people will rejoice to welcome you to your natural position among them, they will only welcome you when you come of your own free will.

"R. E. LEE,
"*General Commanding.*"

The campaign in Maryland was thus undertaken to aid the people of that State in "throwing off the foreign yoke" which had so long weighed down their necks; in "regaining the rights of which they had been despoiled;" "to enable them again to enjoy the inalienable rights of freemen, and restore independence and sovereignty to the State."

No citizen would be coerced; no man's property taken from him; if he joined the Southern army he would be welcome, but if he remained at home he would not be molested. To each and all was accorded the right to "decide his destiny, freely and without constraint."

When the impartial Genius of History comes to survey the events of this period, and compares the infamous *dragoonade* orders of John Pope, with the calm, just, and stately proclamation of Robert E. Lee, what will she say?

When a great cause has such leaders, it is already won.

Certain persons have put themselves to the trouble of attempting to discover a profound *ruse* in this address. Such a construction of the grave and statesmanlike paper is simply absurd. The advance into Maryland was made for the purposes stated by Gen. Lee, and circumstances wholly beyond his control—against the force of which he could not contend—dictated his subsequent operations. What these circumstances were, will be briefly but accurately stated in the ensuing pages of this work.

Gen. Lee had thus advanced without resistance into the enemy's country, and his eagles already began to open their broad wings for flight toward the rich fields of Pennsylvania. But one serious cause of delay existed, which changed the whole face of affairs. This was the fortress, as it may appropriately be called, of Harper's Ferry. At Harper's Ferry, a force of 11,000 of the enemy, with 73 pieces of artillery, remained, directly in Gen. Lee's rear; and it was necessary before proceeding to enter on greater movements, to root out this nest of the enemy, and gain possession of this strong point which they then held.

On his trial, Gen. McClellan, in reply to the question, "Will you give a statement of the principal events connected with the Maryland campaign?" said:

"When at Frederick, we found the original order issued to Gen. D. H. Hill by direction of Gen. Lee, which gave the orders of march for their whole army, and developed their intentions. The substance of the order was, that Jackson was to move from Frederick by the main Hagerstown road, and, leaving it at some point near Middleburg, to cross the Potomac near Sharpsburg, and endeavor to capture the garrison of Martinsburg, and cut off the retreat of the garrison of Harper's Ferry in that direction. Gen. McLaws was ordered, with his own command and the division of General Anderson, to move out by the same Hagerstown road and gain possession of the Maryland Heights, opposite Harper's Ferry. General Walker, who was then apparently somewhere near the mouth of the Monocacy, was to move through Lovettsville and gain possession of Loudoun Heights, thus completing the investment of Harper's Ferry. Gen. Longstreet was ordered to move to Hagerstown, with Hill to serve as a rear-guard. Their reserve trains to Manassas, &c., were ordered to take position either at Boonsboro' or Hagerstown, I have now forgotten which. It was directed in the same order, that after Jackson, Walker, McLaws, &c., had taken Harper's Ferry, they were to rejoin the main army at Hagerstown or Boonsboro'. That order is important in another sense. It shows very clearly that the object of the enemy was to go to Pennsylvania, or at least to remain in Maryland."

Let us see now what movements were made by the enemy to check the advance of Gen. Lee, relieve Harper's Ferry, and defeat the projected invasion of Pennsylvania. After the battle of Manassas, confusion reigned for a brief period in the Federal councils at Washington; and the advance of the Southern army was regarded with a terror which even the official documents betray. Not only the people, but the government also were filled with dire forebodings of the terrible events about to come to pass. Troops were hurried forward from various points in the North; the remnants of the army which had been defeated at Manassas were collected and reorganized; all the reserves which had not arrived in time to participate in those great contests were put in requisition, and another army, heterogeneous in character but vast in numbers, was at once ready to take the field. McClellan was assigned to the command, and the entire force was rapidly sent forward by railway toward Frederick. Never had the enormous resources of men and material of the Federal government been more strikingly displayed; and the Southern army was called upon speedily to meet a new swarm of foes, brought forward to Washington, and thence to the front, from the populous hives in which—the refuse of all nations—they had been harboring. McClellan depended, however, upon his old levies—that reserve which had not been engaged at Manassas—for the hard fighting; and with the huge mass, old soldiers and new, veterans and conscripts, hurried forward toward Hagerstown.

Meanwhile, Gen. Lee had commenced his operations, looking to the reduction of Harper's Ferry. Gen. McLaws was sent to occupy Maryland Heights, a powerful position just opposite the town, and cut off the enemy's retreat if they attempted to fall back toward Frederick; while Gen. Jackson was directed to march straight across the country to Williamsport, take possession of Martinsburg, and intercept their retreat if they moved up the river, or demand the instant surrender of Harper's Ferry. Gen. Jackson could take care of himself, but Gen. McLaws was liable to be assailed in the rear, driven from his position, and the garrison thus relieved. A strong force was accordingly posted at South Mountain, on the main road from Frederick to Boonsboro', under the command of Gen. D. H. Hill, to receive the attack of McClellan, then known to be advancing; and Gen. Longstreet's corps was held in reserve to move in any direction which the exigencies of the occasion demanded.

The enemy appeared in front of the position occupied by Gen. D. H. Hill, on Sunday, Sept. 14th, and immediately assailed him with greatly superior numbers. A severe conflict ensued, the enemy's numbers enabling him to gain possession of the commanding ground on Hill's left, and by overlapping both wings of his force, to press him back. Couriers were immediately sent to Gen. Lee, announcing the position of affairs, and Longstreet was hurried forward to Hill's assistance. His appearance at once changed the face of things, and the enemy who were rapidly driving Hill back, were driven back in turn, and the pass in the mountains held.

Receiving information that Gen. Jackson's movement had entirely succeeded, and that Harper's Ferry would fall on the next morning, Gen. Lee determined to withdraw Gen. Longstreet and Gen. Hill, and retire toward Sharpsburg, where his communications would be uninterrupted, and his army could be concentrated. The trains were accordingly sent forward, and the army followed, entirely unmolested by the enemy, reaching Sharpsburg about daylight on Monday morning.

Gen. McClellan hastened soon after dawn to pass through the mountains, and push forward to the relief of Harper's Ferry. But he was too late. The golden moment had passed away—the strong arm of Jackson had struck.

Gen. Jackson had performed the work allotted to him by his great commander-in-chief, with that rapidity, accuracy, and fatal certainty of calculation and execution which never failed to characterize his movements. While Hill was contending with McClellan near Boonsboro', on Monday evening, Harper's Ferry was already invested. The summons to surrender was at first refused, and time was asked for. But delay was not a favorite word with Gen. Jackson. He posted his guns so as to command the town on every side, and opened upon it with a fire so steady and irresistible that the enemy's guns were soon silenced. The result is told in the following dispatch sent on the next day:

"HEADQUARTERS VALLEY DISTRICT,
September 16, 1862.

"COLONEL,—Yesterday God crowned our arms with another brilliant success on the surrender, at Harper's Ferry, of Brigadier-general White and 11,000 troops, an equal number of small-arms, 73 pieces of artillery, and about 200 wagons.

"In addition to other stores, there is a large amount of camp and garrison equipage. Our loss was very small. The meritorious conduct of officers and men will be mentioned in a more extended report.

"I am colonel,
"Your obedient servant,
"T. J. JACKSON, *Major-general.*

"Col. R. H. CHILTON, *A. A. General.*"

It has been truthfully declared that the capture of Harper's Ferry was worth the entire campaign in Maryland; and the splendid results achieved induced the belief, above alluded to, that General Lee had no other end in view when he advanced into that country. Such a supposition is exceedingly absurd; but the capture of 11,000 prisoners, 73 pieces of artillery, and 200 wagons, is an amount of damage done to an enemy, which few victories result in.

No good fortune, however, is entirely without alloy, and the movement against Harper's Ferry had withdrawn from General Lee a force at that moment infinitely precious. With Jackson's and McLaws' commands detached from the main body, he had been compelled to fall back to Sharpsburg, in order to unite his army, and thus instead of occupying the aggressive attitude of an invader, to stand on the defensive.

General Jackson left a force under General A. P. Hill, to hold Harper's Ferry, and retracing his steps, rapidly hastened to rejoin General Lee near Sharpsburg.

CHAPTER XXVI.

SHARPSBURG.

The battle near Boonsboro' took place on Sunday, September 14th. Harper's Ferry surrendered on the morning of the 15th. Tuesday, the 16th, was occupied by both combatants in concentrating their detached forces, for the great battle which was to ensue.

On Wednesday, September 17th, the two armies were in front of each other, in the valley of Antietam creek. One who was present thus describes the ground:

"The battle was fought in the valley immediately west of that portion of the Blue Ridge known as the South Mountains, and to the east and north of Sharpsburg, almost in a semicircle, the concave side of which is to the town. Unlike most of the valleys in this Blue Ridge country, this valley has not a level spot in it, but rolls into eminences of all dimensions, from the little knoll that your horse gallops easily over, to the rather high hills that make him tug like a mule. Many of the depressions between these hills are dry, and afford admirable cover for infantry against artillery. Others are watered by the deep, narrow, and crooked Antietam, a stream that seems to observe no decorum in respect to its course, but has to be crossed every ten minutes, ride which way you will. Sharpsburg lies on the western side of the valley, and a little to the south from our point of view. Right across the valley from the northeast runs the turnpike from Boonsboro' to Sharpsburg. Two little villages—Poterstown and Keetersville, or Keedysville—lie on the eastern side of the valley, at the foot of the South Mountains. Numerous fine farm-houses dot the valley in every direction, some standing out plainly and boldly on the hill-tops, others half hidden down the little slopes; and with the large, comfortable barns about them, and their orchards of fruit-trees, these hitherto happy and quiet homes greatly enrich the view, at least to the eyes of old campaigners. Nearly every part of the valley is under cultivation, and the scene is thus varied into squares of the light green of nearly ripened corn, the deeper green of clover, and the dull brown of newly ploughed fields. Toward the north are some dense woods. Imagine this scene spread in the hollow of an amphitheatre of hills that rise in terraces around it, and you have the field of last Wednesday's battle."

Such was the field upon which the two leaders who had already met upon the banks of the Chickahominy were again to contend in one of those bloody conflicts, which will throw a glare so lurid and baleful upon the annals of this period. But the circumstances under which the present battle would be fought were very different, at least in reference to the army of Lee. Before Richmond he was in command of a large force, well provisioned, and in good fighting trim. Here he had only the remains of an army, which the immense rapidity of the marches had scattered all along the roads, and not even the whole of this force, from incompetence or neglect of orders, was available. While General Lee was fighting at Sharpsburg, all Northern Virginia was filled with stragglers, preying upon the inhabitants; and if the Maryland campaign achieved no more, it was beyond all value to us in this, that it inaugurated a system which permits to-day *no* stragglers, and has given us *an army.*

But this is not the place for a discussion of the events which took place in Maryland. History will tell the tale—our pages refer only to one actor. Of the battle of Sharpsburg we present the following animated account, taken from the letters of "Personne." This graphic and generally correct writer presents the picture of the eye-witness, and from his narrative an idea may be obtained of the desperate character of the contest:

"With the first break of daylight the heavy pounding of the enemy's guns on their right announced the battle begun, and for an hour the sullen booming was uninterrupted by aught save their own echoes. McClellan had initiated the attack. Jackson and Lawton (commanding Ewell's division), always in time, had come rapidly forward during the night, and were in position on our extreme left. What a strange strength and confidence we all felt in the presence of that man, 'Stonewall' Jackson. Between six and seven o'clock the Federals advanced a large body of skirmishers, and shortly after the main body of the enemy was hurled against the division of General Lawton. The fire now became fearful and incessant. What were at first distinct notes, clear and consecutive, merged into a tumultuous chorus that made the earth tremble. The discharge of musketry sounded upon the ear like the rolling of a thousand distant drums, and ever and anon the peculiar yells of our boys told us of some advantage gained. We who were upon the centre could see little or nothing of this portion of the battle, but from the dense pall of smoke that hung above the scene, we knew too well that bloody work was going on.

"The Federals there outnumbered us three to one. Their best troops were concentrated upon this single effort to turn our left, and for two hours and a half the tide of battle ebbed and flowed alternately for and against us. Still our boys fought desperately, perhaps as they never fought before. Whole brigades were swept away before the iron storm, the ground was covered with the wounded and dead. Ewell's old division, overpowered by superior numbers, gave back. Hood, with his Texans, the 18th Georgia, and the Hampton Legion, rushed into the gap and retrieved the loss. Ewell's men, rallying on this support, returned to the fight, and adding their weight to that of the fresh, enthusiastic troops, the enemy in turn were driven back. Reinforced, they made another desperate effort on the extreme left, and here again was a repetition of the scenes I have described. For a time they flanked us, and our men retired slowly, fighting over every inch of ground. It was a trying hour. The Federals saw their advantage, and pressed it with vigor. Eight batteries were in full play upon us, and the din of heavy guns, whistling and bursting of shells, and the roar of musketry, was almost deafening.

"At this juncture Lee ordered to the support of Jackson the division of General McLaws, which had been held in reserve. And blessing never came more opportunely. Our men had fought, until not only they but their ammunition were well nigh exhausted, and discomfiture stared them in the face. But thus encouraged, every man rallied, and the fight was redoubled in its intensity. Splendidly handled, the reinforcement swept on like a wave, its blows falling thick and fast upon the audacious columns that had so stubbornly forced their way to the position on which we originally commenced the battle. Half an hour later and the enemy were retreating. At one point we pursued for nearly a mile, and last night a portion of our troops on the left slept on the Yankee ground. The success, though not decisive, as compared with our usual results, was complete as it was possible to make it in view of the peculiar circumstances of the battle and the topography of the country. Certain it is, that after the cessation of the fight at half-past ten, the Yankees did not renew it again at this point during the day. They had been defeated, and all they could do thereafter was to prevent us from repeating in turn the experiment which they had attempted on our line. It was beyond all doubt the most hotly contested field on which a battle has taken place during the war.

"*The Fight upon the Centre.*—Soon after the cessation of the fight on the left, the enemy made a strong demonstration upon our centre, in front of the division of Gen. D. H. Hill. Here, for a while, the contest was carried on mainly by artillery, with which both the enemy and ourselves were abundantly supplied. The only difference between the two, if any at all, was in the superiority of their metal and positions, and on our part the lack of sufficient ammunition. Battery after battery was sent to the rear exhausted, and our ordnance wagons, until late in the day, were on the opposite side of the Potomac, blocked by the long commissary trains, which had been ordered forward from Martinsburg and Shepherdstown to relieve the necessities of the army.

"As indicated in the former part of this letter, our artillery was posted on the summits of the line of hills which ran from right to left in front of the town. That of the enemy, with one exception, was on the rising ground at the base of the Blue Ridge, and upon the various eminences this side. A single Federal battery was boldly thrown over the Stone Bridge, on the turnpike, nine hundred or a thousand yards in our front, and held its position until disabled, with a hardihood worthy of a better cause. I cannot now name all the positions of the different batteries—only those which I saw. Altogether, we may have had playing at this time one hundred guns. The enemy having at least an equal number, you may imagine what a horrid concert filled the air, and how unremitting was the hail of heavy balls and shells, now tearing their way through the trees, now bursting and throwing their murderous fragments on every side, and again burying themselves amid a cloud of dust in the earth, always where they were least expected.

"This exchange of iron compliments had been kept up from early morning, but at eleven o'clock the fire began to concentrate and increase in severity. Columns of the enemy could be distinctly seen across the Antietam on the open ground beyond, moving as if in preparation to advance. Others were so far in the distance that you could recognize them as troops only by the sunlight that gleamed upon their arms, while considerable numbers were within cannon-shot defiantly flaunting their flags in our faces. At twelve o'clock the scene from the apex of the turnpike was truly magnificent, and the eye embraced a picture such as falls to the lot of few men to look upon in this age.

"From twenty different stand-points great volumes of smoke were every instant leaping from the muzzles of angry guns. The air was filled with the white fantastic shapes that floated away from bursted shells. Men were leaping to and fro, loading, firing, and handling the artillery, and now and then a hearty yell would reach the ear, amid the tumult, that spoke of death or disaster from some well-aimed ball. Before us were the enemy. A regiment or two had crossed the river, and, running in squads from the woods along its banks, were trying to form a line. Suddenly a shell falls among them, and another and another, until the thousand scatter like a swarm of flies, and disappear in the woods. A second time the effort is made, and there is a second failure. Then there 's a diversion. The batteries of the Federals open afresh; heir infantry try another point, and finally they succeed in effecting a lodgment on this side. Our troops, under D. H. Hill, meet them, and a fierce battle ensues in the centre. Backwards, forwards, surging and swaying like a ship in a storm, the various columns are seen in motion. It is a hot place for us, but is hotter still for the enemy. They are directly under our guns, and we mow them down like grass. The raw levies, sustained by the veterans behind, come up to the work well, and fight for a short time with an excitement incident to their novel experiences of a battle; but soon a portion of their line gives way in confusion. Their reserves came up, and endeavor to retrieve the fortunes of the day. Our centre, however, stands firm as adamant, and they fall back. Pursuit on our part is useless, for if we drove the enemy at all on the other side of the river, it would be against the sides of the mountain, where one man fighting for his life and liberty, disciplined or undisciplined, would be equal to a dozen.

"Meanwhile deadly work has been going on among our artillery. Whatever they may have made others suffer, nearly all the companies have suffered severely themselves. The great balls and shells of the enemy have been thrown with wonderful accuracy, and dead and wounded men, horses, and disabled caissons are visible in every battery. The instructions from General Lee are, that there shall be no more artillery duels. Instead, therefore, of endeavoring to silence the enemy's guns, Col. Walton directs his artillery to receive the fire of their antagonists quietly, and deliver their own against the Federal infantry. The wisdom of the order is apparent at every shot, for with the overwhelming numbers of the enemy, they might have defeated us at the outset, but for the powerful and well-directed adjuncts we possessed in our heavy guns.

"Time and again did the Federals perseveringly press close up to our ranks, so near indeed that their supporting batteries were obliged to cease firing, lest they should kill their own men, but just as often were they driven back by the combined elements of destruction which we brought to bear upon them. It was an hour when every man was wanted. The sharpshooters of the enemy were picking off our principal officers continually, and especially those who made themselves conspicuous in the batteries. In this manner the company of Captain Miller, of the Washington Artillery, was nearly disabled, only two out of his four guns being fully manned. As it occupied a position directly under the eye of General Longstreet, and he saw the valuable part it was performing in defending the centre, that officer dismounted himself from his horse, and assisted by his Adjutant-general, Major Sorrel, Major Fairfax, and General Drayton, worked one of the guns until the crisis was passed. To see a general officer wielding the destinies of a great fight, with its cares and its responsibilities upon his shoulders, performing the duty of a common soldier, in the thickest of the conflict, is a picture worthy of the pencil of an artist.

"The result of this battle, though at one time doubtful, was finally decisive. The enemy were driven across the river with a slaughter that was terrible. A Federal officer who was wounded, and afterward taken prisoner, observed to one of our officers that he could count almost the whole of his regiment on the ground around him. I did not go over the field, but a gentleman who did, and who has been an actor in all our battles, informed me that he never, even upon the bloody field of Manassas, saw so many dead men before. The ground was black with them, and, according to his estimate, the Federals had lost eight to our one. Happily, though our casualties are very considerable, most of them are in wounds.

"There now ensued a silence of two hours, broken only by the occasional discharges of artillery. It was a sort of breathing time, when the panting combatants, exhausted by the battle, stood silently eyeing each other, and making ready—the one to strike, and the other to ward off another staggering blow.

"*The Fight on the Right.*—It was now about three o'clock in the afternoon, but notwithstanding the strange lull in the storm, no one believed it would not be renewed before night. Intelligence had come from the rear that General A. P. Hill was advancing from Harper's Ferry with the force which Jackson had left behind, and every eye was turned anxiously in that direction. In a little while we saw some of his troops moving cautiously under cover of the woods and hills to the front, and in an hour more he was in a position on the right. Here about four o'clock the enemy had made another bold demonstration. Fifteen thousand of their troops, in one mass, had charged our lines, and after vainly resisting them, we were slowly giving back before superior numbers.

"Our total force here was less than six thousand men, and had it not been for the admirably planted artillery, under command of Major Garnett, nothing until the arrival of reinforcements could have prevented an irretrievable defeat. I know less of this portion of the field than any other, but from those who were engaged heard glowing accounts of the excellent behavior of Jenkins' brigade, and the 2d and 20th Georgia, the latter under the command of Colonel Cummings. The last two regiments have been especial subjects of comment, because of the splendid manner in which they successively met and defeated seven regiments of the enemy, who advanced across a bridge, and were endeavoring to secure a position on this side of the river. They fought until they were nearly cut to pieces, and then retreated only because they had fired their last round. It was at this juncture that the immense Yankee force crossed the river, and made the dash against our line, which well nigh proved a success. The timely arrival of General A. P. Hill, however, with fresh troops, entirely changed the fortunes of the day, and after an obstinate contest, which lasted from five o'clock until dark, the enemy were driven into and across the river with great loss. During this fight the Federals had succeeded in flanking and capturing a battery, belonging, as I learn, to the brigade of General Toombs. Instantly dismounting from his horse, and placing himself at the head of his command, the general, in his effective way, briefly told them that the battery must be retaken if it cost the life of every man in his brigade, and then ordered them to follow him. Follow him they did into what seemed the very jaws of destruction, and after a short but fierce struggle, they had the satisfaction of capturing the prize, and restoring it to the original possessors.

"Throughout the day there occurred many instances of personal valor and heroic sacrifice on the part of both officers and men; but at this early hour it is impossible to gather from crude statements, those truthful narratives which ought to adorn the page of history.

"The results of the battle may be briefly summed up. Judged by all the rules of warfare, it was a victory to our arms. If we failed to rout the enemy, it was only because the nature of the ground prevented him from running. Wherever we whipped him, we either drove him against his own masses on the right, left, and centre, or into the mountains; and against the latter position it would have been impossible to operate successfully. Nowhere did he gain any permanent advantage over the Confederates. Varying as may have been the successes of the day, they left us intact, unbroken, and equal masters of the field with our antagonist. Last night we were inclined to believe that it was a drawn battle, and the impression generally obtained among the men, that, because they had not in their usual style got the enemy to running, they had gained no advantage; but to-day the real facts are coming to light, and we feel that we have, indeed, achieved another victory. Twenty thousand additional men could not, under the circumstances, have made it more complete.

"We took few prisoners, not more than six or seven hundred in all. The Federals fought well, and were handled in a masterly manner, but their losses have been immense—probably not less than twenty thousand killed and wounded. They had the advantage not only of numbers, but of a position from which they could assume an offensive or defensive attitude at will; besides which, their signal stations on the Blue Ridge, commanded a view of our every movement. We could not make a manœuvre in front or rear that was not instantly revealed to their keen look-outs, and as soon as the intelligence could be communicated to their batteries below, shot and shell were launched against the moving columns. It was this information conveyed by the little flags upon the mountain top, that no doubt enabled the enemy to concentrate his force against our weakest points, and counteract the effect of whatever similar movements may have been attempted by us. Our loss is variously estimated at from five to nine thousand."

The above narrative sufficiently describes the great battle of Sharpsburg, in which our forces contended against overwhelming odds, but after the long and exhausting conflict, remained in possession of the field. The enemy—great as were their numbers—made no attempt to renew the conflict; and Gen. McClellan's statement on his trial, sufficiently shows how powerless the Federal army was for another assault. "The next morning," says McClellan, "I found that our loss had been so great, and there was so much disorganization in some of the commands, that I did not consider it proper to renew the attack that day." This was the 18th, and during the whole of that day Gen. Lee remained drawn up in line-of-battle, ready to renew the conflict if the enemy advanced. His army had suffered serious loss, however; reinforcements were constantly reaching the Federal commander; and Lee determined to recross the river, and await at his leisure those additions to his own force, which he expected and so much needed.

Accordingly, on the night of the 18th, having previously sent across all his trains, artillery, and stores of every description, he moved his army to the south bank of the Potomac, entirely unmolested; and, taking up a strong position near Shepherdstown, bade the enemy defiance. The army finished crossing on the morning of the 19th, and throughout the day, a heavy cannonade with long-range guns was kept up across the river—Gen. Pendleton commanding our artillery. On the next morning, a considerable force succeeded in crossing, but being promptly met by a portion of Jackson's corps, under A. P. Hill, were utterly routed. "With no stop or hesitation," says an eye-witness, "using no artillery, sending his men in, steadily, Gen. A. P. Hill drove the enemy into and across the river, taking 300 prisoners, and making the river *blue with their dead*."

This engagement was brief, but one of the most deadly of the war. It stunned the enemy, reassured our troops, and discouraged all future attempts to disturb them.

When the army went into camp in the beautiful region along the banks of the Opequon, it did so with the certainty of not being molested—the enemy had learned a lesson, and were quiet.

The Maryland campaign had ended in one of those retreats which ruin an opponent. Gen. Lee had pierced the enemy's territory unresisted; had cut him off when he appeared, from all communication with Harper's Ferry; had captured that place, together with 11,000 prisoners, and 73 pieces of artillery; had defeated his enormous forces in a pitched battle of incredible fury; had remained in line-of-battle during the whole succeeding day; and then, determining of his own motion, to retire, had done so at his ease, without losing a wagon, and wholly unmolested. Such a retreat after such successes, was a victory, and there were many persons at the North even, candid enough to concede the fact. "He leaves us," growled the *N. Y. Tribune*, "the *debris* of his late camps, two disabled pieces of artillery, a few hundred of his stragglers, perhaps two thousand of his wounded, and as many more of his unburied dead. Not a sound field-piece, caisson, ambulance, or wagon; not a tent, box of stores, or a pound of ammunition. He takes with him the supplies gathered in Maryland, and the rich spoils of Harper's Ferry."

Gen. Lee's address to his army upon their return to Virginia, will appropriately conclude our brief account of the great campaign to which he refers:

"HEADQUARTERS ARMY NORTHERN VIRGINIA,
October 2d, 1862.

"*General Orders*, *No.* 116.

"In reviewing the achievements of the army during the present campaign, the Commanding General cannot withhold the expression of his admiration of the indomitable courage it has displayed in battle, and its cheerful endurance of privation and hardship ou the march.

"Since your great victories around Richmond you have defeated the enemy at Cedar Mountain, expelled him from the Rappahannock, and, after a conflict of three days, utterly repulsed him on the Plains of Manassas, and forced him to take shelter within the fortifications around the capital.

"Without halting for repose you crossed the Potomac, storming the heights of Harper's Ferry, made prisoners of more than eleven thousand men, and capturing upwards of seventy pieces of artillery, all their small-arms, and other munitions of war.

"While one corps of the army was thus engaged, the other insured its success by arresting at Boonsboro' the combined armies of the enemy, advancing under their favorite general to the relief of their beleagued comrades.

"On the field of Sharpsburg, with less than one-third his numbers, you resisted, from daylight until dark, the whole army of the enemy, and repulsed every attack along his entire front, of more than four miles in extent.

"The whole of the following day you stood prepared to resume the conflict on the same ground, and retired next morning, without molestation, across the Potomac.

"Two attempts, subsequently made by the enemy, to follow you across the river, have resulted in his complete discomfiture, and being driven back with loss.

"Achievements such as these demanded much valor and patriotism. History records few examples of greater fortitude and endurance than this army has exhibited; and I am commissioned by the President to thank you, in the name of the Confederate States, for the undying fame you have won for their arms.

"Much as you have done, much more remains to be accomplished. The enemy again threatens us with invasion, and to your tried valor and patriotism the country looks with confidence for deliverance and safety. Your past exploits give assurance that this confidence is not misplaced.

R. E. Lee,
General Commanding."

This just ana admirable summary, makes further comment upon the glories of the Army of Northern Virginia, useless.

These words have inscribed its name in fadeless characters upon the eternal tablets of Fame.

CHAPTER XXVII.

THE ARMY RESTING.

General Jackson's corps passed the beautiful month of October in the picturesque Valley of the Shenandoah—that region which their great leader had already made so famous.

There, in the bright October days, the army rested, and recovered its strength and spirits. The bracing mountain breeze, the beautiful skies, the liberty to engage in every species of fun and frolic, within the limits of military discipline, seemed to pour new life-blood into the frames of the men, exhausted and worn down by the immense marches which they had made from Cedar Run to Sharpsburg, and the toils, privations, hardships, and excitements which they had undergone.

Once or twice only in all that time did the enemy appear—at Martinsburg and Leetown, on reconnoissances. But Gen. Stuart drove them back with cavalry and artillery, and a brigade of Gen. Jackson's—thenceforth they did not come. The gay-hearted "boys" of the corps returned to their frolics and camp amusements.

That region must have aroused many memories in the hearts of Jackson's men—especially in the members of the "Old Stonewall Brigade," which had fought the enemy all along from Falling Waters to the sources of the Shenandoah. They had encountered Patterson in one of the earliest engagements of the war, near Martinsburg, but a few miles distant—on the road by the side of which they were now encamped, they had retreated before the huge columns of the same general—and along that road they had pressed after Banks, when, routed and overthrown at Winchester, he had hastened to recross the Potomac. Since those old days, they had fought at Cross Keys, Port Republic, Cold Harbor, Malvern Hill, Cedar Run, Bristow, Manassas, Ox Hill, Harper's Ferry, Sharpsburg, Shepherdstown, and Kerneysville. Comrade after comrade had lain down to die upon those bloody fields—face after face had "gone into the darkness," amid the war smoke hovering above the swamps of the lowland, the pines of Manassas, the Valley of the Antietam. They were still alive, and, after all their wanderings, had returned to the land where they first learned the art of war under their now illustrious chief—returned to it, too, at a season when the face of nature is glorious with that beauty which seems to reach perfection just when it is passing—when the fields and forest, with their tints of gold, and red, and yellow, are more lovely than the dreams of poets. Here, in the fine and beautiful Valley of the Shenandoah, on the banks of the Opequon, which murmurs under its tall trees, as it lapses gently toward the Potomac, did the weary soldiers of the Stonewall Corps find rest and refreshment; and the bracing air, as we have said, made them boys again, filling every pulse with health and joy. The jest, the practical joke, the ready laugh passed around; and for a time the whole army of Northern Virginia was in extravagant spirits, cheering upon the least provocation like a party of boys, and permitting no occasion for indulging in laughter to escape them. We have a letter written by one of the corps about this time, which conveys a very accurate idea of the manner in which Jackson's men amused themselves; and its careless style and homely details may serve to interest the stay-at-home reader, who is not familiar with the "goings on" of an army. Here it is:

"'Cock-a-doodle-doo-oo!' sounded the 'shrill clarion' of a neighboring hen-roost *before* day this morning; a wakeful soldier caught up the strain, and he and a hundred others forthwith repeated bogus cock-a-doodle-doos, until they had effectually 'murdered sleep' throughout the entire regiment.

To pass the time till breakfast (!)—i. e., till some 'solid shot biscuit' and leather steaks of lean kind be cooked—I will 'retaliate' on you and your readers.

"The campaign having apparently ended, there are no moving accidents by flood or field of interest, and therefore, nothing left to record but the routine of daily camp life; this shall be true to history, however, to let the old folks at home know how we live 'sure enough' while here. At this particular season, though, it is particularly dull—

'No mail, no post,
No news from any foreign coast;
No warmth, no cheerfulness, no healthful ease,
No comfortable feel in any member,
No shade, no sunshine, no butterflies, no bees,
November!'

"Our camp not being regulated by military rule for want of material in tents, &c., is left to illustrate the variegated, architectural, and domestic tastes of the thousand different individuals concerned. Hence, although a wall tent or Sibley graces an occasional locality, the most of the men ensconce themselves in bush-built shelters of various shapes, in fence-corners, under gum-blankets eked out by cedar-boughs, or burrow semi-subterraneously, like Esquimaux. If, as is said, the several styles of architecture took their origin from natural circumstances and climate, &c., as the curving oriental roofs, from the long reeds originally in use—the slanting Egyptian, from the necessity of baking their unburnt bricks in the hot sun—the Corinthian, from its own flowery clime, &c., &c.—an architectural genius might find enough original designs in this camp to supply a century to come.

"The only 'useful occupation' of this brigade for some time past has been to destroy all the railroads in reach; apparently, too, for no better reason than the fellow had for killing the splendid Anaconda in the museum, because it was his 'rule to kill snakes wherever found.' A soldier just said, 'Old Jack intends us to tear up all the railroads in the State, and with no tools but our pocket knives.' They have so far destroyed the Baltimore and Ohio from Hedgesville to near Harper's Ferry, the Winchester and Potomac almost entirely, and now the Manassas Gap from Piedmont to Strasburg.

"It is when idle in camp that the soldier is a great institution, yet one that must be seen to be appreciated. Pen cannot fully paint the air of cheerful content, care-hilarity, irresponsible loungings, and practical spirit of jesting that 'obtains,' ready to seize on any odd circumstance in its licensed levity. A 'cavalryman' comes rejoicing in immense top-boots, for which in fond pride he had invested full forty dollars of pay; at once the cry from a hundred voices follows him along th line: 'Come up out o' them boots!—come out!—too soon tr go into winter-quarters! I know you're in thar!—see your arms stickin' out!' A bumpkin rides by in an uncommonly big hat, and is frightened at the shout: 'Come down out o' that hat! Come down! 'Tain't no use to say you ain't up there; I see your legs hanging out!' A fancy staff officer was horrified at the irreverent reception of his nicely twisted moustache—as he heard from behind innumerable trees—'Take them mice out o' yer mouth!—take 'em out!—no use to say they ain't thar—see their tails hanging out!' Another, sporting immense whiskers, was urged to 'Come out of that bunch of har! I know you're in thar! I see your ears a working!' Sometimes a rousing cheer is heard in the distance, it is explained—'Boys, look out!—here comes Old Stonewall, or an old hare, one or t'other'—they being about the only individuals who invariably bring down the house.

"And yet there are no better specimens of the earnest, true soldier, than the men of this brigade. It is known in the army, if not in print, as 'the fighting brigade.' It is now constituted of the 13th, 25th, 31st, 44th, 47th, 52d, and 58th Virginia regiments—the 12th Georgia, one of the most gallant regiments in the service, having, to the regret of all their old comrades of 'the mountain brigade,' been transferred. The brigade has been represented, by some of its regiments, in nearly every battle-field in Virginia,—in Northwest Virginia, in the Valley, on the Peninsula, around Richmond, from Cedar Run to Manassas Plains, at Harper's Ferry, and when reduced to scarce five hundred men, and surrounded by overwhelming numbers, it fought a bloody way clear out through the Yankee lines at Sharpsburg. Four of its brigadiers have been wounded in the service. Generals Ed. Johnson, Elzey, Stuart, and Early. Five of the regiments above-named were united in one command under General Ed. Johnson, whose conspicuous bravery at Greenbrier, Alleghany, and McDowell, has never lost its example upon his men. The 13th and 49th Virginia have been since united with it. It is at present commanded by Col. J. A. Walker, of the 13th, a gallant officer and courteous gentleman, who has well deserved a brigadier's commission.

"But the whole day of camp life is not yet described; the night remains, and latterly it is no unusual scene, as the gloaming gathers, to see a group quietly collect beneath the dusky shadows of the forest trees—'God's first temples'—whence soon arise the notes of some familiar hymn, awaking memories of childhood and of home. The youthful chaplain in earnest tones tells his holy mission; another hymn is heard, and by the waning light of the pine torches, the weird-like figures of the grouped soldiers are seen reverently moving to the night's repose. The deep bass drum beats taps—the sounds die out in all the camps; save at times the sweet strains from the band of the Fifth Stonewall regiment in a neighboring grove, till they, too, fade away into the stilly night, and soon—

'The soldiers lie peacefully dreaming,
Their tents in the rays of the clear autumn moon,
Or the light of the watch-fires are gleaming,
A tremulous sigh as the gentle night wind
Through the forest leaves slowly is creeping,
While the stars up above with their glittering eyes
Keep guard, for the army is sleeping.'"

During these days, General Jackson had his headquarters near Bunker's Hill, and was often seen moving to and fro among his troops on his old sorrel horse with the old uniform. He was always greeted with cheers by his men, and the phrase, "Jackson, or a rabbit," became universal in alluding to these gay sounds, heard in the distance. A hundred anecdotes were told—a hundred witticisms attributed to him. In Maryland, where the ladies crowded around him, he was represented as saying, "Ladies, this is the first time I was ever surrounded," in spite of which, says a letter-writer, "they cut every button off his coat, commenced on his pants, and at one time threatened to leave him in the uniform of a Georgia colonel—shirt-collar and spurs." Another incident was related of him by Colonel Ford, a Federal officer, who conversed with the general at Harper's Ferry:

"While we were in conversation," says Colonel Ford, "an orderly rode rapidly across the bridge, and said to General Jackson, 'I am ordered by General McLaws to report to you that General McClellan is within six miles with an immense army.' Jackson took no notice of the orderly, apparently, and continued his conversation; but when the orderly had turned away, Jackson called after him, with the question, 'Has McClellan any baggage-train or drove of cattle?' The reply was, that he had. Jackson remarked, that *he could whip any army that was followed by a drove of cattle*, alluding to the hungry condition of his men."

These anecdotes, and a thousand others, were passed about from lip to lip, and "Old Jack"—a name by which the general had now become universally known—was immensely popular. We have already referred to other and more solid grounds of popularity in his character; but these familiar anecdotes of his dry humor, truthful or not, had no small influence in rendering him the prime favorite of his men. Certain it is that Jackson was never more popular than after the Maryland campaign; and no doubt this arose in a great measure from the satisfaction which the corps experienced in having secured the really solid results of the movement at Harper's Ferry.

The army remained in the Valley of Virginia, watching the movements of McClellan—who was in front of their position—until November, when the enemy having commenced moving toward the Rappahannock, the troops were put in motion in that direction.

Jackson's corps formed the rear-guard, and slowly moved up toward Millwood, parallel with the Federal advance from Leesburg. His measured and deliberate movements undoubtedly retarded their advance, suspicious as they at all times were of some sudden and dangerous blow from his well-known arm, and General Lee was thus allowed ample time to concentrate his forces behind the Rappahannock.

Jackson remained in the Valley of Virginia until about the

1st of December, when the enemy having developec an intention to cross at Fredericksburg, he was sent for, and speedily appeared. A rapid march brought him to the fir-clad hills around Fredericksburg, and his corps encamped beyond the Massaponnax, entirely out of sight, ready to take part in the events which were soon to follow.

CHAPTER XXVIII.

FREDERICKSBURG.

Foiled and driven back upon every line of advance—by Manassas, the Peninsula, the Valley, the Rapidan—the Federal authorities had determined to try a new route, and assail the Confederate capital from the direction of Fredericksburg.

General McClellan—just superseded in the command of the army by General Ambrose Burnside—had always maintained that this route was impracticable; but President Lincoln and the new commander-in-chief thought differently, and the attempt was now about to be made with all the power of the Federal Government.

Burnside moved his army down to the rear of the Stafford Hills, just opposite Fredericksburg, in the latter part of the month of November; and General Lee, who, until that time, had remained in the vicinity of Culpepper Court-house, watching his opponent, made a correspondent movement, appearing again in front of the Federals, and ready whenever they advanced to give them battle.

The position occupied by the Confederates was a commanding one, and there could be little doubt of the result if the enemy assailed them in their stronghold. General Lee had disposed his forces along the crest of hills which extends from a point on the Rappahannock just above the town, down to Hamilton's Crossing on the railroad to Richmond, about four miles below. Here the crest sinks suddenly into a wide plain, stretching off to the Massaponnax, which shuts it in a mile or two away. In front of the hills occupied by the Southern army, a broad flat reaches to the river, about a mile distant, and upon this, just where the ground begins to rise, the main portion of the battle was to be fought.

Up to the 11th of December, no movement of any importance had taken place, though the enemy had made numerous attempts to produce the impression that they intended to cross below, or above, not at Fredericksburg. Their troops were seen moving to and fro on the Stafford Hills opposite, and the river bank was heavily picketed down to Port Royal, and above United States ford.

The Confederate generals awaited the threatened movement with confidence, and a well-grounded belief, that in spite of the numbers of the Federal army, and the presence of such men as Sumner, Franklin, Hooker, and others in command of grand divisions, they would be able to repulse any attack.

It would seem that the enemy were, on their side, equally confident. The dismissal of McClellan had been very distasteful to the troops, but they were thoroughly disciplined, and ready to fight under any one; and the Northern journals extensively circulated among their camps, had sedulously instilled the conviction that the "On to Richmond" movement was now certain of success. They were the best troops in the Federal service—led by the best generals—in thorough fighting condition, and the Government at Washington appears to have looked forward to a "glorious success" at last, to make amends for all the failures which had preceded it.

The Confederate commander finally received reliable intelligence that the enemy had finished their preparations for crossing, and were putting their troops in motion. General Lee's order of battle had been determined upon. Longstreet's corps was to hold the hills from the extreme left to a point mid-way to Hamilton's Crossing; here Jackson's left would join his right, while the extreme right would be protected by General Stuart with cavalry and horse artillery.

Before daylight, on the morning of Thursday, December 11th, the enemy commenced throwing two pontoons across at Fredericksburg, one above, the other below the destroyed railroad bridge. While engaged in this attempt, and swarming upon the boats like beavers, a destructive fire was opened upon them from the southern bank of the river, where Brigadier-general Barksdale was posted with his Mississippians, and this fire was so deadly, that it at first drove the enemy back. They quickly renewed the attempt, however, and pushed on the work, in spite of the hail-storm of bullets from Barksdale, whose gallant troops fought with desperation. The heavy fog slowly lifted from the scene, and then commenced, and was kept up all day, one of the most terrific bombardments known in history. The writer of these pages had a full view of the entire spectacle from "Lee's Hill," just to the right of the telegraph road, where it descends toward the town; and never before had such a sight greeted him. The enemy had planted more than a hundred pieces of artillery on the hills to the northern and eastern sides of the town, and from an early hour in the forenoon, swept the streets with roundshot, shell, and case-shot—firing frequently a hundred guns a minute. The quick puffs of smoke, touched in the centre with tongues of flame, ran incessantly along the lines of the enemy's batteries on the slopes, and as the smoke slowly drifted away, the bellowing roar came up in one continuous roll. It was a "symphony of hell," truly. The town was soon fired, and a dense cloud of smoke enveloped its roofs and steeples. The white church spires still rose serenely aloft, unharmed by shot or shell, though a portion of one of them was torn off. The smoke was succeeded by lurid flame, and the crimson mass brought to mind the pictures of Moscow burning.

The incessant fire of heavy artillery on the doomed town

was kept up from daylight until dark. Barksdale's gallant troops never flinched, but held the place like heroes, in spite of the terrible enfilading fire sweeping the streets with round-shot, grape, and shell, right and left. Amid houses torn to pieces and burning, chimneys crashing down and burying men in the ruins, amid a fire which might have demoralized the finest soldiers in the world, they still held it.

When night descended on the scene of this barbarity, the flames of burning houses still lit up the landscape, and the roar of the batteries was hushed, except a random gun at intervals, seeming to indicate that their taste for bloodshed and destruction was not glutted.

What had they accomplished? They had gained possession of the town, which may or may not have been intended, and they had driven out and slaughtered citizens, women, and children. One young girl was shot through the hip—hundreds of ladies and children were wandering, homeless and shelterless, over the frozen highway, with bare feet and thin clothing, knowing not where to find a place of refuge. Delicately nurtured girls, with slender forms, upon which no rain had ever beat, which no wind had ever visited too roughly, walked hurriedly, with unsteady feet, upon the road, seeking only some place where they could shelter themselves. Whole families sought sheds by the wayside, or made roofs of fence rails and straw, knowing not whither to fly, or to what friend to have recourse. This was the result of the enemy's bombardment. Night had settled down—the lurid smoke, lit up by burning houses, rested on a torn and shattered Virginia city, filled with Confederate and Yankee bodies—that was the "supreme result."

Such were the results of the cruel bombardment. The enemy held the town, but they had only gained possession of it at a frightful loss of life. Barksdale, fighting from street to street, and disputing every inch of ground, fell back no further than the suburbs; and here, posting himself behind a stone fence, held his ground.

When the morning of Friday dawned, the enemy had thrown across additional pontoons; and their army was nearly over. As yet they had not been saluted by a single shot from our artillery; and they no doubt felicitated themselves, in a very high degree, upon this circumstance. Thus Friday ended—the night passed—the great day arrived.

Gen. Lee had disposed his forces in the manner already indicated. Longstreet's corps was posted on the left, with strong batteries along the hills by Marye's house. Jackson held the right, with Gen. A. P. Hill in front and near Hamilton's Crossing; Gen. Taliaferro, commanding Jackson's old division, in his rear, and Gen. D. H. Hill, behind the crest of hills, in reserve. On the slope of the hill, just where it descends toward the crossing, Colonel Lindsay Walker was posted, with Pegram's, McIntosh's, and sections of Crenshaw's, Latham's, and Johnson's batteries—14 guns. On the left of the line, near the Bernard Cabins, Capt. Davidson was stationed, with Rains', Caskie's, Braxton's, and Davidson's batteries—21 guns. To the right, and two hundred yards in advance of these, Capt. Brockenbrough commanded Carpenter's, Wooding's, and Braxton's batteries—12 guns. On Jackson's left was the right of Gen. Longstreet under Hood; and this was just at the centre of the whole line. On the extreme right, as we have said, beyond Hamilton's Crossing, on the extensive plain, diversified by woods, General Stuart had drawn up his cavalry and horse artillery, ready to assist in repulsing the attack upon what was felt to be the weakest portion of our line.

Soon after daybreak, the troops were all in position, and Gen. Lee rode along the lines accompanied by Gen. Jackson, to inspect in person the disposition of the forces. On the old "Richmond road," leading from the Crossing to the Bowling Green road, Gen. Stuart joined them, and they proceeded to the outer picket lines, close on the enemy. The movement had already begun, and the enemy were seen advancing across the bottom directly upon Gen. Jackson's position. By direction of Gen. Stuart, Major John Pelham, of the Stuart Horse Artillery, immediately brought up a Napoleon gun, and opened on their left flank; three batteries replied, and for many hours this one gun fought them all with unyielding firmness. Major Pelham and Captain Henry, who both superintended the working of the piece, were publicly complimented, and their obstinate stand, in an important position, unquestionably had a most valuable part in demoralizing the Federal forces.

Soon after daylight the enemy began to feel our entire position, from left to right, with infantry and artillery. To one who had witnessed their manner of proceeding, it was evident that the Federal leaders were wandering in the dark, and completely puzzled. There was no generalship displayed, no power of combination or manœuvring. Their lines were pushed forward, and when mowed down by our artillery or musketry, new ones took their places, and the wavering, uncertain character of their movements continued. The fight was on much more equal terms than is supposed—with this important difference, that the enemy very far outnumbered us, opposing two or three to one at every point of attack. Their artillery was most effectively handled, and did us much damage, as the casualties in that arm will show. The writer was present in this portion of the field, and recalls an instance. A Blakely gun was brought up, placed in position, and opened upon the enemy. One of their guns was instantly directed to the point, a shot crashed among the cannoneers, and a boy exclaimed, "General, the very first shot has killed two of our men!"

About ten o'clock the fog lifted, and the enemy were seen rapidly approaching in heavy force—at least 55,000 troops being concentrated upon this important point. They were commanded by Gens. Franklin and Hooker, whose orders were to gain possession of the old "Richmond road," turn the crest of hills at Hamilton's Crossing, and assail our right flank. Encouraged by the silence of our batteries, the enemy pushed forward directly upon Walker's position, and were suffered to come within eight hundred yards before a gun was fired. When they had reached that point, however, the fourteen guns opened suddenly upon them, with terrific effect, and completely broke and repulsed them. No troops could stand before the iron storm, tearing through their ranks, and Franklin could not immediately re-form his men, and bring them again to the assault.

About one o'clock, however, another attempt was made to carry the position—this time preceded by a heavy fire of artillery directed against Col. Walker and Gen. A. P. Hill. Walker opened all his batteries in response, and was assisted by Pelham on the right. The enemy's force, consisting of Franklin's and Hooker's grand divisions, were evidently staggered by the terrible fire; but re-forming, pressed on and closed in upon A. P. Hill in a fierce and bloody struggle. Unfortunately, an interval had been left between Archer's and Lane's brigades, and of this the enemy took instant advantage. Pressing forward, Hill's line was penetrated; Lane's right and Archer's left, turned; and they were forced to fall back, though not without desperate fighting. Gaining thus a position in rear of that occupied by Lane and Archer, the enemy attacked Gregg's brigade; and in this contest Gen. Gregg, while attempting to rally Orr's Rifles, which had given way, fell mortally wounded.

Seeing that his first line was rapidly being forced back by the overwhelming numbers brought against it, Gen. Jackson now ordered up his second line, consisting of the commands of Lawton, Early, Trimble, and Taliaferro. Their appearance upon the scene operated an entire change immediately. In a brief but decisive combat, they repulsed the enemy, and following up their advantage, drove him with great slaughter to the railroad in front of the first position, taking a number of prisoners. So far was the pursuit carried, that Jackson's forces came within full and deadly range of the enemy's artillery, and full upon their strong reserves of infantry. The ground was not yielded, however, on that account; and finding that the enemy did not advance, Gen. Jackson determined to do so himself. Their artillery was so posted as to render the movement an extremely hazardous one, but the stake was great, and Jackson determined to take the risks, and if possible put the force of the enemy directly opposed to him to complete rout. Those who saw him at that hour, will never forget the expression of intense but suppressed excitement which his face displayed. The genius of battle seemed to have gained possession of the great leader, ordinarily so calm; and his countenance glowed as from the glare of a great conflagration. His design was to place his artillery in front, draw up the infantry in rear of it, and make the movement just as night descended, so that if necessary he might fall back under the cover of darkness. This design was destined, however, not to be carried into execution. Delay occurred in making the necessary preparations, and when, finally, the first guns moved forward, the enemy, evidently fearing such a movement, opened a terrific fire of artillery, which caused the abandonment of the project.

We have neglected to speak of the events which occurred on Gen. Jackson's right. The batteries there were a part of his command, though directed by Gen. Stuart, and throughout the day fought with unyielding obstinacy. The enemy handled their guns with skill and nerve, but they were no match for our cannoneers. Their immense reserves of artillery were in vain brought up and put into action—they were encountered and silenced. The duel between the opposing batteries was, during the latter part of the day, most terrific. Col. Walker was particularly exposed, from the position of his guns, to the deadliest fire of the Federal batteries. The enemy directed upon him a storm of shell, which, bursting incessantly around and about him, presented a spectacle at once terrible and sublime. He had a caisson blown up, and many horses killed. His loss was also considerable; but the roar of his guns never slackened. Major Pelham, and his gallant associate, Captain Henry, ably seconded Col. Walker from the right. They returned the compliment by blowing up a caisson of the enemy, and in spite of three batteries in front, and an enfilading fire from heavy guns across the river, the Napoleon and Blakely continued to tear the opposing ranks, and "hold their own" obstinately against the almost overpowering weight of metal brought to bear upon them.

Toward evening the battle at this point became desperate. The enemy seemed to be fighting with the madness of despair, and to be possessed by the devil of carnage. Every species of projectile known to modern warfare was rained upon the fields, from guns of every character, all sizes, and in every position. Round shot, spherical case, rifle, Parrott—projectiles of all classes, and each with a different sound in its passage through the air, showered down. The enormous strength of their artillery arm was never more fully displayed, and they used it with desperation. They had now turned their attention more particularly to our right, where the cavalry were posted, and where they suspected our weakness in artillery. The attempt made to turn our flank was vigorous, and with troops less courageous than ours, might have succeeded. But it utterly failed. In vain did they advance their guns, and open a terrific fire parallel to the railroad, throwing forward sharpshooters at the same moment to pick off our cannoneers. Their challenge was accepted, and our guns were ready to meet them. Pegram's, Latham's, Crenshaw's, Johnson's, McIntosh's, Braxton's, Letcher's, and other batteries, engaged them at close range with unyielding obstinacy. To these were added the second and third companies Richmond Howitzers—

the first company being engaged on our left—the Staunton Artillery, Lieutenant Garber, a section of Poague's battery, Lieutenant Graham, Caskie's, Hardaway's, Louisiana Guard Artillery, Captain D'Aquin, and others—all under the command of Major Pelham, who fought them with heroic firmness and coolness. The whole of the artillery on the right, including Captain Henry's horse artillery, of Major Pelham's battalion, was under the immediate direction of General Stuart, who was everywhere in the thickest of the fight—the target of artillery and sharpshooters alike. The latter had posted themselves two or three hundred yards off, behind a hedge, and no doubt attracted by the plume and uniform of a general officer, directed their fire upon him, striking him twice, but not doing him injury. Meanwhile, the batteries never for an instant relaxed in their fire. All through the afternoon and into the night they continued the fight—those which were disabled, or out of ammunition, retiring, to be replaced by others. As night fell, the work was done. Some of our bravest hearts were cold in death, or were lying with the life-blood welling from their glorious wounds; but the day was ours. The enemy's guns slackened fire, retired, and one after another were silenced—our own batteries regularly advanced, and this whole portion of our line was pushed far toward the front. General Stuart had well redeemed his grim dispatch—that he was "going to crowd them with artillery." The ceremony was too rough for them to stand, and when the voice of the general in the darkness ordered the last advance, the combat had terminated in the silence of the foe.

His shattered columns had disappeared from vision with the advent of darkness, and now no reply came from his guns. In vain did our own send after him shot and shell as before—no answering roar came back. Beaten, driven back, and thoroughly disheartened, the great host which had advanced in the morning with banners flying, and in all the "pride, pomp, and circumstance of glorious war," now sneaked away toward its pontoon bridges, and gave up the "On to Richmond" movement as completely hopeless.

We have spoken of the contest on the Confederate right. On the left, Longstreet had repulsed the enemy with heavy loss; and recoiling from Marye's Hill—from the brigades of Cobb and Cooke, and the batteries of Walton—as from Hill and Walker on the crest to the right—they had fled, shattered and too much disheartened to renew the conflict. Thus the battle had been in every portion of the field a Confederate victory; and it might have been supposed that the enemy would have taken advantage of the darkness to cross the river. For some unaccountable reason, they did not do so, however; and on Sunday were drawn up directly beneath our batteries, and even went through all manner of evolutions, apparently for the amusement of Gens. Lee and Jackson, who looked on in silence from Walker's Hill. On the same day they sent a flag of truce, asking permission to bury their dead. As the application was made by a major-general only, it was immediately sent back; and not until Monday did the paper return signed by Gen. Burnside's A. A. General. The application was then granted, and while the white flag was floating and the dead being borne off, *the enemy commenced recrossing the river.* On Tuesday morning they were gone, and on the vast plain only dead bodies remained, arranged neatly in long rows, and—left for us to bury.

We shall not dwell upon the events which succeeded the great battle of Fredericksburg—upon the howl of rage and anguish which went up throughout the North—the deposition of Burnside—the quarrel among the Federal generals, and the mad resolve of the bankrupt government at Washington to attempt a new advance, destined in its turn to fail as all the rest had done.

We have confined our attention to Gen. Jackson, and now proceed to add, that having thoroughly performed his work, as he always did, he went into retirement at Moss Neck, with his corps hidden in the woods there, and applied himself to a task for which he had never before found leisure—the preparation of his official reports.

NOTE.—Here, and in one or two other places, the writer has, for the sake of convenience, used matter previously contributed by him to the papers of the day. This statement is made to prevent misconception.

CHAPTER XXIX.

WINTER-QUARTERS AT MOSS NECK.

AT "Moss Neck," some ten miles below Fredericksburg, Jackson rested from his toils, during all those months of the winter and spring of 1862–3.

With his headquarters upon the crest of hills which here runs along the right bank of the Rappahannock, dominating the wide low grounds, and affording admirable positions for artillery, if the enemy advanced, he remained for months, watching the hills upon the opposite side of the river, and ready at any moment to hurl his veterans of the old corps upon the advancing Federals. From the hills near headquarters the view was very attractive. To the right and left the wooded range extended toward Fredericksburg on the one hand, and Port Royal on the other; in front, the far-stretching low grounds gave full sweep to the eye; and at the foot of its forest-clad bluffs, or by the margin of undulating fields, the Rappahannock calmly flowed toward the sea. Old mansions dotted this beautiful land—for beautiful it was in spite of the dull influences of winter, with its fertile meadows, its picturesque woodlands, and its old roads skirted by long rows of shadowy cedars, planted with the regularity of ornamental shrubbery in a gentleman's garden.

Headquarters were near the "Corbin House;" in front was "Hayfield," the residence of that Taylor family illustrated in old days by "Colonel John Taylor of Caroline;" near at hand were the hospitable residences of the Baylors, Bernards, and others; and in the distance, toward Fredericksburg, was "St. Julian," the ancient homestead of the Brooke family, which Washington, Randolph, and the great statesmen of the past always paused at on their journeys, to give the news and discuss the men and things of the past century.

Another age had come now; a baser foe than ever had invaded this fair land; and the smiling fields were disfigured by the footprints of war. The meadows were crossed and recrossed by roads which had cut up the soil into ruts and miry holes. The steep banks—as the enemy have had an opportunity of seeing—were fashioned into earthworks for sharpshooters. The beautiful cedars were felled to supply firewood for the troops; and every thing betrayed the presence of the huge, dark, bloody, dirty, brutal genius of battle.

On the crest of hills above, Gen. Jackson, as we have said, had fixed his headquarters, with his brave troops posted in the woods behind, ready at any moment to appear upon the wide low-grounds and repulse the enemy if he attempted to cross. If driven from the line of the river road, they would have fallen back to the hills crowned with artillery, and from that position not all the power of the Federal army could have made them budge one inch.

Gen. Jackson, as stated above, employed himself during these moments of leisure in preparing the official reports of his battles. The embodiment of the facts, as given in the reports of officers engaged, was intrusted to Lieut-col. Faulkner, A. A. G., but Gen. Jackson carefully revised and corrected the statements before his official signature was appended. He was exceedingly careful not to have any thing placed thus upon formal record which was not established by irrefutable proof. *Truth* was with him the jewel beyond all price—and nothing discomposed him more than the bare suspicion that accuracy was sacrificed to effect. He disliked all glowing adjectives in the narratives of his battles; and presented to the members of his staff and all around him, a noble example of modesty and love of truth. He seemed, indeed, to have a horror of any thing like ostentation, boasting, or self-laudation, expressed or implied. Nothing was more disagreeable to him than the excessive praises which reached his ears through the newspapers of the day; and he shrunk from the attempts made to elevate him above his brother commanders with a repugnance which was obvious to every one. His dislike for all popular ovations was extreme. He did not wish his portrait to be taken, or his actions to be made the subject of laudatory comment in the journals of the day. When the publishers of an illustrated periodical wrote to him requesting his daguerreotype and some notes of his battles for an engraving and a biographical sketch, he wrote in reply that he had no picture of himself and *had never done any thing.*

So carefully did he guard all the statements in his reports from error, and such was the rigid censorship which he established in relation to the most minute portions of these narratives, that the official reports revised and signed by him, may be relied upon as the very quintessence of truth, and historians may quote them, through all coming time, as the sworn statements of a man who would have laid down his very life before he would have attached his name to what was partial, unfair, or aught but the simple, absolute truth. Those battles were fought as Jackson's reports declare; and almost the sole merit of this poor record of his career consists in this, that events are stated here, as they are stated there—with nothing added to or taken from the record.*

* The only exceptions to this statement are the narratives of the second battle of Manassas, and the battles of Harper's Ferry and Sharpsburg. The official report of the latter engagements is given in the Appendix. The report of the former is not at this time accessible.

These winter months of 1862–3 were not entirely passed, however, in laborious occupations connected with the general's official position. Many pleasant incidents are related of him, at this period, which we could dwell upon at length, did time and space permit. Those who visited Moss Neck during those days, give a humorous description of the surroundings of the famous General Stonewall. Before his tent was pitched, he established his headquarters in a small out-building of the Corbin House; and all who came to transact business with Lieutenant-general Jackson, were struck by a series of head-quarter ornaments of the most unique and surprising description. On the walls of the apartment were pictures of race-horses, well known and dear in former days to the planters of the neighboring region. Then there was a portrait of some celebrated game-cock, ready trimmed and gaffed for conflict to the death. A companion piece of these, was the picture of a terrier engaged in furious onslaught upon an army of rats, which he was seizing, tearing, and shaking to death as fast as they came. These decorations of headquarters excited the merriment of the general's associates; and one of them suggested to him that a drawing of the apartment should be made, with the race-horses, game-cocks, and terrier in bold relief, the picture to be labelled, "View of the winter-quarters of Gen. Stonewall Jackson, presenting an insight into the tastes and character of the individual."

Hearty laughter on the part of Gen. Jackson greeted this jest from the distinguished brother soldier who had stood beside him upon so many bloody fields—whom he loved and opened his whole heart to—and to whom, when struck down by the fatal ball at Chancellorsville, his mind first turned as his successor.

The children of the house, and in the neighborhood, will long remember the kind voice and smile of the great soldier—his caresses and affectionate ways. A new military cap had been sent him just before the battle of Fredericksburg, which was resplendent with gold braid and all manner of decorations. General Jackson did not admire this fine substitute for that old, sun-scorched head-covering which had so long served him; and when, one day, a little girl was standing at his knee, looking up from her clustering curls at the kindly general, whose hand was caressing her hair, he found a better use for the fine gold braid around the cap. He called for a pair of scissors, ripped it off, and joining the ends, placed it like a coronet upon her head, with smiles and evident admiration of the pretty picture thus presented.

Another little girl, in one of the hospitable houses of that region, told the present writer that when she expressed to a gentleman her wish to kiss Gen. Jackson, and the gentleman repeated her words, the general blushed very much, and turned away with a slight laugh, as if he was confused.

These are trifles, let us agree, good reader; but is it not a pleasant spectacle to see the great soldier amid these kindly, simple scenes—to watch the stern and indomitable leader, whose soul has never shrunk in the hour of deadliest peril, passing happy moments in the society of laughing children?

At the first battle of Manassas, while Jackson's wound was being dressed, some one said, "Here comes the President." He threw aside the surgeons, rose suddenly to his feet, and whirling his old cap around his head, cried, with the fire of battle in his eyes:

"Hurrah for the President? Give me ten thousand men, and I'll be in Washington to-night!"

It was the same man who blushed when a child expressed her wish to kiss him.

The days passed thus quietly at Moss Neck, the enemy making numerous demonstrations, but never crossing. January, February, the greater part of March went by, and Jackson still remained upon his crest of hills above the meadows of the Rappahannock; but late in March he moved his headquarters to a point near Hamilton's Crossing, just in rear of the battle-field of Fredericksburg, on the southern side of the Massaponnax, and not far from Gen. Lee.

The spring was now beginning to advance, and the season for hostilities had returned. Gen. Jackson hastened the preparation of his reports, and had the satisfaction of knowing that at last they were nearly complete.

It was while he was engaged in his revision of the report of the operations of his corps in the Maryland campaign, that the note of battle was again sounded, and from memories of past events, and the battles already fought, he was recalled to the present, and to the still more desperate conflict about to take place—to the last, and what was to prove not the least splendid, of his achievements.

CHAPTER XXX.

HOOKER ADVANCES.

BURNSIDE, defeated and disgraced, had been long since succeeded by Hooker, soon to join in his turn that great procession of Headless Phantoms, the Yankee Generals, on their march toward the River of Oblivion.

Gen. Hooker had noisily declared his ability to defeat the rebel army; had scoffed at McClellan and all preceding generals, as incompetent; and his shameless self-laudation, boasting, and bravado, had reaped from a congenial government their full reward. He was assigned to the command of the Federal army on the Rappahannock—and the time had now come when he was about to exhibit those great qualifications which he had so long and persistently claimed for himself.

The first note of the coming conflict was sounded on the 17th of March, from the upper Rappahannock. On that day Gen. Averill, with three thousand cavalry, crossed the river at Kelly's Ford, for an extensive raid on the communications of the army in the direction of Gordonsville. Hooker's design in ordering this movement was undoubtedly to cut the Central Railroad, and ascertain as far as possible, the strength and position of Gen. Lee.

Bad fortune, however, attended the expedition. The Federal general was met near Kelly's Ford, by Gen. Fitz. Lee, with about eight hundred cavalry, and his advance so obstinately opposed, that, after a day of stubborn and bloody conflict, he was forced to fall back, with heavy loss, and recross the river. Our own loss was considerable; and among the officers killed was Major John Pelham—the "Gallant Pelham," of Gen. Lee's report at Fredericksburg—who was present with Gen. Stuart during the battle. The fall of this great artillerist was an irreparable calamity, but the enemy were completely checked; and the Southern army had the prestige of victory in the first battle of the spring campaign.

After the battle of Kellysville, which for hard and obstinate fighting, has scarcely been excelled by any encounter of the war, the enemy remained quiet until April. Toward the middle of that month, every thing indicated an early advance on the part of the Federal forces. It was known that Gen. Hooker had been making extraordinary exertions to increase the strength of his army, and to place every department of the command upon a thorough "war footing"—these labors were said to have secured the desired result—and, in the month of April, the Northern journals repeatedly and confidently asserted Gen. Hooker's ability to overwhelm Gen. Lee whenever he advanced.

This spirit of vainglorious confidence seems to have been shared by Gen. Hooker and the majority of his officers. Whether deceived by spies, who communicated false intelligence, or misled by his own glowing anticipations, which made "the wish the father of the thought," the Federal commander exhibited, in many ways, the most unhesitating confidence in his ability to defeat Lee, and looked forward to the battle about to take place, as destined to annihilate the Confederate army and terminate the war.

The advance of the Federal forces was preceded as usual by movements of cavalry. The enemy had largely increased their force in this branch, and paid great attention to its armament and equipment. The North had been ransacked for horses; the best patterns of carbines and pistols were furnished in profusion; and great attention was given to the organization of the force, the character of its officers, and its efficiency in every particular. The commanders were given to understand that much was expected of them; and Gen. Pleasanton, to whose command the whole was intrusted, seemed anxious to recover the laurels which Averill had lost in his encounter with Fitz. Lee.

During the month of April, persistent attempts were made by Pleasanton to penetrate into the county of Culpepper, and beat up General Stuart's quarters there: his expectation being to gain information, and unmask General Lee's position. These attempts, however, all failed. Our cavalry, under Gen. Stuart, confronted them at every point, from United States Ford, below the confluence of the rivers, to the upper waters; whenever they crossed they were driven back with considerable slaughter; and up to the moment when General Hooker's army was put in motion, it may be declared with truth, that the enemy's great cavalry force had proved completely useless in gaining for the commanding general information of Gen. Lee's movements, position, or designs.

The position of our forces did not materially differ from what it had been before, and subsequent to the battle of Fredericksburg. The main body of the Southern army confronted the enemy's camps opposite the town—occupying the woods in rear of the old battle-field. A force was posted opposite U. S. Ford, higher up the river, to watch the enemy's movements in that direction; and the various fords from U. S. to Hinson's, far up the Rappahannock, nearly opposite

Orleans, were picketed by Stuart's cavalry, which, under the supervision of that energetic commander, left no avenue of advance unguarded. The exposed left flank was rightly regarded as the direction from which the enemy would attack with a view to turning Gen. Lee's position, and forcing him to fall back. Extreme vigilance was accordingly enjoined upon the cavalry pickets; and no sooner had the Federal forces put themselves in motion on the upper waters than Gen. Stuart telegraphed the fact to Gen. Lee below.

It would seem that General Hooker decided to advance, upon receiving information that "the only army to oppose him was one of forty thousand under Jackson, Lee bein sick, and his army scattered." The presence of Gen. Long street in front of Suffolk was well known to the Federai commander; and it thus appeared that the absence of a very considerable portion of the Confederate force was the circumstance which induced Gen. Hooker, after all his boasts, to undertake an advance.

All things were at last declared to be ready: the organization of the Federal army was completed—that is to say, Gen. Longstreet was absent—and the movement which was to "crush the rebellion" and end the war was commenced. A writer in the *New York World* newspaper, who criticises the operations of Gen. Hooker with great plainness of speech, and apparent truth, says that the Federal plan was as follows

"A portion of the army, about half of it, was to cross the river near Fredericksburg, and pretend to renew the attempt in which Burnside had been previously unsuccessful, and accomplish two objects—first, to hold the enemy's force at that point; and second, to protect our communications and supplies, while the other half of the army should make a crossing above the fortifications, and sweeping down with the greatest rapidity to the rear of Fredericksburg, take a strong position and hold it until they could be reinforced by the portion of the army engaged in making the feint which was to withdraw from its position, take the bridges to the point of the river which had been uncovered by the flank movement, and the whole army was thus to be concentrated in the rear of Fredericksburg."

The writer thus continues:

"On Monday, the 26th, was commenced the execution of this plan. Three corps, the Fifth, Eleventh, and Twelfth, were ordered to march with eight days' rations, to Kelly's Ford, near the Orange and Alexandria Railroad, General Slocum, of the Twelfth Corps, was placed in command, and on Tuesday night the force intrusted with the important part of executing the flank movement had reached the point at which they were ordered to cross the Rappahannock. Tuesday night, also, three other corps, the First, Third, and Sixth, were sent to Franklin's crossing, three miles below Fredericksburg, to be ready to undertake the crossing simultaneously with the other corps at Kelly's Ford on Wednesday morning. The enemy were evidently not prepared to resist the crossing at either point, and the affair was so well managed that both divisions of the army had established themselves on the west bank of the river and covered these bridges without any serious opposition by the enemy.

"Gen. Sedgwick, who commanded the three corps of the left wing, made no forward demonstration, except enough to attract the enemy and prevent them from turning upon the detachment which was forcing its way toward the rear of the enemy's works in command of General Stoneman. General Hooker had personally superintended the passage of the troops at Kelly's Ford, and returned while they pushed on toward the Rapidan at Germania Mills, where they crossed successfully, and made some progress beyond before Wednesday night."

As soon as the designs of the enemy were developed in the direction of Kelly's Ford, Gen. Stuart concentrated his cavalry in front of that point, and observed their further movements, communicating full information of their force and the direction of their march to Gen. Lee. He fell back as the Federal column advanced, and detaching a portion of his command under Gen. W. H. F. Lee to oppose the Federal cavalry under Stoneman, who was moving in the direction of Rapidan

Station, on the Orange and Alexandria Railroad, proceeded with the remainder toward Fredericksburg, hanging on the flank of the enemy, and as far as possible impeding his movements.

The following account of the subsequent operations of the right and left wings of the Federal army, up to the night of Friday, April 30th, is taken from the same journal quoted above, and will throw light upon the designs of Gen. Hooker, which by this time had been completely penetrated by the sagacious and far-seeing commander of the Confederate forces:

"*Thursday.*—Sedgwick still threatened the enemy, and held them near Fredericksburg, while Slocum pressed on from the Rapidan and took his position across the plank-road, the enemy's line of retreat toward Gordonsville, at Chancellorsville. Couch's Second Corps, which had remained at Banks' Ford, now moved up to the United States Ford, and crossed to join General Slocum. General Hooker also rejoined, and took command of the four corps thus concentrated in the rear of Fredericksburg and across the line of the enemy's retreat. It was now time for the detachment to take the defence and hold their position until the other corps should join them, and, the army thus united, be enabled to meet all the forces which the enemy might bring against them. Thursday night there was sharp work on both sides to out-manœuvre each other. The enemy had now learned, with sufficient certainty, that a large force was in their rear in the direction of Chancellorsville, and that Stoneman's cavalry was greatly endangering their railroad communication, and they were moving accordingly away from Sedgwick toward the rear of Hooker, between Chancellorsville and the Rapidan, by the roads at the south of the plank-road, which was in our possession. While leaving Sedgwick's front the enemy made unusual demonstrations of camp fires, as if concentrating there, and similar devices were resorted to on our own side. But neither deceived the other, for both were moving away, and on our side a portion of the bridges were taken up immediately, and the Third corps moved all night toward the United States Ford to join with Gen. Hooker at Chancellorsville.

"*Friday.*—While the First and Third Corps were moving from the left wing to join Gen. Hooker at Chancellorsville,

Sykes, of the Fifth Corps, and Williams, of the Twelfth, pushed on nearer to the rear of Fredericksburg, skirmishing and fighting with the enemy who showed slight resistance in that direction. The enemy were thus driven before them for four miles, when General Hooker, for some reason, ordered them to fall back and rejoin his lines at Chancellorsville. By night his army was all concentrated, except the Sixth corps, an ready for a forward movement to the rear of Fredericksburg heights. The main body of the enemy had now moved away from their works at Fredericksburg, and were preparing to attack our army on the right in a direction from which, if beaten, they could successfully retreat, and from which it was hardly expected they would meet us."

Such was the rather bungling strategy by which General Hooker expected to out-general Lee; turn his left flank; and force him to fall back from his strong position, or fight at an enormous disadvantage. Let us see now what dispositions were made by the commander thus threatened. Our narrative concerns itself mainly, of course, with the operations of Gen. Jackson, the only corps commander on the field; and we shall trace his movements from his camp upon the Massaponnax to the disastrous moment when, amid the dense and lugubrious shades of the Wilderness he fell, at the instant when full victory crowned him.

CHAPTER XXXI.

THE WILDERNESS—CHANCELLORSVILLE.

THE left wing of the Federal army, composed of three grand divisions under General Sedgwick, crossed below Fredericksburg on Wednesday, April 28th, and Gen. Jackson promptly drew up his corps in line of battle to repel the expected attack.

As the enemy did not advance, however, either on that day

or the next, it became apparent that General Sedgwick's orders were to threaten Fredericksburg, while the main body of the Federal army was massed above, and moved down with a view to out-flank General Lee, and drive him from his position.

Jackson was accordingly ordered, on Thursday evening, to leave one division of his corps in front of the enemy at Fredericksburg, and proceed with the three others to the Tabernacle, a point on the road to Chancellorsville, where he would take command of Anderson's and a portion of McLaws' divisions, and "attack and repulse the enemy."

This order reached Jackson about eight o'clock in the evening, and at midnight the three divisions were on the road to Chancellorsville. They were A. P. Hill's division, commanded by that general; D. H. Hill's, commanded by Gen. Rodes; and Trimble's, commanded by Gen. Colston.

On reaching the Tabernacle Church next morning, Anderson's division was added to the command and placed in front, two brigades of McLaws' division being sent forward on the road to U. S. Ford. The march was then resumed—Posey's and Wright's brigades, to which Ramseur's was afterwards added, preceding the column in line-of-battle, on the right and left of the road.

The command proceeded thus until it approached Chancellorsville, when the advance became engaged with the enemy, and was fired upon by a battery masked behind the dense woods, and completely protected from attack by a complicated abatis in front.

Finding the day far spent, and having had no opportunity of observing the ground or ascertaining the enemy's position, General Jackson ordered a halt, and employed the rest of the afternoon in getting up his command, and seeing that all were in place for work the next morning.

At night Gen. Lee arrived, and a consultation was held. The position of affairs was such as to demand the utmost promptness, sagacity, and generalship, to insure the defeat of the enemy's plans. While Sedgwick was threatening Lee's position below, General Hooker with the main body of his army had rapidly advanced to Chancellorsville, a point on the Old Plank-road, between Fredericksburg and Germanna, and opposite U. S. Ford. Here he had formed a double line of battle, resembling the two sides of a square—his right ranging along the plank-road, nearly east and west, his left extending toward the river, nearly north and south—the apex, where the two lines-of-battle joined each other, being near the Old Chancellor House. In front of these lines the dense timber of the region had been felled, so as to form an almost impassable series of abatis: in rear of this were elaborate ranges of earthworks for infantry; and behind, as upon either flank—wherever, indeed, a position could be obtained—the hills bristled with artillery, completely protected by felled timber from attack.

Humanly speaking, Hooker's position was impregnable, except with a frightful loss of life in storming it, and the design of assailing him in front was speedily abandoned.

An attack upon one of his flanks promised better results; and General Jackson's suggestion that he should move well to the left and assail the enemy's right and rear near the Wilderness was speedily assented to by General Lee. By this movement the elaborate series of defences thrown up by the enemy would be rendered useless, their plan of battle reversed, and they would be compelled to face to the rear and fight, if they fought at all, at a fatal disadvantage.

Those who are familiar with the bent of Jackson's genius will easily comprehend the alacrity with which he proceeded to carry out General Lee's orders. These sudden and mortal blows struck at an enemy, rejoicing in the strength of his defences, and prepared to hurl destruction on the assailant, while he himself is protected, always possessed an inexpressible charm for the great leader who had delivered so many such; and General Jackson now saw the field open for a supreme exhibition of military genius, and a decisive blow.

He knew the importance of celerity and secrecy of movement, and every preparation was made for the march at an early hour on the succeeding morning. We have already quoted his words, "Mystery! mystery is the secret of success!"—and on this occasion no precautions were omitted, calculated to mask the movement from the enemy. General Fitz. Lee's brigade of cavalry was disposed in such a manner as to guard the front and flanks of the column as it advanced, from the observation of the Federal commander, by driving off scouting parties, and acting as pioneers; and by this and other precautions General Jackson did not doubt his ability to reach the point where he intended to attack, without having his design discovered by the enemy.

He was early in the saddle, and the march commenced—the cavalry keeping well on the flanks and to the front. Diverging to the left from the plank-road, the command, which now consisted of Jackson's three divisions only, and the cavalry, moved to and passed the point known as "The Furnace," and thence proceeded toward the plank-road from Chancellorsville to Orange Court-house, crossing it near its junction with the road leading up to Germanna Ford. It was along this latter road that the right wing of the enemy's line-of-battle was posted—and to reach their right and rear it was necessary to move still further to the left. The march was accordingly continued, the cavalry moving as well upon the flank as the dense undergrowth which had given the region the name of the Wilderness, permitted; and the head of the column, completely screened from the enemy, thus reached the Germanna Ford road about half a mile east of the Old Wilderness Post-office.

At this point, Gen. Fitz. Lee informed Gen. Jackson that by ascending a neighboring hill, he could obtain a view of the position of the enemy, who would take him for a simple cavalry vidette, and pay no attention to him. He accordingly proceeded to the point indicated, accompanied by one or two of his staff, and saw at a glance the position of the Federal line-of-battle. He turned instantly to one of his aids; said briefly, "Tell my column to cross that road;" and hastening back, placed himself at the head of his command, and advanced without delay to the Old Turnpike running to Chancellorsville.

The movement had been a complete success. Jackson had reached a position where he had the enemy in flank and reverse, and orders were instantly given to prepare the troops for action. The order was promptly obeyed, and the lines formed. Gen. Rodes' division was formed in front; next came Gen. A. P. Hill's, three hundred yards in rear; and Colston's was drawn up the same distance behind Hill. This disposition of the forces was subsequently changed, however, owing to the dense undergrowth, which greatly fatigued the men; and Rodes only advanced in line-of-battle, the two other divisions with the artillery, marching in column along the road. This manner of moving his artillery, by a commander so prudent and skilful as Gen. Jackson, will more than all else serve to show the almost impassable character of the ground over which he now advanced.

The Old Turnpike ran straight into the rear of the enemy, and Jackson followed it, extending his line-of-battle well to the left—his design being to swing round with his left, and thus cut off the enemy from U. S. Ford, and destroy them.

No intimation of the steady, inexorable advance of "Jackson's men" had yet reached the doomed Federals. The movement was so bold and unexpected, and had been accomplished with such consummate skill, that now when the vengeful Confederates were sweeping forward, and had almost come into actual collision with their foes, their presence was not even suspected, and the fate of the corps opposed to them was sealed.

It was the "Eleventh Corps" of the Federal army, celebrated in the Northern journals as "Siegel's Veterans," before whose onslaught the Southern troops would melt away as frost before the flame. It was now commanded by Gen Howard—and Fate that day decreed for it and him the unenviable notoriety of receiving the last assault of Jackson.

That assault was sudden, unlooked for, terrible. From the first instant it was a rout—perfect, decisive, ignominious. The mercenaries who composed the corps, fled before the onset of their enemies with a precipitation which was ludicrous. Whole regiments ran without firing a shot. Batteries went off at a gallop, ran into trees and fences, and were captured and turned upon the enemy. At one blow, Gen. Jackson had paralyzed a powerful portion of the Federal force, and they were rushing, mad with terror, upon the reserves. Let their own friends describe the scene. A writer in a Northern journal, says:

"The flying Germans came dashing over the field in crowds, stampeding and running as only men do run when convinced that sure destruction is awaiting them. I must confess that I have no ability to do justice to the scenes that followed. It was my lot to be in the centre of that field when the panic burst upon us. May I never be a witness to another such scene. On one hand was a solid column of infantry retreating at double quick; on the other was a dense mass of beings who were flying as fast as their legs could carry them, followed up by the rebels, pouring their murderous volleys in upon us, yelling and hooting, to increase the confusion; hundreds of cavalry horses, left riderless at the first discharge from the rebels, dashing frantically about in all directions; scores of batteries flying from the field; battery wagons, ambulances, horses, men, cannon, caissons, all jumbled and tumbled together in one inextricable mass—and the murderous fire of the rebels still pouring in upon them! To add to the terror of the occasion, there was but one means of escape from the field, and that through a little narrow neck or ravine washed out by Scott's creek. Toward this, the confused mass plunged headlong. For a moment it seemed as if no power could avert the frightful calamity that threatened the entire army. On came the panic-stricken crowd, terrified artillery riders spurring and lashing their horses to their utmost; ambulances upsetting and being dashed to pieces against trees and stumps; horses dashing over the field; men flying and crying with alarm—a perfect torrent of passion apparently uncontrollable. The men ran in all directions. They all seemed possessed with an instinctive idea of the shortest and most direct line from the point whence they started to the United States Mine Ford, and the majority of them did not stop until they had reached the ford. Many of them, on reaching the river, dashed in and swam to the north side, and are supposed to be running yet. The stampede was universal; the disgrace general."

Jackson saw at a glance the immense results to be achieved by vigorously following up this success. The enemy were pressed toward Chancellorsville, and A. P. Hill's division was ordered to hasten forward and take the place of Rodes's. The wood of this strange Wilderness was so thick, however, that to advance in line-of-battle, was impracticable, and Gen. Hill's forces were accordingly disposed in and on each side of the road, in the best manner possible, for attack.

We now approach the fatal moment; the hour of sorrow and loss to all this nation. God had limited the great man's days; had decreed that his career should here end; and it is not without a sort of awe that we proceed to record, in a few brief sentences, the details of this irreparable public calamity.

Gen. Jackson ordered Gen. Hill to advance with his division in the manner described, reserving his fire *unless cavalry approached from the direction of the enemy;* and then, with that burning and intense enthusiasm for conflict which lay under his calm exterior, hastened forward to the line of skirmishers who were hotly engaged in front. Such was his ardor, at this critical moment, and his anxiety to penetrate the movements of the enemy, doubly screened as they were by the dense forest and gathering darkness, that he rode ahead of his skirmishers, and exposed himself to a close and dangerous fire from the enemy's sharpshooters, posted in the timber.

So great was the danger which he thus ran, that one of his staff said: "General, don't you think this is the wrong place for you?" He replied quickly: "The danger is all over; the enemy is routed. Go back and tell A. P. Hill to press right on!" Soon after giving this order, General Jackson turned, and accompanied by his staff and escort, rode back at a trot, on his well-known "Old Sorrel" toward his own men. Unhappily in the darkness—it was now nine or ten o'clock at night—the little body of horsemen was mistaken for Federal cavalry charging, and the regiments on the right and left of the road fired a sudden volley into them with the most lamentable results. Capt. Boswell of Gen. Jackson's staff was killed, and borne into our lines by his horse; Col. Crutchfield, Chief of Artillery, was wounded; and two couriers were killed. Gen. Jackson received one ball in his left arm, two inches below the shoulder joint, shattering the bone and severing the chief artery; a second passed through the same arm, between the elbow and wrist, making its exit through the palm of the hand; a third ball entered the palm of his right hand, about the middle, and passing through, broke two of the bones.

He fell from his horse, and was caught by Capt. Wormly, to whom he said, "All my wounds are by my own men."

The firing was responded to by the enemy, who made a sudden advance, and, the Confederates falling back, their foes actually charged over Jackson's body. He was not discovered, however, and the Federals being driven back in turn, he was rescued. Ready hands placed him upon a litter, and he was borne to the rear, amid a heavy fire from the enemy. One of the litter-bearers was shot down, and the general fell from the shoulders of the men, receiving a severe contusion, adding to the injury of the arm and injuring the side severely. The enemy's fire of artillery on the point was terrible. General Jackson was left for five minutes until the fire slackened, then placed in an ambulance and carried to the field-hospital at Wilderness Run. He lost a large amount of blood, and at one time told Dr. McGuire he thought he was dying, and would have bled to death, but a tourniquet was immediately applied. For two hours he was nearly pulseless from the shock. As he was being carried from the field, frequent inquiries was made by the soldiers, "Who have you there?" He told the doctor, "Do not tell the troops I am wounded."

To conceal his fall from the troops was important; but there was a more important point still—the officer to succeed to the command. Gen. Hill had also been wounded, and the brigadiers were inexperienced in such great commands. General Jackson immediately expressed a desire that General Stuart should direct the subsequent movements of his corps; and by a coincidence of sentiment Gen. Rodes, to whom the command fell when Gen. Hill was wounded, had already dispatched a messenger to Stuart. When he arrived, General Stuart requested Major Pendleton, A. A. Gen., to go to Gen. Jackson and ask what his dispositions and plans were, as he "knew that what Gen. Jackson had designed was the very best that could be done." When this message was delivered to the wounded hero, he replied, "Go back to General Stuart and tell him to act upon his own judgment, and do what he thinks best; I have implicit confidence in him."*

General Stuart assumed command of the corps, and was busily engaged throughout the night in preparing for a continuation of the conflict on the morrow. The battle of the Wilderness had been fought, and the battle of Chancellorsville was to succeed, though it is probable that in spite of the separate scenes and days, the whole will hereafter be known by the latter name. The exertions of Stuart were unceasing throughout the night, and when the signal for the advance

* These details are given upon the authority of Major A. H. Pendleton, who recalls the exact words used by General Jackson.

was given on the following morning, it was the prelude of victory.

No official reports of these great battles have yet been made, and in the absence of detailed and strictly reliable accounts, we present the following narrative from the *New York World*. It is the enemy who speaks, and when he describes the Confederates under Stuart "sweeping slowly, but confidently, determinedly, and surely through the clearings," and acknowledges "their superiority in the open field to our men"—that is the Federals—we cannot attribute these statements to the partiality of a Southerner, who feels bound to commend his own people, and uphold them under all circumstances. The writer speaks first of the movements on Saturday, which we have just described:

"*Saturday.*—General Hooker occupied the day in awaiting the attack of the enemy, which was evidently expected in front. The movements of the enemy seemed to indicate that they were retreating, and as the main line of their retreat was occupied by our forces, an attack to recover that line was confidently expected. What was the surprise, then, to find Stonewall Jackson, on Saturday afternoon, upon our extreme right and rear, between Chancellorsville and Germania Mills? A most furious and desperate attack was made, and the right of our lines, which was held by the Eleventh Corps, was almost instantly broken, and the *panic-stricken men*, in *utter confusion*, with and without muskets, hats, and coats, rushed headlong from under fire down the only road which led to the bridges, and *no power on earth could have stopped or prevented the complete and disgraceful rout of the soldiers* who have hitherto shown better qualities under their former commander. General Howard could have no control over the *cowardly fugitives*, who stopped not to look back until they reached the Rappahannock. *So disgraceful a panic has not been seen in this army.*

"The Third Corps, under General Sickles, was interposed in the breach thus made, and the excellent coolness of this officer, with the better qualities which his corps exhibited, saved the further progress of the panic and the rout, and the evil was temporarily stayed. But the poison was infused; the other corps had witnessed the utter confusion and panic of one full corps, and their enthusiasm was from that moment dampened, and the confidence they had hitherto felt in their success under General Hooker was lost in the reflection that they could place little confidence in one another.

"But a little ground was lost in this event, yet all had an ill-boding sense of fear that our men would not prove reliable, and that our successes thus far were but to prove fruitless in the end. This rout of the Eleventh (formerly Siegel's) Corps *was* the crisis. This was the turning point, from which our succeeding misfortunes can be most distinctly traced. Saturday closed the operations of the first week, with doubtful prospects of the final result, and the previous successes of the right wing seemed destined to end in disaster.

"Sedgwick, with the Sixth Corps, had, at this time, withdrawn to the east bank of the river, taken up his bridges, and replaced them again directly in front of Fredericksburg, and prepared for an assault on the morrow of the earthworks back of the town.

"*Sunday.*—The assault of General Sedgwick upon the heights of Fredericksburg was commenced on Sunday morning. A more determined and desperate attack has not been made. No man ever attacked the fortifications of an enemy with more enthusiasm or vigor. The bank was steep, the fire of shot and shell was terrific, and the slaughter of General Sumner's Corps, four months ago, gave little promise of success. To almost certain death the men charged up and carried the works, driving the artillerists from their guns, captured twelve pieces of the best and heaviest artillery, and many prisoners of war in their trenches. With the heaviest losses, Sedgwick followed up his success with the boldest energy, and pursued the enemy toward Chancellorsville with the purpose of uniting with General Hooker at that place.

"But this brilliant success came too late, for the enemy held the plank-road which the rout of the Eleventh Corps had yielded to them on the previous night, and the enemy was enabled to throw any sufficient force against him to prevent his junction with Hooker. This was speedily done, and soon Sedgwick's fine corps, the largest, and perhaps the best of the army, was cut off from communication either with Hooker or with Fredericksburg, and, thus isolated, was compelled to fall back upon the river at Banks' Ford, where bridges had been thrown over, by which, if severely pressed, he could make safe his retreat across the Rappahannock again. Thus followed misfortune on misfortune, not for lack of skill or bravery, but for the conduct of the miscreants who had fled from their position on the previous night almost upon the first attack of the enemy.

"But another repulse was sustained on Sunday morning by the army near Chancellorsville. The enemy renewed the attack, and again drove back our lines for half a mile. From the large brick house, which gives the name to this vicinity, the enemy could be seen sweeping slowly, but confidently, determinedly, and surely, through the clearings which extended in front. Nothing could excite more admiration for the best qualities of the veteran soldier than the manner in which the enemy swept out, as they moved steadily onward, the forces which were opposed to them. We say it reluctantly, and for the first time, that the enemy have shown the finest qualities; and we acknowledge, on this occasion, their superiority in the open field to our own men.

"They delivered their fire with precision, and were apparently inflexible and immovable under the storm of bullets and shell which they were constantly receiving. Coming to a piece of timber, which was occupied by a division of our own men, half the number were detailed to clear the woods. It seemed certain that here they would be repulsed, but they marched right through the wood, driving our own soldiers out, who delivered their fire and fell back, halted again, fired and fell back as before, seeming to concede to the enemy, as a matter of course, the superiority which they evidently felt themselves. Our own men fought well. There was no lack of courage, but an evident feeling, apparently the result of having been so often whipped, or of having witnessed the rout on the night previous, that they were destined to be beaten, and the only thing for them to do was to fire and retreat. The enemy felt confident that they were to be victorious, and our men had, from some occasion, imbibed the same impression. Our men showed lack of earnestness and enthusiasm, but no want of courage. All that they needed was the inspiration of a series of victories to look back upon, and an earnestness and confidence in the success of the cause for which they were fighting. Thus ended the Sabbath and another chapter in the series of our disasters.

"*Monday*—Another day of misfortune; and the day was hardly ushered in before the enemy in force came down upon the detachments which had been thought sufficient to hold the works upon the heights of Fredericksburg. First a brigade, then a division, then a larger force came in upon them, and, after strongly contesting the position, they were compelled to yield and fall back under the protection of the town. The enemy formed their line of battle on the outskirts, and within the town the two brigades of General Gibbon held them in check as long as could be. Many wounded men were here in the hospitals, and the position was maintained as long as possible. At length the ground was given up, the troops were withdrawn, the bridges taken up, and Fredericksburg was given back to the enemy.

"They were now at liberty to turn their attention to Sedgwick, and they lost no time in concentrating their forces against him. They were too strong for him.

"After a most obstinate fight, in which the enemy almost were successful in destroying his bridges, and the possibility of his escape, he made good his retreat also to the east bank of the Rappahannock. His losses were appalling. He suffered terribly, and in their retreat there was much confusion and disorder among the troops. A few at the first onset laid down their arms and yielded themselves up prisoners without firing a musket, but generally the men of this corps displayed the greatest gallantry in fighting, and only yielded when overpowered by superior numbers.

"*Tuesday*—By this time the aspect of affairs had become exceedingly dark. The troops were much dispirited, and although they had held their position on Monday, the prospect of meeting the combined forces of the enemy with large reinforcements, which they were known to have received, was exceedingly unpromising. A severe storm appeared also on Tuesday afternoon, swelling the Rappahannock to a torrent, and threatening to carry away the bridges. Tuesday night the army of the Rappahannock was withdrawn, and our entire force brought again to this side cf the river, with the exception of many dead and wounded, who were left behind to the tender mercies of the enemy."

Such is the history of the battle of Chancellorsville given in a Northern journal. Let us conclude with the comment of the editor of that journal—the *New York World.* It is a morsel which should not be lost; and we rescue it from the oblivion of newspaper literature for the benefit of the future historians of this epoch. Here is the criticism:

"In view of the pleasing delusions which the administration is now endeavoring to propagate, it would be well, perhaps, to outline some of the leading facts in this short campaign, from which the reader can draw his own moral:

"1. It is not true that Lee was surprised or deceived by Hooker's movement across the Rappahannock. From the Richmond papers of last Saturday, it is clear that the Confederate military leaders understood it perfectly, and deliberately allowed our army to cross, confident of their ability to defeat, if not destroy it. Forney, in the *Philadelphia Press*, states that Hooker was induced to cross by the assurances of his spies and scouts that the only army to oppose him was one of forty thousand under Jackson, Lee being sick and his army scattered. The Baltimore Secessionists had the same report, and believed it. Gen. Hooker, therefore, at the very start, was the deceived party, and walked straight into the trap prepared for him.

"2. The great cavalry raid, which was an entire success, did Gen. Hooker no good, because it did not preceed instead of accompanying his movements. Lee's reinforcements had all arrived before the destruction of the railroads and bridges. To him this is now only a temporary inconvenience. Had Hooker retained his cavalry with his army, it would have been far better for him. He could have captured several housand more prisoners when Fredericksburg was taken, and, more than all, could have prevented Jackson's surprise of his flank and rear. They might have changed the complexion of the fight.

"Gen. Hooker's division of his army was as disastrous in this instance as have been all such in former military history. It is known that Gen. Halleck utterly disapproved of this dispersion of the Union forces, and the result proved that in this case, at least, he was right. If Lee had furnished Hooker with a plan, it could not have been more to his liking. He first hurled all his forces upon Hooker, and beat him; this was on Saturday and Sunday, and then on Monday he repossessed the heights of Fredericksburg, and drove Sedgwick across the river, with the loss of one-third of his force. Thus Lee, with one great army, beat two smaller armies in detail.

"4. The battles of Saturday and Sunday were indisputable rebel victories, as the enemy's attack upon Sedgwick on Monday proved. The latter was defeated almost before Hooker's eyes, and the latter could not even make a diversion to save him. Lee and Jackson drove our army steadily from point to point until it was crowded back upon the south bank of the river. Our artillery, which, according to the rebel accounts, was splendidly served, no doubt saved what remained of the army.

"5. The retreat across the river, according to Lee's dispatch to Jeff. Davis, commenced on Sunday night, and was in consequence of his signal victory. The administration's statement is that it was commenced on Tuesday night, simply as a matter of precaution on account of the storm and the rising stream. Lee's account has all the known facts and the probabilities on its side. The Union correspondents all agree that the stores and baggage were moved to the north bank on Monday, leaving nothing but the artillery and infantry to cross on Tuesday. The fierce storm of that day probably saved the bulk of our army, which was passed over at night.

"6. Gen. Hooker's statement of his losses reads as if it was made by Gen. Wadsworth. He says his total loss in killed, wounded, and missing, will not be more than ten thousand men. If this be true, there are several circumstances that need explaining badly. Gen. Sedgwick alone, all the accounts agree, lost one-third his force, or about six thousand men; but call it five thousand. The capture of Fredericksburg, and the storming of the heights in its rear on Sunday, lost us eight hundred men in killed and wounded. This would leave but little over four thousand to have been killed, wounded, and captured in the tremendous battles of Saturday and Sunday, when, at the very least, one hundred and fifty thousand men met in deadly conflict. If Hooker and Lee commanded Chinese armies, this might have been possible; but as they were Americans on both sides, it is simply incredible. The rout of the Eleventh Corps, and the driving back of our whole lines for two days in succession, must have cost us —we will not say how many men, but certainly more than four thousand. Judged by the other battles of the war, this fight ought to have put twenty-five thousand men *hors du combat*. Gen. Hooker may be right in his estimate, but if he is, the fighting on both sides was disgraceful.

"But the theme is too painful to dwell upon. The whole management of the campaign shows a painful lack both of capacity and true courage, of mental force and a high sense of honor. Our rulers are alike incapable and unveracious."

Such was the epitaph of Gen. Hooker!

CHAPTER XXXII.

"IT IS ALL RIGHT."

ALL day long on Sunday, while the great conflict was roaring around Chancellorsville, Jackson lay at Wilderness Run, faint, motionless, but thrilling at this sound so long familiar to his ears.

Never before had the famous soldier been compelled to retire from the field—for at Manassas, though wounded, he still retained the command of his brigade; and it must have stirred his fiery soul to its very depths to find himself thus prostrate and powerless as an infant while the great battle, big with weal or woe for his beloved country, was being fought a few miles distant from the couch on which he lay.

But there was no choice left him. The fatal balls had torn through flesh, and muscle, and artery. His life was even then ebbing away; and he could only submit his spirit humbly to the decree of that merciful God who had never deserted him, and to whom he bowed with simple, childlike humility.

He had lost so much blood before a surgeon could be found in the confusion and darkness, that he was for a long time nearly pulseless. But reaction finally took place; he revived; and a thorough examination was made of the nature and extent of his injuries. They were found to be very serious, and the result of a consultation between Drs. McGuire, Black,

Coleman and Walls, was that amputation of the arm should be immediately resorted to.

This decision of the surgeons was guardedly communicated to him. He was asked—"If we find amputation necessary shall it be done at once?" He replied with alacrity and that cheerful disregard of pain which was a part of his manly spirit:

"Yes! certainly. Dr. McGuire do for me whatever you think right."

Preparations were accordingly made for performing the operation, and the patient having been put under the influence of chloroform, his arm was taken off without subjecting him, apparently, to very great pain. He slept well after the operation, and when he woke asked for Mrs. Jackson, and requested that she might be sent for.

His thoughts then turned to the battle which was at the time in progress, and he seemed to have no doubt that it would result in victory for the Confederates. He spoke of the attack which he had made on the preceding evening, and said with a glow of martial ardor and a proud smile:

"If I had not been wounded, or had had one hour more of daylight, I would have cut off the enemy from the road to United States Ford; we would have had them entirely surrounded; and they would have been obliged to surrender or cut their way out—they had no other alternative. My troops may sometimes fail in driving an enemy from a position; but the enemy always fails to drive my men from a position."

He did not complain of his wounds, and never referred to them unless a direct question was addressed to him on the subject by some one. He spoke, however, of the fall from the litter as he was being borne from the field; and, although no contusion or abrasion was perceptible from this accident, declared that it had done him injury.

About this time he had the great satisfaction of receiving from the commander whom he loved and admired so warmly that note which we have placed as a motto on the title page of this book. It was in these words:

"I have just received your note, informing me that you were wounded. I cannot express my regret at the occurrence. Could I have directed events, I should have chosen, for the good of the country, to have been disabled in your stead. I congratulate you on the victory which is due to your skill and energy."

This supreme recognition from his commanding general of the loss which the cause had sustained when he was wounded, proved most grateful to his feelings, and will remain his noblest epitaph.

The regret of Gen. Lee at this deplorable event was indeed poignant. The soul of the great commander was moved to its depths; and he who had so long learned to conceal emotion, could not control his anguish. "Jackson will not—he *cannot* die!" General Lee exclaimed, in a broken voice, and waving every one from him with his hand—"he *cannot* die!"

But the hours were hastening on—Sunday passed; the wounded man sleeping well in the afternoon; and Monday came.

His physicians now deemed it advisable to remove him to some point where he could be more quiet; and, accordingly, he was carried to Mr. Chancellor's, near Guinea's Depot, on the Richmond, Fredericksburg, and Potomac Railroad, about eight miles from Hamilton's Crossing, where every arrangement was made to insure his comfort and careful treatment. During the ride from the Wilderness to Guinea's, he complained greatly of the heat of the day, and in addition to the wet applications applied to his wound, begged that a wet cloth might be laid upon his stomach. He declared that this gave him great relief, and on Monday night he slept well, and ate with relish in the morning.

During the ride to Guinea's, he had maintained his serene and cheerful bearing, and talked much in reference to the battle of Saturday. He spoke of the gallant bearing of Gen. Rodes, and said that his commission as Major-general ought to date from that day; and of the grand charge of the old Stonewall Brigade in the battle of Sunday, which he had heard of. He asked after all his officers, and said:

"The men who live through this war will be proud to say, 'I was one of the Stonewall Brigade!' to their children."

With that grand modesty which ever characterized him, he hastened, however, to guard this declaration even from the appearance of egotism; and earnestly declared that the name of "Stonewall" did not belong to *him;* it was the name given to his old brigade, and their property alone.

On Tuesday his wounds were doing very well, and he evidently looked forward to a speedy recovery. He said to his physician: "Can you tell me, from the appearance of my wounds, how long I will be kept from the field?" and when told that they were doing remarkably well, he exhibited very great satisfaction. He had no pain in the side, and thought himself well enough to see and converse with his staff; but he was advised against this by his attendants, and did not persist.

On Wednesday, his wounds continued to look remarkably well, and he was now regarded as so far out of danger, that preparations were made to carry him by railroad to Richmond. A rain, however, which had set in, prevented this design, and he was not removed. On this night, while Dr. McGuire, who had not closed his eyes for three nights, was snatching a little rest, the general complained of nausea, and ordered his body-servant, Jim, to place a wet towel on his stomach. This was done, but with bad results. The surgeon was waked by Jim at daylight, and informed that his master was suffering very much. The pain was in the right side, and was due partly to the heavy fall from the litter while being borne from the battle-field, and partly to incipient pneumonia, which now began to develop itself.

This was on the morning of Thursday, and later in the day

Mrs. Jackson arrived. The presence of his wife seemed to afford the general very great joy, and thenceforth she nursed him to the moment of his death.

The remainder of the sorrowful record will not fill much space, or occupy the attention of the reader many moments. The Supreme Ruler of the destinies of humanity, had decreed that this pure and majestic spirit should pass from earth to a happier and more peaceful realm; the hours of the great soldier were numbered; he had fought his last battle, finished his work, and now was about to receive that crown laid up for those who believe in Him who governs all things.

On Thursday evening all pain had ceased; but a mortal prostration came on, from which he never recovered. He still conversed feebly, and said:

"I consider these wounds a blessing; they were given me for some good and wise purpose, and I would not part with them if I could."

From this time he continued to sink, and on Sunday morning it was obvious that he could only live a few hours longer. His mind was still clear, however, and he asked Major Pendleton, his adjutant-general, "who was preaching at headquarters on that day?" Mrs. Jackson was with him during his last moments, and conversed with him fully and freely. She informed him that he was about to die, and his reply was:

"*Very good, very good; it is all right!*"

He then sent messages to all his friends, the generals and others, and murmured in a low voice his wish to be buried in "Lexington, in the Valley of Virginia."

His mind then began to wander; and that delirium which seizes upon the most powerful minds, the most vigorous brains, at the mysterious moment when the last sands fall from the glass, began to affect him. He gave orders to the commissary of his corps, the surgeons, and the commanders. Among the last words which escaped his lips were:

"A. P. Hill, prepare for action!"

After this, he speedily sank; and at fifteen minutes past three in the evening, he tranquilly expired.

Such was the death of Jackson; serene, resigned, hopeful. He who had passed through a thousand perils expired of disease upon his bed, surrounded by weeping friends, who were taught by that august spectacle how a Christian soldier can die.

The body of the dead hero was conveyed to Richmond; and here a great and solemn pageant marked the universal sense of loss. The body, embalmed and prepared during the night, was placed in a metallic coffin in the reception-room at the Governor's. Bouquets of flowers, and wreaths, the tributes of the tender hearts of women, covered the pall; and around the coffin was wrapped the snow-white banner of the Confederate States.

At the hour appointed the coffin was borne to the hearse, a signal gun was fired from near the Equestrian Statue in the Square, and the great procession began to move to the solemn strains of the Dead March in Saul. The hearse was preceded by two regiments of General Pickett's division, with arms reversed; that general and his staff; the Fayette artillery, and Wrenn's company of cavalry. Behind came the horse of the dead soldier, caparisoned for battle, and led by a groom; his staff officers; members of the Old Stonewall Brigade, invalids and wounded, with downcast looks; and then a vast array of officials, President Davis, members of the Cabinet, Generals Longstreet, Elzey, Winder, Garnett, Kemper, Corse, Commodore Forrest, with the judges, citizens, and good people generally of the city.

The procession, nearly a mile in length, moved down Governor's-street, and up to the head of Main-street, whence it returned to the western gate of the Capitol Square, where a countless multitude had assembled to see it enter. The hearse moved to the steps of the Capitol, the band playing a low dirge; and lifting the coffin, the pall-bearers, General Longstreet and others, bore it into the hall of the House of Representatives, where it was deposited upon a sort of altar, covered with white linen, looped up with crape, in front of the Speaker's chair. The crowd was then admitted; and old and young, the gray-haired man and the child—20,000 persons it was estimated—looked upon the wan countenance of the great soldier.

"The face of the dead," says a writer in one of the journals, "displayed the same indomitable lines of firmness, with the long, slightly aquiline nose, and high forehead, of marble whiteness; but the cheeks presented a deep pallor. The eyelids were firmly closed, the mouth natural, and the whole contour of the face composed, the full beard and moustache remaining. The body was dressed in a full citizen's suit, it being the object of his friends, and we doubt not, the nation's wish, to preserve the uniform in which he fought and fell."

From the Capitol the remains of Jackson were borne to Lexington, where he had lived so long, passed so many happy hours in other years, and to which his thoughts went back in those last moments when he murmured, "Bury me in Lexington, in the Valley of Virginia."

"Lexington!" That town has witnessed the peaceful labors of the professor; the calm researches of the quiet student; the serene enjoyments of the good husband and friend. Thence he had departed to enter upon the career which was to make his name a famous one forever, in the annals of a mighty nation and a tragic epoch—to crown him with glory and honor as the right arm and chief hope of a great people. From Lexington, where he had been so happy, he went upon that path of danger and trial which was to render him so famous. He murmured "Lexington! Lexington!" as the German exiles are said to murmur, "The Rhine! the Rhine!"

"The Valley of Virginia!" Those words too had, doubtless, a magical influence upon the stern and unimaginative soul of the celebrated leader. They conjured up visions of his chief glories won upon that old familiar, long-loved soil. They meant Kernstown! McDowell! Winchester! Cross Keys! Port Republic! There was scarce a foot of the great highways of that region but had been trodden by him and his soldiers; scarce a mile over which he had not fought. There his steps had been clogged with battles—and almost every encounter was a victory. For that sacred earth he had fought so long and persistently; thence he had so frequently driven the hireling invader; every foot was dear to him from the mouth of the beautiful Shenandoah to its source; and for its freedom he had cheerfully risked all that man possesses. He had delivered that lovely land from all its foes; and, lying powerless there near Fredericksburg, his heart turned fondly to the scene of his happiness and his fame. In that earth which he had redeemed—the soil of the Valley of Virginia—he desired his ashes to repose.

There they now rest. The same great honors which had saluted the remains of the famous general in Richmond, were paid them at Lexington; and there his body was committed to the mother-earth.

The journals report that some loving hand planted on his grave a piece of laurel brought from the grave of Napoleon at St. Helena; and if a comparison of the military genius of the two was meant, the tribute was not inappropriate. But a greater than Napoleon slept in the graveyard near the quiet Virginia town—one allied to him in capacity for making war, nor his inferior;—in all else wholly and incomparably superior.

On their death-beds, these two men, Napoleon and Jackson, displayed their radical difference of character and sentiment.

Napoleon died with the fierce cry, "*Tête d'armée!*" upon his lips.

Almost the last words of Jackson were, "It is all right!" As long as his thought went wandering to the field of battle, his muttered words were busy with those scenes of duty. "A. P. Hill, prepare for action!" came from the dying man; but soon a greater subject absorbed his attention.

"It is all right," expressed his sublime trust in God: his submission to the divine decree which had struck him down.

Napoleon trusted in his star—Jackson in God. Napoleon was a pure and simple fatalist: Jackson's motto was, "Do your duty, and leave the rest to Providence."

One was a great soldier of imperial genius—but no more. The other was a mighty leader, but an humble, faithful child of God, as well.

He accepted the lot decreed him by the Almighty Father with submission and an humble hope, believing that whatever God permitted was the best.

Let us, too, trust that all is well, and look beyond the storm—beyond the darkness, blood, and mourning of the present—with serene trust in Him who rules the destinies of men and nations.

CHAPTER XXXIII.

JACKSON, THE SOLDIER AND THE MAN.

Our poor, brief record of this splendid career is finished. "Would it were worthier!"—but one merit it at least posseses, that of truth.

Thus fought and fell the great leader who had attracted to himself so much of the affection, the respect, the admiration of his countrymen—thus passed before the eyes of the world, and into the shadow of the tomb, the lofty figure which will live forever in the memories of the Southern people, as in every heart.

It is hard to convey an adequate idea of the effect produced by the death of the illustrious general. When the "invincible Stonewall Jackson" was thus conquered by a stronger enemy than man, something of strength, of hope, of life appeared to be removed from every heart. Falling, he seemed to take away the charm and prestige of victory. The sunshine seemed less bright, the future dark with clouds and gloom. His name had been a tower of strength to all, and when this mighty bulwark of the Southern cause was overthrown, Heaven seemed to frown upon us, and to punish us.

It was not the loss of the leader only that men mourned; it was the friend, the benefactor, the father who was taken from the people. No one remembered that Jackson was not forty when he died—nor regarded him otherwise than as the mature patriot of age and experience, with all the wisdom of gray hairs. Men looked up to him, as of old the Greeks did to the wise Ulysses or the thoughtful Nestor—as to one who was competent to hear and decide, as well as to act, in every emergency. There was something childlike in the sentiment with which the whole nation mourned his death. They listened to the announcement with a hush of awe, with that silence which salutes a great and irreparable public calamity. Strong men wept for him, with a sense of loss and desolation, as children weep for the great head of their house, who crowned with honors, and in the fulness of age, descends into the tomb. His veterans mourned as men do rarely—dumb and still before this terrible fatality; and General Lee, who knew his incomparable value more than all other men, exclaimed, with tears in his eyes, "He is better off than I am. *He* lost his *left* arm, but *I* have lost my *right!*" All classes shared this sentiment. "Jackson is dead!" sounded like the tolling of great bells, like the death-knell to every heart. Dead? He who had been so long the King of combat?—upon whose banner victory had perched whenever he delivered battle?—the invincible Stonewall Jackson dead and gone like a common every-day mortal? The truth could scarcely be realized! Who could supply his place? Who could lead his veterans to victory as he had led them? His form had towered in the van so long, that men began to look upon him as the man of Fate, predestined not to fall until his work was finished, and seeing that the conflict was not ended, they were struck with wonder.

Did God decree his death to administer a rebuke to this man-worship?—to show that all men were His instruments, and that He could raise them up or strike them down? We cannot solve the problem, and bow in humble submission to the inexplicable decree, well satisfied that "all is right." We only know that the hand of God beckoned to him, and he went from us—humble, childlike, with supreme trust in Him whom he had so long looked to. Let us take comfort from the circumstances of his death, and be glad that he thus passed away—that the hero of a hundred battles died in his bed, with loving friends around him—not upon some wild stricken field—died very tranquilly, without the racking pains of dissolution, but as calmly as a child, his great life ebbing wave after wave away.

The aim of this sketch has been to supply in a convenient form, and without delay, the facts of the illustrious soldier's career. The full delineation of the individual in his characters of soldier and citizen—husband, father, and friend—must be left to other times and more competent hands. It will not be inappropriate, however, to hazard, even here, and pressed by the emergencies of the moment, some notices of the peculiarities of Gen. Jackson's character and genius.

Where the opposing forces are any thing like equal, war is a contest of brains. It is the generals who do the fighting, so to speak, and not the soldiers. If one overcomes the other, and defeats or destroys his army, the inquirer will not have to go very far to discover the reason. One side is victor because the general was a better master of the art of making war than his opponent—because his plans were deeper, his insight into those of the enemy more penetrating, his execution more rapid, or his nerve more steady and indomitable. As at chess

—the opponents may start equal, without advantage on either side; but the brain of Morphy will easily win the game. Advance another step: let us say that the armies, instead of equal, are greatly unequal--that humanly speaking, one is sure to be defeated by the other, unless some force sufficient to turn the balance be thrown into the scale against numbers. Then the general who wins the day is a general indeed!

"*These were soldiers indeed!*" Jackson said at Cold Harbor, as he looked at the ditch and abatis over which the Texans charged on the enemy's batteries, and took them, at the point of the bayonet. "*He was a soldier indeed!*" will be the verdict of history in summing up the career and character of Jackson.

The fate of many distinguished soldiers had been his. *Colonel* Jackson of the early days of Patterson in the Valley was acknowledged to be a hard man to deal with at close quarters, and all that was necessary it was said, was a brain to think for him—a competent superior to plan his movements and tell him when to attack or retire. That opinion lasted for some time. Colonel Jackson could fight harder than any other man—was a veritable bull-dog indeed, and invaluable in his place—but he was in his proper place, and should be kept there.

Then he fought his way to the command of a brigade. The old criticism followed him. *Brigadier-general* Jackson was an excellent officer, had handled his command with distinguished success, but he had now, it was certain, touched his limit. A few regiments were not beyond his faculties, and his success with this "Stonewall Brigade," which people began to hear about, was unquestionable; but the command of a division was quite another thing—above all, of a division detached from the rest of the army, and constituting an army in itself. The responsibility would be far too great for the man; he could not safely be intrusted with *that* command. He *was* soon intrusted with it, however, and how he deported himself in his new sphere is well known. The critics began to discover that this eccentric, erratic Colonel Jackson had been misunderstood, under-estimated, and when the appointment of Lieutenant-general was sent to him, they found it perfectly natural and proper.

In every sphere of action, and under ever-increasing command and responsibility, General Jackson had proved himself equal, and more than equal, to the call upon his faculties, and the fashion of talking about his being "only a fighter" became, somehow, obsolete.

The truth is that the great soldier shone conspicuously wherever he was placed. He was a good Colonel, a better Brigadier, and as Major and Lieutenant-general, best of all. His entire campaign against Banks in the lower Valley—the execution of the plans of General Lee on the Chickahominy and Rapidan—and the splendid manœuvring of his corps before Pope at Manassas, when he retired in face of the enormous columns of the enemy, chose his ground to fight, and, while waiting for General Longstreet, turned savagely, like a lion at bay—these movements undoubtedly reveal military genius of the first order, and vindicate the claim of the leader who executed them to the title of a great general.

In that noble letter which he wrote to President Davis just before his death, Gen. Sydney Johnston declared that, after all, he agreed with the popular verdict, that success was the test of merit. If Jackson's career be subjected to that test, his excellence will be established. No soldier of the war was more uniformly successful in his undertakings. He never failed to achieve his object, from the day when, with 2,700 men, he held in check 11,000 at Kernstown, to the moment when, moving by that bold and stealthy march through the Wilderness, he struck the enemy with the suddenness of the thunderbolt, and determined the fate of Gen. Hooker's advance. Such successes as those which mark the career of Jackson, are not accidental. They are the tests of generalship, and indicate the possession of faculties which God vouchsafes to few of his creatures. General Jackson was undoubtedly a man of very extraordinary military genius; and in his whole career, it will be difficult, if not impossible, to find a serious error of judgment or fault of execution. The old faded cap of the general covered a brain which revolved deep thoughts—the penetrating eyes beneath could not be deceived. The wiliest foe could not outwit the simple-looking personage; no feint or trick mislead the clear judgment presiding serenely over the fiery soul. Indeed, the enemy who tried to undermine him, secretly, found a mine beneath *him*—which, almost before he knew of its existence, was sprung upon him. It is not too much to say that the victor of Port Republic was more than a match for all his foes combined, in strategy, and their best friends might have advised them to depend upon numbers and hard fighting, rather than military manœuvre, if they wished to snatch laurels from Jackson.

Unfortunately, however, that very "last resort" of *hard fighting* was the strong point of this general. If Jackson was famous for any thing at all, it was for an inborn and ineradicable tendency to stubborn, unyielding combat, against any odds. Of this there is no question. He had little of the fiery dash of Rupert, at the head of his cavaliers—but the very bull-dog pertinacity and iron nerve of Cromwell—sworn to conquer or die. He was in favor of advancing upon McClellan at Harrison's Landing; on Burnside at Fredericksburg—he was always in favor of advancing. To advance and fight appears to have been the military philosophy of General Jackson—and to go on fighting until the enemy was whipped.

The extraordinary success of his career can only be explained upon one hypothesis. He was a born soldier. This he showed in all that he undertook; more especially in that brief but decisive campaign of the Valley, to which we have so frequently referred. The details of his movements at this time cannot be too attentively studied—and it is difficult to conceive of a campaign more consummately skilful in design and execution. Hopelessly outnumbered by the Federal forces, beset by a swarm of foes in front, and hemmed in by a vast cordon on every side, he defeated or eluded them with matchless skill, and bore off all the most substantial fruits of victory. Nothing but the possession of incomparable military genius could have made this campaign the magnificent success which it proved; it is doubtful if any other general on the continent could have conducted it, through obstacles apparently so overwhelming, to an issue so triumphant. The more deeply it is studied by the military student, the more wonderful will that famous series of manœuvres appear. It will be understood how critical the situation was—how nice were the calculations of time, of material, of chances. One broken link would have burst the great chain—one wheel neglected would have thrown into disorder the complicated machinery of Jackson's movements. After Kernstown, he fell back step by step—but it was to fight the battle of McDowell. After Winchester, he pressed on to the Potomac, but victory had not lulled him into fatal security; and when Fremont and McDowell clashed together near Strasburg to cut him off, they struck only his rear-guard—his main force having marched away with all the prisoners and captured stores to the upper Valley. At Port Republic, he terminated this immortal campaign by whipping his enemy in detail—and then descended to his great work in the lowlands at Cold Harbor, Cedar Run, and the second Manassas.

This campaign of the Valley, and the march to Manassas, will remain the crowning glories of Jackson's career; and they display a genius for war which will rank him with the greatest generals of history. He was possessed by nature of the distinguishing characteristics of the Leader of men—of Alexander, of Cæsar, of Napoleon. To make war against wily and powerful enemies, was the occupation for which, by his distinctive genius, he was fitted. He was an intense man—

concentrating all his faculties upon the object in view, and striking heavy blows when once the combat began. To go on striking with all his force—to advance, to be the aggressor, to fight to the death, was, as we have said, his philosophy of war. His military calculations omitted no element of strategy, but to the wise counsel was added indomitable combativeness. His designs had a grand simplicity about them—"Advance and fight," seemed to be his motto. Personally, he loved excitement—even thirsted at times for battle; and he once told a distinguished officer of the cavalry, that he longed to accompany him upon one of his raids, and share the perils and excitements of the occasion.

We have said that General Jackson was *an intense man.* We mean that what he did, he did with all his might. When he put his hand to the plough he never looked back, but bent all his energies to the work before him. His will was enormous, his strength of purpose invincible. He never paused, or could tolerate the thought of pausing, until all opposition was shattered, and the enemy overwhelmed and driven from the field. At Winchester, his cry to the weary troops was, "Press right on to the Potomac!" At Fredericksburg, after the prostrating conflict of that hard-fought day, Jackson thought of one thing only—an advance before night, and a more desperate attack than before. At Chancellorsville, the very last words which he uttered before he fell, were, "Tell A. P. Hill to press right on!"

The unconquerable will of the man seemed to defy all opposing forces, and to wring victory from the very jaws of Fate. Under the calm exterior, the sweet womanly smile, was a tenacity of purpose so unbending—a resolution so stern and obdurate, a will so gigantic—that to the present writer, as to others who saw this great man at critical moments, he seemed to possess the power of overwhelming all human opposition, and compelling Destiny to crouch before him, and obey him.

He was a man of earnestness and singleness of purpose. He did not fritter away his strength upon small objects, or unimportant things. He had the faculty which has characterized the great judicial minds of the statesmen and lawyers of England,—the power of discerning the main obstacle in his path, and of so disposing his forces as to assail it to the best advantage. The fortress once overcome, the surrounding country he knew must fall into his hands; and he did not trouble himself in reducing the villages.

He knew what was necessary to insure victory—was fertile in resource—of unfailing prudence in guarding against disaster, never leaving unstrengthened that fatal weak point in the dam, through which the flood will slowly but surely work its way, sweeping every thing eventually before it. With him there were no trifles—nothing was too small or unimportant to guard against. Like the painter, who, when criticised for his multitudinous touches, replied, "These may seem trifles, but they secure perfection, and perfection is no trifle"—he never rested until he had seen in person that all things were attended to, down to the minutest details; rightly thinking that the grand result was worth any amount of trouble. He never failed to keep his line of retreat open, and left nothing to good fortune. All was calculation of forces, time, and material.

His dispositions for attack were always perfect, thorough and the very best that the time and place would admit of. He uniformly proceeded on the hypothesis that the assailing force possessed from that circumstance an enormous advantage; and, once in motion, he advanced with the utmost rapidity, and struck with all his strength. If one blow failed, another was delivered; if that was unsuccessful, every available force which he could control was concentrated for another and another. It was only when the overpowering numbers of the enemy made the encounter hopeless, that he retired with dogged, sullen deliberation—as dangerous in retreating as when advancing.

His tenacity of purpose was invincible. Never has a soul of more stubborn nerve been born into the world. He refused to recognize the possibility of defeat, and never knew when he was whipped. At Kernstown he was firmly convinced that if daylight had continued, his little handful of weary troops, worn down by exhausting marches, and shattered by a day of terrible conflict, would have put to rout the fourfold forces of Federals in front of them. At Manassas, he believed that with 10,000 men he could have captured Washington. In Charles City he was confident that if McClellan was attacked in his defences near Harrison's Landing, his army would be forced to surrender. At Fredericksburg he projected and nearly executed an audacious assault, with the bayonet, upon Burnside's entire force in front of our position at nightfall. Who shall say that on any of these occasions Jackson miscalculated his strength, or over-estimated his ability? History has recorded the battles which he won. Who shall say that those which he declared his ability to win would have resulted in defeat?

He struck boldly, but formed his plans in secret. Mystery is the favorite resort of charlatans; but with Jackson it was the herald of victory. He talked little, and measured his words when speaking of military affairs. No one knew whither he was going; what he designed. He proceeded upon the sound and excellent maxim that a secret is always guarded from indiscretion when confined to a single person—and the person whom he selected as the sole repository of his plans was himself. He even put himself to great trouble to mask his designs—camping often when he arrived at cross-roads, and leaving thus that body of quidnuncs, which are found in every army, profoundly puzzled as to what direction he would take with his command upon the morrow. On one occasion he reprimanded an officer on the march for engaging dinner for headquarters at a house a few miles in advance, upon the highway which the troops were pursuing; it afforded information of his line of march to that extent, and so was reprehensible. A favorite device with him was to institute inquiries in the presence of the crowd around him as to roads and watercourses in a direction which he did *not* intend to take; even to order maps to be prepared, and roads laid down, as though for instant use. Having thus set every gossip talking and predicting his intentions, he would calmly march directly in the opposite direction.

"Mystery, mystery, is the secret of success!"

He was just to his officers and men, taking up prejudices rarely for or against persons, and measuring out equal justice to all. No man could say that he had treated him with conscious unfairness; and if a calm examination of those cases wherein he is said to have acted from personal dislike, be instituted, it will be found that he proceeded upon grounds which appeared to him incontrovertible, and not from haste and ill-temper. Ill-tempered, in the proper meaning of the phrase, he never was. He was stern, abrupt, harsh at times, but the occasion always demanded plain speech—and his object of reprimand, correction, or repulse of ill-advised interference once attained, the offence was entirely forgotten, and the offender restored completely to his former position.

He had the faculty of calculating forces, rarely developed. He always knew his strength and his weakness. When he attacked, it was because he knew that victory was, humanly speaking, in his grasp. He based his calculations not upon numbers only, but upon position, material, the morale of his troops, and the effect of the situation upon the morale of the enemy. He estimated to their full extent the decisive character of a sudden, bold, and obstinate attack. He trusted most to the bayonet, but had a marked fondness for artillery. He did not overestimate its value in inflicting injury upon the enemy, but he trusted greatly to its influence upon the morale of his opponents. To "demoralize" the enemy was a large part of his military philosophy, and he rightly thought that a foe disheartened is a foe half beaten.

In summing up, briefly and generally, the peculiarities of Jackson's military genius, it may be said, without unmeaning panegyric, or the least disposition to over-estimate his faculties as a leader, that he was profound and comprehensive in his plans—as rapid and mortal as a thunderbolt in execution; that he possessed a courage in the face of danger which no peril could affect, no possible reverse, however sudden, unexpected, and disheartening, deprive him of; that he was cautious, prudent, judicious in all his dispositions; lastly, that he possessed the native faculty of penetrating the intentions of the enemy, of guarding himself wholly from surprise, of delivering his blows upon the weakest point, and of making war on all occasions and against the most dangerous opponents, with the mastery, precision, and success of the greatest leaders which the world has yet produced. This illustrious soldier is just dead, and little of sound criticism has been published in relation to him—few estimates of his genius have been made. The present writer, though an humble and obscure soldier of the Southern army, had the inestimable privilege of knowing this great man, and seeing him in battle; and the profound conviction of his mind is expressed in the statement that Gen. Jackson was one of the three or four great masters of the art of war which the world has known. The century, the material, the field of operations were all different, but this was Alexander, the conqueror of the East; Cæsar, the greatest leader of all ages; Napoleon, the supreme master of the art of fighting armies—contending with a little army, and against mighty disadvantages, for the liberty of his country. It was the New World and the Nineteenth Century which saw this struggle, and the force with which the great Virginian operated was small; but the mastery of his art was just the same, the faculty of the brain as perfect in proportion and as great as in his predecessors—the result the same. Jackson overcame his enemies as Cæsar and Napoleon did, by inexhaustible resources both of brain and nerve: by that superiority which God had given him for His own wise purposes; and if he was not spared to exhibit greater faculties upon a larger arena, it was because the Almighty, in His wisdom, thought best to remove him, leaving the great struggle in the hands of his associates.

To-day, when the smoke has scarcely lifted from the field, and forms are seen but dimly, these words may appear absurd, and dictated by a weak spirit of eulogy and hero-worship; but the time will come when the immense military genius of the Conqueror of the Valley will be accurately estimated, and his statue placed beside those of the greatest captains of history.

Personally, General Jackson was awkward, and, in his movements, constrained and ungraceful. He was tall, raw-boned, and had a peculiar stride in walking. He was absent-minded: would often pause suddenly and fix his eyes upon the ground; and in riding had a habit of slapping his side and raising his arm aloft—whether from some physical ailment which he thus relieved, or in prayer, is not known. His address wanted ease; his manner was shy and constrained, like that of a student who has so long secluded himself in libraries that the faces of men annoy and discompose him. He talked little with strangers, and was brief of speech, but never failed to return the salute of the humblest person, treating all men with the most kindly courtesy. His eyes were dark, penetrating, and had a peculiar brightness when he was aroused, which the most casual observer noticed. The remainder of the countenance was not remarkable, but his smile was very sweet—a lady who had conversed with him, applied to it the word "angelic." It was, indeed, full of attraction, and indicated the wealth of kindness which lay under the calm, somewhat cold exterior.

The result of the great soldier's immense popularity lay in

the universal conviction of his simplicity and goodness. Sincerity, purity, truthfulness in thought and word and deed, lit up the path upon which he walked, and made him beautiful in the eyes of the good men and women of the land. The people, generally, admired him for his military successes; but the character of the individual was the passport to that truly extraordinary love and admiration which saluted him where-ever he moved. His enemies even shared this sentiment; and gentlemen who remained in Winchester during the Federal occupation of that town, assure us that the enemy uniformly spoke of him with the utmost admiration, and declared that nothing could induce them to kill a man like Stonewall Jackson. Some singular details are given of the feeling of the Federals toward him in that region. We are told that they regarded it as Jackson's property, his private domain; and believed that he would return at any moment to "his own again." He had told the people, in his cool, brief speech, "that he would come again, and as certainly as now"—and when the enemy were informed of this, they gave implicit credence to the promise, and were seen on more than one occasion to start suddenly at the very report that "Jackson was coming."

But all these anecdotes must be reserved for another occasion. We hasten to the end of our sketch.

Few human beings have been purer, or more guileless. H had the simplicity of a child; and the renown, which ever increased as his great services were more fully recognized, seemed only to make him more modest and retiring. All the ends he aimed at were his country's; and that profound affection and respect which all the world had for him will last always, for it was based upon the eternal foundations of truth and goodness.

To say that he was a pure and humble Christian is unnecessary. Piety was the absorbing and controlling sentiment of his being. He seemed to look to God in all that he did, and thought, and uttered. He was a member of the Presbyterian Church, but no sectarian. So great a spirit could not be tinged with bigotry; and a gentleman of high character, long serving on his staff, assured the present writer that he was wholly free from any trace of illiberality or dogmatism in his religious creed. His "fatalism" has been dwelt upon persistently; his cool, brave bearing in the heat of battle, set down as the result of some strange Oriental fatalistic sentiment, which made him insensible to fear.

Such was the idle talk of those who did not know the great soldier. The truth may be stated in very few words: Jackson believed in the doctrine of predestination, as all rational minds believe in it. Looking fervently to an overruling Providence, and trusting to the goodness of an omnipotent Creator, he gave himself no concern, except as to the performance of his duty. The issues of life and death, he felt, were in a mightier hand than man's; and to that omnipotent Power—to the "King eternal, unchangeable, invisible"—he was content to leave the decision whether he was to live or die. The shell that burst in iron spray around him did not move the stern, calm nerve; the storm of bullets which he passed so often through was powerless to shake the heroic courage of the soldier of God. Whatever was, was best with him; and when they told him he was going to die, his words, "Very good, very good; it is all right!" expressed the deep and changeless faith of one who left all issues to the King of kings and Lord of lords with calm and abiding trust.

Prayer was the breath in his nostrils, and he never failed in going into battle to raise his heart to the Lord of Hosts, beseeching him on bended knee to prosper the cause of truth and right. This phase of the great leader's character need be only touched upon here. The world has been glad to hear that a competent writer, possessed of ample materials will ere long present a full and complete view of the religious character of General Jackson. Let us here say, in concluding our sketch, that profound submission of his whole heart to the will of God, was Jackson's never-failing sentiment in all the scenes of his arduous and exciting career—that the great lieutenant-general was as humble, simple, and confiding as a child who reaches out weak hands for help toward its father; and that the mighty intellect, the stern, unshrinking will bent with humility before that God in whom he trusted with supreme faith in every hour of trial.

For such a man to die was gain. Through the Valley of Shadows his path led surely to that realm where neither wars nor rumors of wars—nor wounds, or suffering, or anxiety—can ever come. In the darkness of the trying hour the rod and the staff of the Almighty Father comforted him. He had no regrets, no longing for life. Earth possessed for this sublime and noble soul no attractions which could blind him to the greater joys which awaited him. He had fought the good fight, had finished his course, and kept the faith. God called him in the hour of victory; and his pure and childlike spirit passed away in the tranquil hours of that Sabbath season which he had so long loved.

The poet paints the happiness of his hero dying "in the arms of victory;" but the lot of Jackson, the patriot, the hero, the humble Christian, was far better. He fell asleep with the "everlasting arms beneath him," in the assurance of blessed immortality.

APPENDIX.

I.

OPERATIONS OF GENERAL JACKSON'S COMMAND FROM SEPTEMBER 5TH TO SEPTEMBER 27TH, 1862.—OFFICIAL REPORT.

HEADQUARTERS 2D CORPS A. N. V.,
April 23d, 1863.

General,—I have the honor to submit a report of the operations of my command from the 5th to the 27th of September, 1862, embracing the capture of Harper's Ferry, the engagement at Shepherdstown, and so much of the battle of Sharpsburg as was fought by my command.

My command comprised A. P. Hill's Division, consisting of the Brigades of Branch, Gregg, Field, (Colonel Brockenbrough commanding,) Pender, Archer, and Colonel Thomas, with the Batteries of the Division, under Lieutenant-colonel R. L. Walker; Ewell's Division, under Brigadier-general Lawton, consisting of the Brigades of Early, Hays, (Colonel Strong,) Trimble, (Colonel Walker,) and Lawton, (Colonel Douglas,) with the Artillery under Major Courtney; and Jackson's Division, under Brigadier-general Starke, consisting of the Brigades of Winder, (Colonel Grigsby,) Jones, (Colonel B. T. Johnson,) Taliaferro, (Colonel Warren,) and Starke, (Colonel Stafford,) with the Artillery under Major Shumaker, Chief of Artillery.

On the 5th of September my command crossed the Potomac at White's Ford, and bivouacked that night near the three springs in the State of Maryland. Not having any cavalry with me except the Black Horse, under Captain Randolph, I directed him, after crossing the Potomac, to take a part of his company and scout to the right, in order to prevent a surprise of the column from that direction. For the thorough and efficient manner in which this duty was performed, and for the valuable service rendered generally whilst attached to my headquarters, I desire to make special mention of this company and of its officers, Captain Randolph, and Lieutenants Paine, Tyle, and Smith, who frequently transmitted orders in the absence of staff-officers.

The next day we arrived in the vicinity of Frederick City. Jackson's division encamped near its suburbs, except the brigade of General Jones, (Colonel Bradley T. Johnson commanding,) which was posted in the city as a Provost Guard. Ewell's and Hill's divisions occupied positions near the railroad bridge, on the Monocacy, guarding the approaches from Washington City. In obedience to instructions from the commanding general, and for the purpose of capturing the Federal forces and stores then at Martinsburg and Harper's Ferry, my command left the vicinity of Frederick City on the 10th, and passing rapidly through Middletown, Boonsborough, and Williamsport, recrossed the Potomac into Virginia at Light's Ford, on the 11th. General Hill moved with his division on the turnpike direct from Williamsport to Martinsburg. The divisions of Jackson and Ewell proceeded toward the North Mountain depot, on the Baltimore and Ohio Railroad, about seven miles northwest of Martinsburg. They bivouacked that night in the vicinity of the depot. In order to prevent the Federal forces then at Martinsburg from escaping westward unobserved, Major Myers, commanding the cavalry, sent part of his troops as far south as the Berkeley and Hampshire turnpikes. Brigadier-general White, who was in command of the Federal forces at Martinsburg, becoming advised of our approach, evacuated the place on the night of the 11th, and retreated to Harper's Ferry. On the morning of the 12th our cavalry entered the town, as in the course of the day did the main body of my command. At this point, abandoned quartermaster, commissary, and ordnance stores fell into our hands. Proceeding thence toward Harper's Ferry, about 11 o'clock, A. M., on the following morning (13th), the head of our column came in view of the enemy drawn up in force at Bolivar Heights. General Hill, who was in the advance, went into camp near Hallstown, about two miles from the enemy's position. The two other divisions encamped near by.

The commanding general, having directed Major-general McLaws to move with his own and General R. H. Anderson's divisions, to take possession of the Maryland Heights overlooking Harper's Ferry, and Brigadier-general J. G. Walker, pursuing a different route, to cross the Potomac and move up that river on the Virginia side, and occupy the Loudoun Heights, both for the purpose of co-operating with me, it became necessary, before making the attack, to ascertain whether they were in position. Failing to learn the fact by signals, a courier was dispatched to each of these points for the required information. During the night the courier from the Loudoun Heights returned, with a message from General Walker, that he was in position. In the mean time, General McLaws had attacked the Federal forces posted to defend the Maryland Heights, had routed it, and taken possession of that commanding position. The Potomac river flowed between the positions respectively occupied by General McLaws and myself, and the Shenandoah separated me from General Walker; and it became advisable, as the speediest mode of communication, to resort to signals. Before the necessary orders were thus transmitted, the day was far advanced. The enemy had, by fortifications, strengthened the naturally strong position which he occupied along Bolivar Heights, extending from near the Shenandoah to the Potomac. McLaws and Walker, being thus separated from the enemy by intervening rivers, could afford no assistance, beyond the fire of their artillery, and guarding certain avenues of escape to the enemy. And from the reports received from them by signals, in consequence of the distance and range of their guns, not much could be expected from their artillery, so long as the enemy retained his advanced position on Bolivar Heights.

In the afternoon (14th), General Hill was ordered to move along the left bank of the Shenandoah, turn the enemy's left, and enter Harper's Ferry. General Lawton, commanding Ewell's division, was directed to move along the turnpike for the purpose of supporting General Hill, and of otherwise operating against the enemy to his left.

General J. R. Jones, commanding Jackson's division, was directed, with one of his brigades, and a battery of artillery, to make a demonstration against the enemy's right, whilst the remaining part of his command, as a reserve, moved along the turnpike. Major Massie, commanding the cavalry, was directed to keep upon our left flank for the purpose of preventing the enemy from escaping. Brigadier-general Walker guarded against an escape across the Shenandoah river. Fearing lest the enemy should attempt to escape across the Potomac, by means of signals I called the attention of Major-general McLaws, commanding on the Maryland Heights, to the propriety of guarding against such an attempt. The demonstration on the left against the enemy's right was made by Winder's brigade (Colonel Grigsby commanding). It was ordered to secure a commanding hill to the left of the heights, near the Potomac. Promptly dispersing some cavalry, this eminence, from which the batteries of Poague and Carpenter subsequently did such admirable execution, was secured without difficulty. In execution of the orders given Major-general Hill, he moved obliquely to the right until he struck the Shenandoah river. Observing an eminence, crowning the extreme left of the enemy's line, occupied by infantry, but without artillery, and protected only by an abatis of fallen timber, Pender, Archer, and Brockenbrough were directed to gain the crest of that hill, while Branch and Gregg were directed to march along the river, and during the night to take advantage of the ravines, cutting the precipitous banks of the river, and establish themselves on the plain to the left and rear of the enemy's works. Thomas followed as a reserve. The execution of the first movement was intrusted to Brigadier-general Pender, who accomplished it with slight resistance; and, during the night, Lieutenant-colonel Walker, Chief of Artillery of Hill's division, brought up the batteries of Captains Pegram, McIntosh, Davidson, Braxton, and Crenshaw, and established them upon the position thus gained. Branch and Gregg also gained the positions indicated for them, and daybreak found them in rear of the enemy's line of defence.

As directed, Brigadier-general Lawton, commanding Ewell's division, moved on the turnpike in three columns—one on the road, and another on each side of it—until he reached Hallstown, when he formed line of battle, and advanced to the woods on School-house Hill. The division laid on their arms during the night, Lawton and Trimble being in line on the right of the road, and Hays on his left, with Early immediately in his rear. During the night, Colonel Crutchfield, my Chief of Artillery, crossed ten guns of Ewell's division over the Shenandoah, and established them on its right bank so as to enfilade the enemy's position on Bolivar Heights, and take his nearest and most formidable fortifications in reverse. The other batteries of Ewell's division were placed in position on School-house Hill, on each side of the road.

At dawn, September 15th, Gen. Lawton advanced his division to the front of the woods, Lawton's brigade (Colonel Douglas commanding) moved by flank to the bottom between School-house Hill and Bolivar Heights, to support the advance of Major-general Hill.

Lieutenant-colonel Walker opened a rapid enfilade fire from all his batteries at about one thousand yards' range. The batteries on School-house Hill attacked the enemy's line in front. In a short time the guns of Captains Brown, Garber, Latimer, and Dement, under the direction of Colonel Crutchfield, opened from the rear. The batteries of Poague and Carpenter opened fire upon the enemy's right. The artillery upon the Loudoun Heights of Brigadier-general Walker' command, under Captain French, which had silenced the enemy's artillery near the superintendent's house, on the preceding afternoon, again opened upon Harper's Ferry, and also some guns of Major-general McLaws, from the Maryland Heights. In an hour the enemy's fire seemed to be silenced, and the batteries of General Hill were ordered to cease their fire, which was the signal for storming the works. General Pender had commenced his advance, when, the enemy again opening, Pegram and Crenshaw moved forward their batteries and poured a rapid fire into the enemy. The white flag was now displayed, and shortly afterwards, Brigadier-general White (the commanding officer, Colonel D. S. Miles having been mortally wounded), with a garrison of about 11,000 men, surrendered as prisoners of war.

Under this capitulation we took possession of 73 pieces of artillery, some 13,000 small-arms, and other stores. Liberal terms were granted General White and the officers under his command in the surrender, which, I regret to say, do not seem, from subsequent events, to have been properly appreciated by their government.

Leaving General Hill to receive the surrender of the Federal troops and take the requisite steps for securing the captured stores, I moved, in obedience to orders from the commanding general, to rejoin him in Maryland with the remaining divisions of my command. By a severe night's march, we reached the vicinity of Sharpsburg on the morning of the 16th.

By direction of the commanding general I advanced on the enemy, leaving Sharpsburg to the right, and took position to the left of Gen. Longstreet, near a Dunkard church, Ewell's division, (Gen. Lawton commanding,) forming the right, and Jackson's division, (Gen. J. R. Jones, commanding,) forming the left of my command. Major-general Stuart, with the cavalry, was on my left.

Jackson's division, (Gen. Jones commanding,) was formed partly in an open field and partly in the woods, with its right resting upon the Sharpsburg and Hagerstown turnpike, Winder's and Jones's brigades being in front, and Taliaferro's and Starke's brigades a short distance in their rear, and Poague's battery on a knoll in front.

Ewell's division followed that of Jackson to the wood on the left of the road near the church. Early's brigade was then formed on the left of the line of Jackson's division to guard its flank, and Hays's brigade was formed in its rear; Lawton's and Trimble's Brigades remaining during the evening with arms stacked near the church.

A battery of the enemy, some five hundred yards to the front of Jackson's division, opening fire upon a battery to the right, was silenced in twenty minutes by a rapid and well-directed fire from Poague's battery; other batteries of the enemy opened soon after upon our lines and the firing continued until after dark.

About 10 P. M., Lawton's and Trimble's brigades advanced to the front to relieve the command of Brigadier-general Hood, (on the left of Major-general D. H. Hill,) which had been more or less engaged during the evening. Trimble's brigade was posted on the right, next to Ripley's, of D. H. Hill's division, and Lawton's on the left.

The troops slept that night upon their arms, disturbed by the occasional fire of the pickets of the two armies, who were in close proximity to each other. At the first dawn of day, skirmishing commenced in front, and in a short time the Federal batteries, so posted on the opposite side of the Antietam as to enfilade my line, opened a severe and damaging fire.

This was vigorously replied to by the batteries of Poague, Carpenter, Brockenbrough, Raine, Caskie, and Wooding. About sunrise the Federal infantry advanced in heavy force to the edge of the wood on the eastern side of the turnpike, driving in our skirmishers. Batteries were opened in front from the wood with shell and canister, and our troops became exposed, for near an hour, to a terrific storm of shell, canister, and musketry. Gen. Jones having been compelled to leave the field, the command of Jackson's division devolved upon Gen. Starke. With heroic spirit our lines advanced to the conflict and maintained their position in the face of superior numbers. With stubborn resolution, sometimes driving the enemy before them and sometimes compelled to fall back, before their well-sustained and destructive fire. Fresh troops from time to time relieved the enemy's ranks, and the carnage on both sides was terrific. At this early hour Gen. Starke was killed, Col. Douglas, (commanding Lawton's brigade,) was also killed, Gen. Lawton, commanding division, and Col. Walker, commanding brigade, were severely wounded. More than half of the brigades of Lawton and Hays were either killed or wounded, and more than a third of Trimble's, and all the regimental commanders in those brigades except two were killed or wounded. Thinned in their ranks and exhausted of their ammunition, Jackson's division and the brigades of Lawton, Hays, and Trimble retired to the rear, and Hood, of Longstreet's command, again took the position from which he had been before relieved.

In the mean time, Gen. Stuart moved his artillery to a position nearer to the main command and more in our rear. Early being now directed, in consequence of the disability of Gen. Lawton, to take command of Ewell's division, returned with his brigade (with the exception of the 13th Virginia regiment, which remained with Gen. Stuart,) to the piece of wood where he had left the other brigades of his division when he was separated from them. Here he found that the enemy had advanced his infantry near the wood in which was the Dunkard church, and had planted a battery across the turnpike near the edge of the wood and an open field, and that the brigades of Lawton, Hays, and Trimble, had fallen back some distance to the rear. Finding here Cols. Grigsby and Stafford with a portion of Jackson's division, which formed on his left, he determined to maintain his position there if reinforcements could be sent to his support, of which he was promptly assured. Col. Grigsby, with his small command, kept in check the advance of the enemy on the left flank, while General Early attacked with great vigor and gallantry the column on his right and front. The force in front was giving way under this attack, when another heavy column of Federal troops were seen moving across the plateau on his left flank. By this time the expected reinforcements, consisting of Semmes' and Anderson's brigades, and a part of Barksdale's of McLaw's division arrived, and the whole, including Grigsby's command, now united, charged upon the enemy, checking his advance, then driving him back with great slaughter entirely from and beyond the wood, and gaining possession of our original position. No further advance, beyond demonstrations, was made by the enemy on the left. In the afternoon, in obedience to instructions from the commanding general, I moved to the left with a view of turning the Federal right, but I found his numerous artillery so judiciously established in their front and extending so near to the Potomac, which here makes a remarkable bend, which will be seen by reference to the map herewith annexed, as to render it inexpedient to hazard the attempt. In this movement Major-general Stuart had the advance and acted his part well. This officer rendered valuable service throughout the day. His bold use of artillery secured for us an important position, which, had the enemy possessed, might have commanded our left. At the close of the day my troops held the ground which they had occupied in the morning. The next day we remained in position awaiting another attack. The enemy continued in heavy force west of the Antietam on our left, but made no further movement to the attack.

I refer you to the report of Major-general A. P. Hill for the operations of his command in the battle of Sharpsburg. Arriving upon the battle-field from Harper's Ferry at half-past two o'clock of the 17th, he reported to the commanding general, and was by him directed to take position on the right. I have not embraced the movements of his division, nor his killed and wounded of that action in my report.

Early on the morning of the 19th we recrossed the Potomac river into Virginia, near Shepherdstown. The promptitude and success with which this movement was effected reflected the highest credit upon the skill and energy of Major Harman, chief quartermaster. In the evening the command moved on the road leading to Martinsburg, except Lawton's brigade (Colonel Lamar, of the 61st Georgia, commanding), which was left on the Potomac Heights.

On the same day the enemy approached in considerable force on the northern side of the Potomac, and commenced planting heavy batteries on its heights. In the evening the Federals commenced crossing under the protection of their guns, driving off Lawton's brigade and General Pendleton's artillery. By morning a considerable force had crossed over. Orders were dispatched to Generals Early and Hill, who had advanced some four miles on the Martinsburg road, to return and drive back the enemy.

General Hill, who was in the advance, as he approached the town, formed his line of battle in two lines, the first composed of the brigades of Pender, Gregg, and Thomas, under the command of General Gregg; and the second, of Lane's, Archer's, and Brockenbrough's brigades, under command of General Archer. General Early, with the brigades of Early,

Trimble, and Hays, took position in the wood on the right and left of the road leading to the ford. The Federal infantry lined the high banks of the Virginia shore, while their artillery, formidable in numbers and weight of metal, crowned the opposite heights of the Potomac. General Hill's division advanced with great gallantry against the infantry, in the face of a continued discharge of shot and shell from their batteries. The Federals massing in front of Pender, poured a heavy fire into his ranks, and then extending with a view to turn his left. Archer promptly formed on Pender's left, when a simultaneous charge was made, which drove the enemy into the river, followed by an appalling scene of the destruction of human life. Two hundred prisoners were taken. This position on the banks of the river we continued to hold that day, although exposed to the enemy's guns and within range of his sharpshooters posted near the Chesapeake and Ohio Canal. Our infantry remained at the river until relieved by cavalry under General Fitzhugh Lee.

On the evening of the 20th the command moved from Shepherdstown and encamped near the Opequon, in the vicinity of Martinsburg. We remained near Martinsburg until the 27th, when we moved to Bunker Hill, in the county of Berkeley. The official lists of the casualties of my command during the period embraced in this report, will show that we sustained a loss of 38 officers killed, 171 wounded; of 313 non-commissioned officers and privates killed, 1,859 wounded; and missing 57—making a total loss of 2,438, killed, wounded, and missing.

For these great and signal victories our sincere and humble thanks are due unto Almighty God. Upon all appropriate occasions we should acknowledge the hand of Him who reigns in heaven and rules among the powers of the earth. In view of the arduous labors and great privations which the troops were called on to endure, and the isolated and perilous position which the command occupied while engaged with the greatly superior force of the enemy, we feel the encouraging consolation that God was with us and gave to us the victory, and unto His holy name be all gratitude and praise.

I am, general, very respectfully,

Your obedient servant,

T. J. Jackson,

Lieutenant-general.

II.

"THE OLD STONEWALL BRIGADE."

A WRITER in the "Southern Illustrated News" has the following paragraph in reference to the Stonewall Brigade, so long commanded by Jackson:

"*The Old Stonewall Brigade!* What a host of thoughts, memories, and emotions do these words excite! How like a call to the charge sounds the simple mention of the famous band! These veterans have fought and bled and conquered on so many battle-fields, that memory grows weary almost of recalling their glories. Gathering around Jackson in the old days of Patterson in the Valley, when Stuart had but a handful of cavalry to watch the whole border, and Ashby, our dead hero, was a simple captain—they held in check an enemy twenty times their number, and were moulded by the hand of their great leader into that stern phalanx which no bayonet could break, and no odds intimidate. They were boys and old men, the humblest of the sons of toil, and the flower of the land—but united, trained, and looking with supreme confidence to their commander.

"And then commenced their long career of glory—their wonderful marches over thousands of miles—their incessant combats against odds that seemed overpowering—their contempt of snow and rain, and cold and hunger, and want of rest. The soul of their leader seemed to have entered into every breast—and 'Stonewall's Band' became the terror of the enemy. To meet that enemy, was to conquer him, it might almost be said, so obstinately did the eagles of victory continue to perch upon the old battle-flag. The laws of the human body seemed to have been reversed for these men. They marched, and fought, and triumphed, like war machines, which felt no need of rest, or food, or sleep.

"In one day they marched from Harper's Ferry to Strasburg, nearly fifty miles. On the advance to Romney they walked—many without shoes—over roads so slippery with ice that men were falling and their guns going off all along the column—and at night lay down, without blankets, on the snow, with no camp-fires and no food.

"At the first great battle of Manassas they were nearly starved, but fought with desperation. At the last battles there I saw them by the road-side, where they had halted, and one of my friends, a brave young officer of the command, thanked me for a biscuit.

"The very rapidity of their marches separates them from all soldier-comforts—often from their very blankets, however cold the weather; and any other troops but these and their Southern comrades would long since have mutinied and demanded bread and rest. But the shadow of disaffection never flitted over forehead in that command. Whatever discontent may be felt at times at the want of attention on the part of subordinate officers to their necessities, the 'long roll' has only to be beaten—they have only to see the man in the old faded uniform appear, and hunger, cold, fatigue, are forgotten. The Old Brigade is ready—'Here!' is the answer to the roll-call, all along the line—and though the eye is dull from want of food and rest, the arm is strong, and the bayonet is sharp and bright. Before those bayonets no foe shall stand—to pass them, is to advance over the bodies of dead heroes, grasping still the trusty musket, even in death.

"The campaigns of the Valley; the great flank movement of the Chickahominy; the masterly advance upon Manassas in the rear of Pope—these are the fadeless glories of the Old Brigade. Their path has been strewed all over with battles. Incredible have been their marches; countless their combats—almost always against overpowering numbers. The scythe of death has mowed down whole ranks of them; but the Old Brigade still marches on, and fights and conquers. The war-worn veterans still confront the foe, though the thinned ranks tell the tale of their glories and their losses. Many brave souls have poured out their blood and fallen; but they are conquerors, and more than conquerors, in the world's great eye.. The comrades of these heroes hold their memory sacred, and have offered bloody sacrifices to their manes. 'Steady! Close up!' were the last words echoed in the dying ears—and the aim of the survivors was only more steady, the charge with the bayonet more deadly.

"Those survivors may be pardoned if they tell their children, when the war is ended, that they fought under Jackson, in the 'Old Stonewall Brigade.' They may be pardoned even if they boast of their exploits—their wonderful marches—their constant and desperate combats—the skill and nerve which snatched victory from the jaws of defeat, and, even when they were retiring before overwhelming numbers, made it truly better that the foe had 'ne'er been born,' than meet their bayonet charge.

"In speaking of this veteran legion, 'praise is virtue.' Their history is blazoned all over with glory. They are 'happy names, beloved children'—the favorites of fame, if not of fortune. In their dingy uniforms, lying stretched beneath the pines, or by the road-side, they are the mark of many eyes which see them not—the absorbing thought in the breast of beauty, and the idols of the popular heart. In line before the enemy, with their bristling bayonets, they are the terror of the foe, and the life-guard of their dear old mother, Virginia.

"The heart that does not thrill at sight of the worn veterans, is cold indeed. To him who writes, they present a spectacle noble and heroic; and their old tattered, ball-pierced flag is the sacred ensign of liberty.

"Their history and all about them is familiar to me. I have seen them going into action—after fighting four battles in five days—with the regularity and well-dressed front of holiday soldiers on parade. There was no straggling, no lagging—every man stood at his work, and advanced with the steady tramp of the true soldier. The ranks were thin, and the faces travel-worn, but the old flag floated in the winds of the Potomac as defiantly as on the banks of the Shenandoah. That bullet-torn ensign might have been written all over, on both sides, with the names of battles, and the list have then been incomplete. Manassas, Winchester, Kernstown, Front Royal, Port Republic, Cold Harbor, Malvern Hill, Slaughter Mountain, Bristow Station, Groveton—Ox Hill, Sharpsburg, Fredericksburg, were to follow. And these were but the larger names upon the roll of their glory. The numberless engagements of minor character are omitted—but in these I have mentioned they appear to the world, and sufficiently vindicate their claim to the title of heroes.

"I seemed to see these great names, as the Old Brigade advanced that day; and my whole heart went to greet them. Every heart that is true to our great cause, and loves its defenders, will do as much.

"For these men of the Old Stonewall Brigade have been brave among the bravest—with their noble comrades of Gen. Jackson's corps, they have turned the tide of battle upon many hard-fought fields.

"They have 'done well for the Republic'—and let their names be honored. Let the public salutation greet them—salutation by the lip and pen, no less than by the heart—meet them and greet them, and call them glorious—children of glory marching on to the Pantheon of Fame, in a great and peaceful land!"

THE END.

www.ingramcontent.com/pod-product-compliance
Lightning Source LLC
LaVergne TN
LVHW020240110826
845151LV00003B/986

* 9 7 8 1 4 2 5 5 2 9 8 4 0 *